SHAKESPEARE'S

TRAGEDY OF

KING LEAR

EDITED, WITH NOTES

BY

WILLIAM J. ROLFE, Litt.D.

FORMERLY HEAD MASTER OF THE HIGH SCHOOL
CAMBRIDGE, MASS.

ILLUSTRATED

WILDSIDE PRESS

PREFACE

THIS edition of *King Lear* was first published in 1880. As now revised, it is substantially a new edition on the same general plan as the revised *Merchant of Venice*, *Macbeth*, *Hamlet*, and other plays that have preceded it.

Many of the notes on *textual variations* have been either omitted or abridged. Those that have been retained are mostly on the passages (particularly numerous in this play) in which different readings from the folio or the quarto have been adopted in the more important modern editions. For further information on this subject Dr. Furness's edition may be consulted. No teacher or critical student can afford to do without his encyclopedic volumes, in which all the readings and notes of the early and standard modern editions are recorded or epitomized, together with large extracts from the best commentators and much admirable criticism from Dr. Furness himself.

I have also omitted most of the " Critical Comments " from the introduction, as the books from which they were taken are now to be found in public or school libraries. For these extracts I have substituted familiar comments of my own, and have added more of the same kind in the Appendix. A concise account of Shakespeare's metre has also been inserted as an introduction to the Notes.

Minor changes have been made throughout the Notes. Some have been abridged, some have been expanded, and new ones have been added, including a considerable number in place of those referring to my editions of other plays. The book is now absolutely complete in itself.

I believe that the new edition will be generally preferred to the old one ; but both can be used, without serious inconvenience, in the same class or club.

CONTENTS

COUNTRY NEAR DOVER

LEAR (*Sir Joshua Reynolds*)

INTRODUCTION TO KING LEAR

THE HISTORY OF THE PLAY

King Lear was first published in quarto form in 1608, with the following title-page : —

" M. William Shak-speare : His True Chronicle Historie of the life and death of King Lear and his three Daughters. With the vnfortunate life of Edgar, sonne and heire to the Earle of Gloster, and his sullen and assumed humor of Tom of Bedlam : As it was played

9

before the Kings Maiestie at Whitehall vpon S. Stephans night in Christmas Hollidayes. By his Maiesties seruants playing vsually at the Gloabe on the Banckeside. London, Printed for Nathaniel Butter, and are to be sold at his shop in Pauls Church-yard at the signe of the Pide Bull neere St. Austins Gate. 1608."

A second quarto edition was issued by the same publisher in the same year, the title-page of which is similar, except that it omits " and are to be sold . . . St. Austins Gate."

The text of the folio of 1623 is generally regarded as better than that of the quartos, and appears to have been printed from an independent manuscript. Each text, however, is valuable as supplying the deficiencies of the other. The quartos, according to Furness, contain about two hundred and twenty lines that are not in the folios, and the folios fifty lines that are not in the quartos. One entire scene (iv. 3) is omitted in the folios. This discrepancy in the texts has been the subject of much investigation and discussion ; and the critics differ widely in their explanations of it.

The date of the play cannot be earlier than 1603 nor later than 1606. The former limit is fixed by the publication of Dr. Harsnet's *Declaration of Popish Impostures*, from which Shakespeare got the names of some of the devils mentioned by Edgar in iii. 4 ; and the latter by the entry of the play in the Stationers' Registers, dated November 26, 1607, which states that it was performed " before the kinges maiestie at Whitehall vppon Sainct Stephens night at Christmas Last," that is, upon the 26th of December, 1606.

THE SOURCES OF THE PLOT

The story of King Lear and his three daughters is one of the oldest in English literature. It is told by Geoffrey of Monmouth in his *Historia Britonum*, by Layamon in his *Brut*, by Robert of Gloucester, by Fabyan in his *Chronicle*, by Spenser in the *Faerie Queene*, by Holinshed in his *Chronicle*, by Camden in his *Remaines*, in the *Mirrour for Magistrates*, in Warner's *Albion's England*, and elsewhere in prose and verse. It had also been dramatized in the *Chronicle History of King Leir*, which is probably the same play that was entered in the Stationers' Register in 1594, and that was reprinted in 1605 — possibly on account of the success of Shakespeare's *Lear*, then just brought out. The author of this old play probably took the story from Holinshed, and Shakespeare drew either from the same source or from the old play. The portion of the plot in which Gloster figures was derived from Sir Philip Sidney's *Arcadia*. But the poet's real debt to his predecessors is so insignificant that it is scarce worth tracing or recording. As Furness well says, "the distance is always immeasurable between the hint and the fulfilment; what to our purblind eyes is a bare, naked rock, becomes, when gilded by Shakespeare's heavenly alchemy, encrusted thick all over with jewels. When, after reading one of his tragedies, we turn to what we are pleased to call the 'original of his plot,' I am reminded of those glittering gems, of which Heine speaks, that we see at night in lovely gardens, and think must have been left there by kings' children at play ; but when we look for these jewels by day we see only wretched little worms which, crawl painfully away, and which the foot forbears to crush only out of strange pity."

The old play of *King Leir* is not so poor a thing as some of the critics have represented. Though almost infinitely below Shakespeare's tragedy, it has some features that place it above the average of contemporary dramatic productions. Campbell the poet, who was an excellent critic, calls it "simple and touching." He adds : "There is one scene in it, the meeting of Cordelia with her father in a lonely forest, which, with Shakespeare's *Lear* in my heart, I could scarcely read with dry eyes." Nevertheless, as Campbell says, Shakespeare "has sublimated the old tragedy into a new one by an entire originality in the spiritual portraiture of its personages. . . . Wherever Shakespeare works on old materials, you will find him, not wiping dusted gold, but extracting gold from dust, where none but himself could have made the golden extraction."

One scene in the old play reminds me of Longfellow's *Miles Standish*, and Priscilla's "Why don't you speak for yourself, John ? " The King of France and one of his nobles, disguised as pilgrims, fall in with Cordelia after her father has cast her off. They tell her that the King, whom she has not seen, is a suitor for her hand. But Cordelia says that she will not have him, adding with characteristic frankness : —

> "Then be advised, palmer, what to do:
> Cease for thy king, seek for thyself to woo.
>> *King.* Your birth 's too high for any but a king.
>> *Cordelia.* My mind is low enough to love a palmer."

The King soon reveals himself, and Cordelia gets a royal husband after all.

GENERAL COMMENTS ON THE PLAY

If Lear was an historical character, he is supposed to have lived in the eighth century, and that may well be the time of the dramatic action. Shakespeare appears to have purposely taken us back into heathen and barbarous times. The whole atmosphere is pagan. There is not a single deliberate reference to Christianity or its institutions. Occasionally, as in the Roman plays, we meet with a careless or accidental allusion to something associated with Christian times — like the mention of a " godson " — but this is simply an illustration of the poet's unscholarly habits, which lead him into anachronisms. They do not make the play Christian any more than the allusion to " holy churchyards " in *Coriolanus* or to nunneries in the *Midsummer-Night's Dream.* Lear himself is a barbarian monarch ; Goneril,

Regan, and Edmund are savages. The plucking out of
Gloster's eyes is a piece of savagery in keeping with the
times. Even the better characters, like Kent, have a
certain uncivilized impetuosity about them. The gods
of the play are heathen gods. Astrology, though Edmund sneers at it, being an atheist, is a part of the general faith. As Kent says, —

> " It is the stars,
> The stars above us, govern our conditions."

Lear swears by —

> "the sacred radiance of the sun,
> The mysteries of Hecate and the night,
> By all the operation of the orbs,
> From whom we do exist and cease to be."

It is also the Celtic race that we have to deal with,
not the Saxon—a race "highly inflammable, headstrong,
flushed with sudden angers, and breaking out into wild
violences, but also, in its better children at least, of a
deep tenderness and sincerity; in short, a highly emotional race, quickly stirred to good and to evil; swift
to love, swift to hate; blessing and cursing with the
same breath ; with eyes, now full of a gentle solicitude
and regard, now flashing into an intolerable frenzy of
detestation ; a blind, hysterical race, if not wisely coun-
selled and judiciously led; but under good auspices
springing forward with a splendid vivacity to the highest prizes of glory and honour." Lear himself is the
very type of this race : so is Kent; so is Cornwall : —

"You know the fiery quality of the duke,
How unremovable and fix'd he is
In his own course."

And in Cordelia we see the same Celtic impulsiveness. She cannot control the indignation kindled in her soul by the false protestations of her sisters.

But to presume to comment upon *Lear* seems little short of profanity. One cannot but agree with Hazlitt, who says, in his *Characters of Shakespeare's Plays:* "We wish that we could pass this play over and say nothing about it. All that we can say must fall far short of the subject, or even of what we ourselves conceive of it. To attempt to give a description of the play itself, or of its effect upon the mind, is mere impertinence; yet we must say something. It is, then, the best of all Shakespeare's plays, for it is the one in which he was the most in earnest. He was here fairly caught in the web of his own imagination. The passion which he has taken as his subject is that which strikes its root deepest into the human heart, of which the bond is the hardest to be unloosed, and the cancelling and tearing to pieces of which gives the greatest revulsion to the frame. This depth of nature, this force of passion, this tug and war of the elements of our being, this firm faith in filial piety, and the giddy anarchy and whirling tumult of the thoughts at finding the prop failing it; the contrast between the fixed, immovable basis of natural affection and the rapid, irregular starts of imagination, suddenly wrenched from all its accustomed holds and resting-places in the soul — this is what Shakespeare has given, and what nobody else but he could give."

Coleridge remarks: "In the Shakespearian drama there is a vitality which grows and evolves itself from within, a key-note which guides and controls the harmonies throughout. What is *Lear?* It is storm and tempest — the thunder at first grumbling in the far horizon, then gathering around us, and at length bursting in fury over our heads — succeeded by a breaking of the clouds for a while, a last flash of lightning, the closing-in of night, and the single hope of darkness."

KING LEAR

DRAMATIS PERSONÆ

LEAR, king of Britain.
KING OF FRANCE.
DUKE OF BURGUNDY.
DUKE OF CORNWALL.
DUKE OF ALBANY.
EARL OF KENT.
EARL OF GLOSTER.
EDGAR, son to Gloster.
EDMUND, bastard son to Gloster.
CURAN, a courtier.
OSWALD, steward to Goneril.
Old Man, tenant to Gloster.
Doctor.
Fool.
A Captain employed by Edmund.
Gentleman attendant on Cordelia.
A Herald.
Servants to Cornwall.

GONERIL,
REGAN,   } daughters to Lear.
CORDELIA,

Knights of Lear's train, Captains, Messengers, Soldiers, and Attendants.

SCENE: *Britain.*

ACT I

SCENE I. *King Lear's Palace*

Enter KENT, GLOSTER, *and* EDMUND

Kent. I thought the king had more affected the Duke of Albany than Cornwall.

Gloster. It did always seem so to us ; but now, in the division of the kingdom, it appears not which of the dukes he values most, for qualities are so weighed

19

that curiosity in neither can make choice of either's
moiety.

Kent. Is not this your son, my lord?

Gloster. His breeding, sir, hath been at my charge;
I have so often blushed to acknowledge him that now 10
I am brazed to 't. Do you smell a fault?

Kent. I cannot wish the fault undone, the issue of
it being so proper.

Gloster. But I have a son, sir, by order of law,
some year elder than this, who yet is no dearer in
my account; though this knave came something
saucily into the world before he was sent for, yet was
his mother fair, and the whoreson must be acknowledged. — Do you know this noble gentleman, Edmund?   20

Edmund. No, my lord.

Gloster. My lord of Kent. Remember him here-
after as my honourable friend.

Edmund. My services to your lordship.

Kent. I must love you, and sue to know you better.

Edmund. Sir, I shall study deserving.

Gloster. He hath been out nine years, and away
he shall again. — The king is coming.   [*Sennet within.*

Enter one bearing a coronet, KING LEAR, CORNWALL,
ALBANY, GONERIL, REGAN, CORDELIA, *and* Attendants

  Lear. Attend the lords of France and Burgundy,
  Gloster.

Gloster. I shall, my liege. 30

> [*Exeunt Gloster and Edmund.*

Lear. Meantime we shall express our darker pur-
    pose. —
Give me the map there. — Know that we have
    divided
In three our kingdom; and 't is our fast intent
To shake all cares and business from our age,
Conferring them on younger strengths, while we
Unburthen'd crawl toward death. — Our son of Corn-
    wall, —
And you, our no less loving son of Albany,
We have this hour a constant will to publish
Our daughters' several dowers, that future strife
May be prevented now. The princes, France and
    Burgundy, 40
Great rivals in our youngest daughter's love,
Long in our court have made their amorous sojourn,
And here are to be answer'd. — Tell me, my daughters,
Since now we will divest us both of rule,
Interest of territory, cares of state,
Which of you shall we say doth love us most?
That we our largest bounty may extend
Where nature doth with merit challenge. — Goneril,
Our eldest-born, speak first.
    Goneril. Sir, I love you more than word can wield
    the matter; 50
Dearer than eyesight, space, and liberty;
Beyond what can be valued, rich or rare;

No less than life, with grace, health, beauty, honour ;
As much as child e'er lov'd or father found ;
A love that makes breath poor and speech unable ;
Beyond all manner of so much I love you.
    Cordelia. [*Aside*] What shall Cordelia speak ?   Love,
        and be silent.
    Lear. Of all these bounds, even from this line to this,
With shadowy forests and with champaigns rich'd,
With plenteous rivers and wide-skirted meads,   60
We make thee lady.   To thine and Albany's issue
Be this perpetual. — What says our second daughter,
Our dearest Regan, wife of Cornwall?
    Regan. I am made of that self metal as my sister,
And prize me at her worth.   In my true heart
I find she names my very deed of love,
Only she comes too short ; that I profess
Myself an enemy to all other joys
Which the most precious square of sense professes,
And find I am alone felicitate   70
In your dear highness' love.
    Cordelia.   [*Aside*] Then poor Cordelia !
And yet not so, since I am sure my love's
More ponderous than my tongue.
    Lear. To thee and thine hereditary ever
Remain this ample third of our fair kingdom,
No less in space, validity, and pleasure,
Than that conferr'd on Goneril. — Now, our joy,
Although our last and least, to whose young love
The vines of France and milk of Burgundy

Strive to be interess'd, what can you say to draw   80
A third more opulent than your sisters?   Speak.
 Cordelia. Nothing, my lord.
 Lear. Nothing?
 Cordelia. Nothing.
 Lear. Nothing will come of nothing; speak again.
 Cordelia. Unhappy that I am, I cannot heave
My heart into my mouth.   I love your majesty
According to my bond, no more nor less.
 Lear. How, how, Cordelia! mend your speech a little,
Lest it may mar your fortunes.
 Cordelia.   Good my lord,   90
You have begot me, bred me, lov'd me; I
Return those duties back as are right fit,
Obey you, love you, and most honour you.
Why have my sisters husbands, if they say
They love you all?   Haply, when I shall wed,
That lord whose hand must take my plight shall carry
Half my love with him, half my care and duty.
Sure, I shall never marry like my sisters,
To love my father all.
 Lear. But goes thy heart with this?
 Cordelia.   Ay, my good lord.
 Lear. So young, and so untender?   101
 Cordelia. So young, my lord, and true.
 Lear. Let it be so; thy truth then be thy dower!
For, by the sacred radiance of the sun,
The mysteries of Hecate and the night,
By all the operation of the orbs

From whom we do exist and cease to be,
Here I disclaim all my paternal care,
Propinquity and property of blood,
And as a stranger to my heart and me   110
Hold thee from this for ever.   The barbarous Scythian,
Or he that makes his generation messes
To gorge his appetite, shall to my bosom
Be as well neighbour'd, pitied, and reliev'd,
As thou my sometime daughter.
    Kent.   Good my liege, —
    Lear. Peace, Kent !
Come not between the dragon and his wrath.
I lov'd her most, and thought to set my rest
On her kind nursery. — Hence, and avoid my sight ! —
So be my grave my peace, as here I give   120
Her father's heart from her ! — Call France. Who stirs ?
Call Burgundy. — Cornwall and Albany,
With my two daughters' dowers digest the third.
Let pride, which she calls plainness, marry her.
I do invest you jointly with my power,
Pre-eminence, and all the large effects
That troop with majesty.   Ourself, by monthly course,
With reservation of an hundred knights,
By you to be sustain'd, shall our abode
Make with you by due turn.   Only we shall retain   130
The name and all the addition to a king ;
The sway, revenue, execution of the rest,
Beloved sons, be yours, — which to confirm,
This coronet part between you.

Kent.   Royal Lear,
Whom I have ever honour'd as my king,
Lov'd as my father, as my master follow'd,
As my great patron thought on in my prayers, —
    Lear. The bow is bent and drawn; make from the
      shaft.
    Kent. Let it fall rather, though the fork invade
The region of my heart! Be Kent unmannerly   140
When Lear is mad. What wouldst thou do, old
      man ?
Think'st thou that duty shall have dread to speak
When power to flattery bows ? To plainness honour 's
      bound
When majesty falls to folly. Reserve thy state,
And in thy best consideration check
This hideous rashness. Answer my life my judgment,
Thy youngest daughter does not love thee least ;
Nor are those empty-hearted whose low sound
Reverbs no hollowness.
    Lear.   Kent, on thy life, no more !
    Kent. My life I never held but as a pawn   150
To wage against thy enemies, nor fear to lose it,
Thy safety being the motive.
    Lear.   Out of my sight !
    Kent. See better, Lear, and let me still remain
The true blank of thine eye.
    Lear. Now, by Apollo, —
    Kent.   Now, by Apollo, king,
Thou swear'st thy gods in vain.

Lear. O, vassal ! miscreant!
[*Laying his hand on his sword.*

Albany.
Cornwall. } Dear sir, forbear.

Kent. Kill thy physician, and the fee bestow
Upon the foul disease. Revoke thy gift;
Or, whilst I can vent clamour from my throat, 160
I 'll tell thee thou dost evil.

Lear. Hear me, recreant!
On thine allegiance, hear me !
That thou hast sought to make us break our vow,
Which we durst never yet, and with strain'd pride
To come betwixt our sentence and our power,
Which nor our nature nor our place can bear,
Our potency made good, take thy reward.
Five days we do allot thee, for provision
To shield thee from diseases of the world,
And on the sixth to turn thy hated back 170
Upon our kingdom; if on the tenth day following
Thy banish'd trunk be found in our dominions,
The moment is thy death. Away ! By Jupiter,
This shall not be revok'd.

Kent. Fare thee well, king; sith thus thou wilt
appear,
Freedom lives hence, and banishment is here. —
The gods to their dear shelter take thee, maid,
That justly think'st and hast most rightly said ! —
And your large speeches may your deeds approve,
That good effects may spring from words of love. — 180

Thus Kent, O princes, bids you all adieu;
He 'll shape his old course in a country new.　　[*Exit.*

Flourish.　Re-enter GLOSTER, *with* FRANCE, BURGUNDY,
and Attendants.

　Gloster.　Here 's France and Burgundy, my noble
　　lord.
　Lear.　My lord of Burgundy,
We first address toward you, who with this king
Hath rivall'd for our daughter; what, in the least,
Will you require in present dower with her,
Or cease your quest of love?
　Burgundy.　　　　　　　Most royal majesty,
I crave no more than hath your highness offer'd,
Nor will you tender less.
　Lear.　　　　　　Right noble Burgundy,　　190
When she was dear to us we did hold her so,
But now her price is fallen. Sir, there she stands.
If aught within that little-seeming substance,
Or all of it, with our displeasure piec'd,
And nothing more, may fitly like your grace,
She 's there, and she is yours.
　Burgundy.　　　　　　　I know no answer.
　Lear.　Will you, with those infirmities she owes,
Unfriended, new-adopted to our hate,
Dower'd with our curse and stranger'd with our oath,
Take her or leave her?
　Burgundy.　　　　　Pardon me, royal sir;　　200
Election makes not up on such conditions.

Lear. Then leave her, sir; for, by the power that
    made me,
I tell you all her wealth. — [*To France*] For you,
    great king,
I would not from your love make such a stray
To match you where I hate, therefore beseech you
To avert your liking a more worthier way
Than on a wretch whom nature is asham'd
Almost to acknowledge hers.
    France.   This is most strange,
That she who even but now was your best object,
The argument of your praise, balm of your age,   210
The best, the dearest, should in this trice of time
Commit a thing so monstrous to dismantle
So many folds of favour.   Sure, her offence
Must be of such unnatural degree
That monsters it, or your fore-vouch'd affection
Fallen into taint; which to believe of her
Must be a faith that reason without miracle
Should never plant in me.
    Cordelia.   I yet beseech your majesty, —
If for I want that glib and oily art
To speak and purpose not, since what I well intend   220
I 'll do 't before I speak, — that you make known
It is no vicious blot, nor other foulness,
No unchaste action, or dishonour'd step,
That hath depriv'd me of your grace and favour;
But even for want of that for which I am richer, —
A still-soliciting eye, and such a tongue

That I am glad I have not, though not to have it
Hath lost me in your liking.
    Lear.   Better thou
Hadst not been born than not to have pleas'd me better.
    France. Is it but this? a tardiness in nature,   230
Which often leaves the history unspoke
That it intends to do? — My lord of Burgundy,
What say you to the lady? Love 's not love
When it is mingled with regards that stands
Aloof from the entire point. Will you have her?
She is herself a dowry.
    Burgundy.   Royal Lear,
Give but that portion which yourself propos'd,
And here I take Cordelia by the hand,
Duchess of Burgundy.
    Lear. Nothing. I have sworn ; I am firm.   240
    Burgundy. I am sorry then you have so lost a father
That you must lose a husband.
    Cordelia.   Peace be with Burgundy !
Since that respects of fortune are his love,
I shall not be his wife.
    France. Fairest Cordelia, that art most rich being
        poor,
Most choice forsaken, and most lov'd despis'd,
Thee and thy virtues here I seize upon ;
Be it lawful I take up what 's cast away.
Gods, gods ! 't is strange that from their cold'st neglect
My love should kindle to inflam'd respect.—   250
Thy dowerless daughter, king, thrown to my chance,

Is queen of us, of ours, and our fair France.
Not all the dukes of waterish Burgundy
Can buy this unpriz'd precious maid of me. —
Bid them farewell, Cordelia, though unkind;
Thou losest here, a better where to find.

Lear. Thou hast her, France; let her be thine, for
    we
Have no such daughter, nor shall ever see
That face of hers again. — Therefore be gone
Without our grace, our love, our benison. —   260
Come, noble Burgundy.

        [*Flourish. Exeunt all but France, Goneril,
                Regan, and Cordelia.*

France. Bid farewell to your sisters.
Cordelia. Ye jewels of our father, with wash'd eyes
Cordelia leaves you.   I know you what you are,
And, like a sister, am most loath to call
Your faults as they are nam'd.   Love well our father.
To your professed bosoms I commit him;
But yet, alas! stood I within his grace,
I would prefer him to a better place.
So farewell to you both.   270

Regan. Prescribe not us our duty.
Goneril.   Let your study
Be to content your lord, who hath receiv'd you
At fortune's alms. You have obedience scanted,
And well are worth the want that you have wanted.

Cordelia. Time shall unfold what plighted cunning
        hides;

Who cover faults, at last shame them derides.
Well may you prosper !
    France.   Come, my fair Cordelia.
                  [*Exeunt France and Cordelia.*

  Goneril. Sister, it is not little I have to say of
what most nearly appertains to us both. I think our
father will hence to-night.   280

  Regan. That's most certain, and with you; next
month with us.

  Goneril. You see how full of changes his age is ;
the observation we have made of it hath not been
little. He always loved our sister most; and with
what poor judgment he hath now cast her off appears
too grossly.

  Regan. 'T is the infirmity of his age ; yet he hath
ever but slenderly known himself.

  Goneril. The best and soundest of his time hath 290
been but rash ; then must we look from his age
to receive, not alone the imperfections of long-
ingraffed condition, but therewithal the unruly way-
wardness that infirm and choleric years bring with
them.

  Regan. Such unconstant starts are we like to have
from him as this of Kent's banishment.

  Goneril. There is further compliment of leave-
taking between France and him. Pray you, let us
hit together ; if our father carry authority with such 300
disposition as he bears, this last surrender of his will
but offend us.

Regan. We shall further think of it.

Goneril. We must do something, and i' th' heat.
　　　　　　　　　　　　　　　　　　[*Exeunt.*

SCENE II. *The Earl of Gloster's Castle*

Enter EDMUND, *with a letter*

Edmund. Thou, Nature, art my goddess; to thy law
My services are bound.　Wherefore should I
Stand in the plague of custom, and permit
The curiosity of nations to deprive me,
For that I am some twelve or fourteen moonshines
Lag of a brother?　Why bastard? wherefore base?
When my dimensions are as well compact,
My mind as generous and my shape as true,
As honest madam's issue?　Why brand they us
With base? with baseness? bastardy? base, base?　10
Legitimate Edgar, I must have your land.
Our father's love is to the bastard Edmund
As to the legitimate; fine word, ' legitimate '!
Well, my legitimate, if this letter speed
And my invention thrive, Edmund the base
Shall top the legitimate.　I grow, I prosper; —
Now, gods, stand up for bastards!

Enter GLOSTER

Gloster. Kent banish'd thus! and France in choler
　　　parted!
And the king gone to-night! subscrib'd his power!

Confin'd to exhibition!   All this done   20
Upon the gad! — Edmund, how now! what news?
    Edmund. So please your lordship, none.
                              [*Putting up the letter.*
    Gloster. Why so earnestly seek you to put up that
letter?
    Edmund. I know no news, my lord.
    Gloster. What paper were you reading?
    Edmund. Nothing, my lord.
    Gloster. No? What needed then that terrible dis-
patch of it into your pocket? the quality of nothing
hath not such need to hide itself. Let 's see; come, 30
if it be nothing, I shall not need spectacles.
    Edmund. I beseech you, sir, pardon me: it is a
letter from my brother, that I have not all o'er-read;
and for so much as I have perused, I find it not fit
for your o'erlooking.
    Gloster. Give me the letter, sir.
    Edmund. I shall offend, either to detain or give it.
The contents, as in part I understand them, are to
blame.
    Gloster. Let 's see, let 's see.   40
    Edmund. I hope, for my brother's justification, he
wrote this but as an essay or taste of my virtue.
    Gloster. [Reads] ' *This policy and reverence of age
makes the world bitter to the best of our times, keeps our
fortunes from us till our oldness cannot relish them. I
begin to find an idle and fond bondage in the oppression
of aged tyranny, who sways, not as it hath power, but*

KING LEAR — 3

as it is suffered. Come to me, that of this I may speak
more. If our father would sleep till I wake him, you
should enjoy half his revenue for ever, and live the be- 50
loved of your brother, EDGAR.'
Hum! — Conspiracy! — '*Sleep till I wake him, you*
should enjoy half his revenue.' — My son Edgar!
Had he a hand to write this? a heart and brain
to breed it in? — When came this to you? who
brought it?

Edmund. It was not brought me, my lord; there 's
the cunning of it. I found it thrown in at the case-
ment of my closet.

Gloster. You know the character to be your 60
brother's?

Edmund. If the matter were good, my lord, I
durst swear it were his; but, in respect of that, I
would fain think it were not.

Gloster. It is his.

Edmund. It is his hand, my lord, but I hope his
heart is not in the contents.

Gloster. Hath he never before sounded you in this
business?

Edmund. Never, my lord; but I have heard him 70
oft maintain it to be fit that, sons at perfect age and
fathers declined, the father should be as ward to the
son, and the son manage his revenue.

Gloster. O villain, villain! His very opinion in
the letter! Abhorred villain! Unnatural, detested,
brutish villain! worse than brutish! — Go, sirrah,

seek him ; I 'll apprehend him. Abominable villain !
Where is he ?

Edmund. I do not well know, my lord. If it shall
please you to suspend your indignation against my 80
brother till you can derive from him better testimony
of his intent, you should run a certain course ; where,
if you violently proceed against him, mistaking his
purpose, it would make a great gap in your own honour and shake in pieces the heart of his obedience.
I dare pawn down my life for him that he hath writ
this to feel my affection to your honour, and to no
other pretence of danger.

Gloster. Think you so ?

Edmund. If your honour judge it meet, I will 90
place you where you shall hear us confer of this, and
by an auricular assurance have your satisfaction ;
and that without any further delay than this very
evening.

Gloster. He cannot be such a monster —

Edmund. Nor is not, sure.

Gloster. To his father, that so tenderly and entirely loves him. Heaven and earth ! Edmund, seek
him out ; wind me into him, I pray you ; frame the
business after your own wisdom. I would unstate 100
myself to be in a due resolution.

Edmund. I will seek him, sir, presently, convey
the business as I shall find means, and acquaint you
withal.

Gloster. These late eclipses in the sun and moon

portend no good to us. Though the wisdom of nature can reason it thus and thus, yet nature finds itself scourged by the sequent effects. Love cools,
friendship falls off, brothers divide ; in cities, muti-
nies ; in countries, discord ; in palaces, treason ; and 110
the bond cracked 'twixt son and father. This villain of mine comes under the prediction ; there 's
son against father : the king falls from bias of nature ; there 's father against child. We have seen
the best of our time ; machinations, hollowness,
treachery, and all ruinous disorders follow us disquietly to our graves. Find out this villain, Edmund ; it shall lose thee nothing ; do it carefully.
And the noble and true-hearted Kent banished ! his
offence, honesty ! 'T is strange.   [*Exit.*

Edmund. This is the excellent foppery of the 121
world, that, when we are sick in fortune — often the
surfeit of our own behaviour — we make guilty of
our disasters the sun, the moon, and the stars : as if
we were villains on necessity, fools by heavenly
compulsion ; knaves, thieves, and treachers, by spherical predominance ; drunkards, liars, and adulterers,
by an enforced obedience of planetary influence ;
and all that we are evil in, by a divine thrusting on.
Edgar —   130

Enter EDGAR

and pat he comes, like the catastrophe of the old
comedy. My cue is villanous melancholy, with a

sigh like Tom o' Bedlam.   O, these eclipses do portend these divisions ! fa, sol, la, mi.

Edgar. How now, brother Edmund ! what serious
contemplation are you in ?

Edmund. I am thinking, brother, of a prediction I
read this other day, what should follow these eclipses.

Edgar. Do you busy yourself with that ?

Edmund. I promise you, the effects he writes of 140
succeed unhappily : as of unnaturalness between the
child and the parent; death, dearth, dissolutions
of ancient amities; divisions in state, menaces and
maledictions against king and nobles ; needless diffidences, banishment of friends, dissipation of cohorts,
nuptial breaches, and I know not what.

Edgar. How long have you been a sectary astro-
nomical ?

Edmund. Come, come ; when saw you my father
last ?   150

Edgar. The night gone by.

Edmund. Spake you with him ?

Edgar. Ay, two hours together.

Edmund. Parted you in good terms ?   Found you
no displeasure in him by word nor countenance ?

Edgar. None at all.

Edmund. Bethink yourself wherein you may have
offended him ; and at my entreaty forbear his presence
till some little time hath qualified the heat of his displeasure,which at this instant so rageth in him that with 160
the mischief of your person it would scarcely allay.

Edgar. Some villain hath done me wrong.

Edmund. That 's my fear. I pray you, have a continent forbearance till the speed of his rage goes slower; and, as I say, retire with me to my lodging, from whence I will fitly bring you to hear my lord speak. Pray ye, go; there 's my key; if you do stir abroad, go armed.

Edgar. Armed, brother !

Edmund. Brother, I advise you to the best; go 170 armed. I am no honest man if there be any good meaning toward you. I have told you what I have seen and heard, but faintly, nothing like the image and horror of it; pray you, away.

Edgar. Shall I hear from you anon ?

Edmund. I do serve you in this business. —

                              [Exit Edgar.

A credulous father, and a brother noble,
Whose nature is so far from doing harms
That he suspects none ; on whose foolish honesty
My practices ride easy. I see the business.   180
Let me, if not by birth, have lands by wit;
All with me 's meet that I can fashion fit.   *[Exit.*

       SCENE III. *The Duke of Albany's Palace*

       Enter GONERIL *and* OSWALD, *her steward*

Goneril. Did my father strike my gentleman for chiding of his fool?

Oswald. Ay, madam.

Goneril. By day and night he wrongs me; every
　hour
He flashes into one gross crime or other
That sets us all at odds.　I 'll not endure it.
His knights grow riotous, and himself upbraids us
On every trifle.　When he returns from hunting
I will not speak with him; say I am sick.
If you come slack of former services,　　　　　　10
You shall do well; the fault of it I 'll answer.
　　Oswald. He 's coming, madam; I hear him.
　　　　　　　　　　　　　　　　　[Horns within.
　　Goneril. Put on what weary negligence you please,
You and your fellows; I 'd have it come to question.
If he distaste it, let him to my sister,
Whose mind and mine, I know, in that are one,
Not to be over-rul'd.　Idle old man,
That still would manage those authorities
That he hath given away!　Now, by my life,
Old fools are babes again, and must be us'd　　　20
With checks as flatteries, when they are seen abus'd.
Remember what I have said.
　　Oswald.　　　　　　　　Well, madam.
　　Goneril. And let his knights have colder looks
　　among you.
What grows of it, no matter; advise your fellows so.
I would breed from hence occasions, and I shall,
That I may speak.　I 'll write straight to my sister
To hold my very course.　Prepare for dinner.
　　　　　　　　　　　　　　　　　　[Exeunt.

Scene IV. *A Hall in the Same*

Enter Kent, *disguised*

Kent. If but as well I other accents borrow,
That can my speech diffuse, my good intent
May carry through itself to that full issue
For which I raz'd my likeness.   Now, banish'd
    Kent,
If thou canst serve where thou dost stand con-
    demn'd,
So may it come, thy master, whom thou lov'st,
Shall find thee full of labours.

Horns within.   Enter Lear, Knights, *and* Attendants

   Lear. Let me not stay a jot for dinner; go get it
ready. — [*Exit an Attendant.*]   How now ! what art
thou ?   10
   Kent. A man, sir.
   Lear. What dost thou profess ? what wouldst thou
with us ?
   Kent. I do profess to be no less than I seem; to
serve him truly that will put me in trust; to love
him that is honest; to converse with him that is wise
and says little; to fear judgment; to fight when I
cannot choose; and to eat no fish.
   Lear. What art thou ?
   Kent. A very honest-hearted fellow, and as poor 20
as the king.

Lear. If thou be'st as poor for a subject as he is
for a king, thou art poor enough. What wouldst thou?

Kent. Service.

Lear. Who wouldst thou serve?

Kent. You.

Lear. Dost thou know me, fellow?

Kent. No, sir; but you have that in your countenance which I would fain call master.

Lear. What 's that?   30

Kent. Authority.

Lear. What services canst thou do?

Kent. I can keep honest counsel, ride, run, mar a
curious tale in telling it, and deliver a plain message
bluntly; that which ordinary men are fit for, I am
qualified in, and the best of me is diligence.

Lear. How old art thou?

Kent. Not so young, sir, to love a woman for singing, nor so old to dote on her for any thing; I have
years on my back forty-eight.   40

Lear. Follow me; thou shalt serve me. If I like
thee no worse after dinner, I will not part from thee
yet. — Dinner, ho, dinner! Where 's my knave?
my fool? — Go you, and call my fool hither. —

                    [*Exit an Attendant.*

Enter OSWALD

You, you, sirrah, where 's my daughter?

Oswald. So please you, —   [*Exit.*

Lear. What says the fellow there? Call the clot-

poll back. —[*Exit a Knight.*] Where 's my fool, ho?
I think the world 's asleep. —[*Re-enter Knight.*] How
now! where 's that mongrel? 50

Knight. He says, my lord, your daughter is not
well.

Lear. Why came not the slave back to me when I
called him?

Knight. Sir, he answered me in the roundest manner, he would not.

Lear. He would not!

Knight. My lord, I know not what the matter is;
but, to my judgment, your highness is not entertained with that ceremonious affection as you were 60
wont. There 's a great abatement of kindness appears as well in the general dependants as in the
duke himself also and your daughter.

Lear. Ha! sayest thou so?

Knight. I beseech you, pardon me, my lord, if I
be mistaken; for my duty cannot be silent when I
think your highness wronged.

Lear. Thou but rememberest me of mine own
conception. I have perceived a most faint neglect
of late, which I have rather blamed as mine own 70
jealous curiosity than as a very pretence and purpose
of unkindness. I will look further into 't. But
where 's my fool? I have not seen him this two
days.

Knight. Since my young lady 's going into France,
sir, the fool hath much pined away.

Lear. No more of that; I have noted it well. —
Go you, and tell my daughter I would speak with
her. — [*Exit an Attendant.*]   Go you, call hither my
fool. —   [*Exit an Attendant.*

Re-enter OSWALD

O, you sir, you, come you hither, sir.   Who am I, sir? 81
   Oswald. My lady's father.

   Lear. My lady's father! my lord's knave.   You
whoreson dog! you slave! you cur!

   Oswald. I am none of these, my lord; I beseech
your pardon.

   Lear. Do you bandy looks with me, you rascal?
                                  [*Striking him.*

   Oswald. I 'll not be strucken, my lord.

   Kent. Nor tripped neither, you base foot-ball
player.   [*Tripping up his heels.*

   Lear. I thank thee, fellow; thou servest me, and 91
I 'll love thee.

   Kent. Come, sir, arise, away!   I 'll teach you differences; away, away!   If you will measure your lub-
ber's length again, tarry; but away!   Go to; have
you wisdom? so.   [*Pushes Oswald out.*

   Lear. Now, my friendly knave, I thank thee.
There 's earnest of thy service.

Enter Fool

   Fool. Let me hire him too. — Here 's my coxcomb.   100

Lear. How now, my pretty knave! how dost thou?

Fool. Sirrah, you were best take my coxcomb.

Kent. Why, fool?

Fool. Why? for taking one's part that 's out of favour. Nay, an thou canst not smile as the wind sits, thou 'lt catch cold shortly. There, take my coxcomb. Why, this fellow has banished two on 's daughters, and did the third a blessing against his will; if thou follow him, thou must needs wear my coxcomb. — How now, nuncle! Would I had 110 two coxcombs and two daughters!

Lear. Why, my boy?

Fool. If I gave them all my living, I 'd keep my coxcombs myself. There 's mine; beg another of thy daughters.

Lear. Take heed, sirrah; the whip.

Fool. Truth 's a dog must to kennel; he must be whipped out, when Lady the brach may stand by the fire and stink.

Lear. A pestilent gall to me!   120

Fool. Sirrah, I 'll teach thee a speech.

Lear. Do.

Fool. Mark it, nuncle:

>   Have more than thou showest,
>   Speak less than thou knowest,
>   Lend less than thou owest,
>   Ride more than thou goest,
>   Learn more than thou trowest,
>   Set less than thou throwest;

And thou shalt have more   130
Than two tens to a score.

Kent. This is nothing, fool.

Fool. Then 't is like the breath of an unfee'd lawyer; you gave me nothing for 't. — Can you make no use of nothing, nuncle?

Lear. Why, no, boy; nothing can be made out of nothing.

Fool. [*To Kent*] Prithee, tell him, so much the rent of his land comes to; he will not believe a fool.

Lear. A bitter fool!   140

Fool. Dost thou know the difference, my boy, between a bitter fool and a sweet fool?

Lear. No, lad; teach me.

Fool.   That lord that counsell'd thee
                To give away thy land,
            Come place him here by me,
                Do thou for him stand:
            The sweet and bitter fool
                Will presently appear;
            The one in motley here,   150
                The other found out there.

Lear. Dost thou call me fool, boy?

Fool. All thy other titles thou hast given away; that thou wast born with.

Kent. This is not altogether fool, my lord.

Fool. No, faith, lords and great men will not let me. If I had a monopoly out, they would have part on 't; and ladies too, they will not let me have

all the fool to myself; they'll be snatching. Nuncle,
give me an egg, and I'll give thee two crowns.   160
    Lear. What two crowns shall they be?
    Fool. Why, after I have cut the egg i' the middle
and eat up the meat, the two crowns of the egg.
When thou clovest thy crown i' the middle, and
gav'st away both parts, thou borest thy ass on thy
back o'er the dirt; thou hadst little wit in thy bald
crown when thou gav'st thy golden one away. If I
speak like myself in this, let him be whipped that
first finds it so.

    [Sings] *Fools had ne'er less grace in a year;*   170
           For wise men are grown foppish,
           And know not how their wits to wear,
           Their manners are so apish.

    Lear. When were you wont to be so full of songs,
sirrah?
    Fool. I have used it, nuncle, e'er since thou mad-
est thy daughters thy mothers; for when thou gav'st
them the rod, and put'st down thine own breeches,

    [Sings] *Then they for sudden joy did weep,*
           And I for sorrow sung,   180
           That such a king should play bo-peep,
           And go the fools among.

Prithee, nuncle, keep a schoolmaster that can teach
thy fool to lie. I would fain learn to lie.
    Lear. An you lie, sirrah, we'll have you whipped.
    Fool. I marvel what kin thou and thy daughters
are; they'll have me whipped for speaking true,

thou 'lt have me whipped for lying, and sometimes
I am whipped for holding my peace. I had rather
be any kind o' thing than a fool : and yet I would 190
not be thee, nuncle ; thou hast pared thy wit o' both
sides, and left nothing i' the middle. Here comes
one o' the parings.

Enter GONERIL

Lear. How now, daughter ! what makes that
frontlet on ? Methinks you are too much of late i'
the frown.

Fool. Thou wast a pretty fellow when thou hadst
no need to care for her frowning ; now thou art an
O without a figure. I am better than thou art now ;
I am a fool, thou art nothing. — [*To Goneril*] Yes, 200
forsooth, I will hold my tongue ; so your face bids
me, though you say nothing. Mum, mum ;

> *He that keeps nor crust nor crum,*
> *Weary of all, shall want some. —*

That 's a shealed peascod.

Goneril. Not only, sir, this your all-licens'd fool,
But other of your insolent retinue
Do hourly carp and quarrel, breaking forth
In rank and not-to-be-endured riots. Sir,
I had thought, by making this well known unto you, 210
To have found a safe redress, but now grow fearful,
By what yourself too late have spoke and done,
That you protect this course, and put it on
By your allowance ; which if you should, the fault
Would not scape censure, nor the redresses sleep,

Which, in the tender of a wholesome weal,
Might in their working do you that offence,
Which else were shame, that then necessity
Will call discreet proceeding.

    Fool. For, you know, nuncle,   220
        The hedge-sparrow fed the cuckoo so long,
        That it 's had it head bit off by it young.
So out went the candle, and we were left darkling.

    Lear. Are you our daughter?

    Goneril. Come, sir,
I would you would make use of that good wisdom
Whereof I know you are fraught, and put away
These dispositions which of late transport you
From what you rightly are.

    Fool. May not an ass know when the cart draws 230
the horse? Whoop, Jug! I love thee.

    Lear. Does any here know me? This is not Lear.
Does Lear walk thus? speak thus? Where are his
       eyes?
Either his notion weakens, his discernings
Are lethargied — Ha! waking? 't is not so.
Who is it that can tell me who I am?

    Fool. Lear's shadow.

    Lear. I would learn that; for, by the marks of
sovereignty, knowledge, and reason, I should be false
persuaded I had daughters.   240

    Fool. Which they will make an obedient father.

    Lear. Your name, fair gentlewoman?

    Goneril. This admiration, sir, is much o' the savour

Of other your new pranks.   I do beseech you
To understand my purposes aright ;
As you are old and reverend, you should be wise.
Here do you keep a hundred knights and squires ;
Men so disorder'd, so debosh'd and bold,
That this our court, infected with their manners,
Shows like a riotous inn ; epicurism and lust   250
Makes it more like a tavern or a brothel
Than a grac'd palace.   The shame itself doth **speak**
For instant remedy.   Be then desir'd
By her that else will take the thing she begs,
A little to disquantity your train ;
And the remainder, that shall still depend,
To be such men as may besort your age,
Which know themselves and you.
    Lear.   Darkness and devils ! —
Saddle my horses ! call my train together ! —
Degenerate bastard ! I 'll not trouble thee.   260
Yet have I left a daughter.
    Goneril. You strike my people, and your disorder'd
        rabble
Make servants of their betters.

Enter ALBANY

    Lear. Woe, that too late repents. — O, sir, are you
        come ?
Is it your will ?   Speak, sir. — Prepare my horses. —
Ingratitude, thou marble-hearted fiend,
      KING LEAR — 4

More hideous when thou show'st thee in a child
Than the sea-monster !
   Albany.   Pray, sir, be patient.
   Lear. Detested kite ! thou liest ;
My train are men of choice and rarest parts,   270
That all particulars of duty know,
And in the most exact regard support
The worships of their name. — O most small fault,
How ugly didst thou in Cordelia show !
Which, like an engine, wrench'd my frame of nature
From the fix'd place, drew from my heart all love,
And added to the gall.   O Lear, Lear, Lear !
Beat at this gate, that let thy folly in, [*Striking his head.*
And thy dear judgment out ! — Go, go, my people.
   Albany. My lord, I am guiltless, as I am ignorant
Of what hath mov'd you.
   Lear.   It may be so, my lord. — 281
Hear, Nature, hear ; dear goddess, hear !
Suspend thy purpose, if thou didst intend
To make this creature fruitful ;
Into her womb convey sterility ;
Dry up in her the organs of increase,
And from her derogate body never spring
A babe to honour her ! If she must teem,
Create her child of spleen, that it may live
And be a thwart disnatur'd torment to her !   290
Let it stamp wrinkles in her brow of youth,
With cadent tears fret channels in her cheeks,
Turn all her mother's pains and benefits

To laughter and contempt; that she may feel
How sharper than a serpent's tooth it is
To have a thankless child ! — Away, away !   [*Exit.*
   Albany. Now, gods that we adore, whereof comes this ?
   Goneril. Never afflict yourself to know the cause,
But let his disposition have that scope
That dotage gives it.   300

Re-enter LEAR

   Lear. What, fifty of my followers at a clap !
Within a fortnight !
   Albany.   What 's the matter, sir?
   Lear. I 'll tell thee. — Life and death ! I am asham'd
That thou hast power to shake my manhood thus ;
That these hot tears, which break from me perforce,
Should make thee worth them. Blasts and fogs upon thee !
Th' untented woundings of a father's curse
Pierce every sense about thee ! — Old fond eyes,
Beweep this cause again, I 'll pluck ye out,
And cast you, with the waters that you lose,   310
To temper clay. — Ha ! is it come to this ?
Let it be so. I have another daughter,
Who, I am sure, is kind and comfortable.
When she shall hear this of thee, with her nails
She 'll flay thy wolvish visage. Thou shalt find
That I 'll resume the shape which thou dost think
I have cast off for ever ; thou shalt, I warrant thee.
            [*Exeunt Lear, Kent, and Attendants.*
   Goneril. Do you mark that, my lord ?

Albany. I cannot be so partial, Goneril,
To the great love I bear you, —   320
    Goneril. Pray you, content. — What, Oswald, ho ! —
You, sir, more knave than fool, after your master.
    Fool. Nuncle Lear, nuncle Lear, tarry ; take the
fool with thee. —

> A fox, when one has caught her,
> And such a daughter,
> Should sure to the slaughter,
> If my cap would buy a halter.
> So the fool follows after.   [*Exit.*

    Goneril. This man hath had good council ! A hun-
        dred knights !   330
'T is politic and safe to let him keep
At point a hundred knights ; yes, that, on every dream,
Each buzz, each fancy, each complaint, dislike,
He may enguard his dotage with their powers,
And hold our lives in mercy. — Oswald, I say !
    Albany. Well, you may fear too far.
    Goneril.   Safer than trust too far.
Let me still take away the harms I fear,
Not fear still to be taken.   I know his heart.
What he hath utter'd I have writ my sister ;
If she sustain him and his hundred knights,   340
When I have show'd the unfitness, —

Re-enter OSWALD

                        How now, Oswald !
What, have you writ that letter to my sister ?

Oswald. Ay, madam.

Goneril. Take you some company, and away to horse ;
Inform her full of my particular fear,
And thereto add such reasons of your own
As may compact it more.   Get you gone ;
And hasten your return. — [*Exit Oswald.*] No, no, my
      lord,
This milky gentleness and course of yours
Though I condemn not, yet, under pardon,   350
You are much more at task for want of wisdom
Than prais'd for harmful mildness.

Albany. How far your eyes may pierce I cannot tell ;
Striving to better, oft we mar what 's well.

Goneril. Nay, then —

Albany. Well, well ; the event.   [*Exeunt.*

SCENE V. Court before the Same

Enter LEAR, KENT, and Fool.

Lear. Go you before to Gloster with these letters.
Acquaint my daughter no further with any thing you
know than comes from her demand out of the letter.
If your diligence be not speedy, I shall be there afore
you.

Kent. I will not sleep, my lord, till I have delivered your letter.   [*Exit.*

Fool. If a man's brains were in 's heels, were 't
not in danger of kibes ?

Lear. Ay, boy.   10

Fool. Then, I prithee, be merry; thy wit shall ne'er go slipshod.

Lear. Ha, ha, ha!

Fool. Shalt see thy other daughter will use thee kindly; for though she 's as like this as a crab 's like an apple, yet I can tell what I can tell.

Lear. What canst tell, boy?

Fool. She will taste as like this as a crab does to a crab. Thou canst tell why one's nose stands i' the middle on 's face?   20

Lear. No.

Fool. Why, to keep one's eyes of either side 's nose, that what a man cannot smell out, he may spy into.

Lear. I did her wrong —

Fool. Canst tell how an oyster makes his shell?

Lear. No.

Fool. Nor I neither; but I can tell why a snail has a house.

Lear. Why?   30

Fool. Why, to put 's head in; not to give it away to his daughters, and leave his horns without a case.

Lear. I will forget my nature. So kind a father! — Be my horses ready?

Fool. Thy asses are gone about 'em. The reason why the seven stars are no moe than seven is a pretty reason.

Lear. Because they are not eight?

Fool. Yes, indeed; thou wouldst make a good fool.

Lear. To take 't again perforce ! Monster in- 40
gratitude !

Fool. If thou wert my fool, nuncle, I 'd have thee
beaten for being old before thy time.

Lear. How 's that?

Fool. Thou shouldst not have been old till thou
hadst been wise.

Lear. O, let me not be mad, not mad, sweet heaven !
Keep me in temper ; I would not be mad ! —

Enter Gentleman

How now ! are the horses ready ?

Gentleman. Ready, my lord. 50

Lear. Come, boy. [*Exeunt.*

ACT II

SCENE I. *The Earl of Gloster's Castle*

Enter EDMUND *and* CURAN, *meeting*

Edmund. Save thee, Curan.

Curan. And you, sir. I have been with your father, and given him notice that the Duke of Cornwall and Regan his duchess will be here with him this night.

Edmund. How comes that?

Curan. Nay, I know not. You have heard of the news abroad; I mean the whispered ones, for they are yet but ear-kissing arguments ?

Edmund. Not I; pray you, what are they ?   10

Curan. Have you heard of no likely wars toward, 'twixt the Dukes of Cornwall and Albany?

Edmund. Not a word.

Curan. You may do then in time.   Fare you well, sir.

[*Exit.*

Edmund. The duke be here to-night?   The better !
          best !
This weaves itself perforce into my business.
My father hath set guard to take my brother ;
And I have one thing, of a queasy question,
Which I must act.   Briefness and fortune, work !—
Brother, a word ; descend !   Brother, I say !   20

Enter EDGAR

My father watches !   O sir, fly this place !
Intelligence is given where you are hid ;
You have now the good advantage of the night.
Have you not spoken 'gainst the Duke of Cornwall?
He 's coming hither, now, i' the night, i' the haste,
And Regan with him ; have you nothing said
Upon his party 'gainst the Duke of Albany?
Advise yourself.

Edgar.   I am sure on 't, not a word.

Edmund. I hear my father coming.   Pardon me ;
In cunning I must draw my sword upon you.   30

Draw ; seem to defend yourself ; now quit you well.
Yield ! come before my father ! — Light, ho, here ! —
Fly, brother ! Torches, torches ! — So, farewell.
[Exit Edgar.
Some blood drawn on me would beget opinion
Of my more fierce endeavour. I have seen drunkards
Do more than this in sport. — Father, father ! —
Stop, stop ! — No help ?

Enter GLOSTER, *and* Servants *with torches*

Gloster. Now, Edmund, where 's the villain ?
Edmund. Here stood he in the dark, his sharp sword
out,
Mumbling of wicked charms, conjuring the moon   40
To stand auspicious mistress.
Gloster.   But where is he ?
Edmund. Look, sir, I bleed.
Gloster.   Where is the villain, Edmund ?
Edmund. Fled this way, sir, when by no means he
could —
Gloster. Pursue him, ho ! Go after. — *[Exeunt some*
Servants.] By no means what ?
Edmund. Persuade me to the murther of your lord-
ship ;
But that I told him the revenging gods
'Gainst parricides did all the thunder bend,
Spoke with how manifold and strong a bond
The child was bound to the father ; — sir, in fine,   50

Seeing how loathly opposite I stood
To this unnatural purpose, in fell motion
With his prepared sword he charges home
My unprovided body, lanc'd mine arm.
But when he saw my best alarum'd spirits
Bold in the quarrel's right, rous'd to the encounter,
Or whether gasted by the noise I made,
Full suddenly he fled.
    Gloster.   Let him fly far.
Not in this land shall he remain uncaught;
And found — dispatch.   The noble duke my master,
My worthy arch and patron, comes to-night.   61
By his authority I will proclaim it
That he which finds him shall deserve our thanks,
Bringing the murtherous coward to the stake;
He that conceals him, death.
    Edmund. When I dissuaded him from his intent,
And found him pight to do it, with curst speech
I threaten'd to discover him; he replied:
' Thou unpossessing bastard ! dost thou think,
If I would stand against thee, would the reposal   70
Of any trust, virtue, or worth in thee
Make thy words faith'd ?   No ; what I should
        deny —
As this I would, — ay, though thou didst produce
My very character — I 'd turn it all
To thy suggestion, plot, and damned practice;
And thou must make a dullard of the world,
If they not thought the profits of my death

Were very pregnant and potential spurs
To make thee seek it.'

    Gloster.   Strong and fasten'd villain !
Would he deny his letter ?   I never got him. —   80
                             [*Tucket within*.
Hark, the duke's trumpets !   I know not why he comes.
All ports I 'll bar, the villain shall not scape ;
The duke must grant me that.   Besides, his picture
I will send far and near, that all the kingdom
May have due note of him ; and of my land,
Loyal and natural boy, I 'll work the means
To make thee capable.

    Enter CORNWALL, REGAN, *and* Attendants

    Cornwall. How now, my noble friend ! since I came
         hither,
Which I can call but now, I have heard strange news.
    Regan. If it be true, all vengeance comes too short 90
Which can pursue the offender.   How dost, my lord ?
    Gloster. O, madam, my old heart is crack'd, — it 's
         crack'd !
    Regan. What, did my father's godson seek your life ?
He whom my father nam'd ? your Edgar ?
    Gloster. O, lady, lady, shame would have it hid !
    Regan. Was he not companion with the riotous
         knights
That tend upon my father ?
    Gloster. I know not, madam.— 'T is too bad, too bad.
    Edmund. Yes, madam, he was of that consort.

Regan. No marvel then, though he were ill affected ;
'T is they have put him on the old man's death,   101
To have th' expense and waste of his revenues.
I have this present evening from my sister
Been well inform'd of them, and with such cautions
That if they come to sojourn at my house,
I 'll not be there.
    Cornwall.   Nor I, assure thee, Regan.—
Edmund, I hear that you have shown your father
A child-like office.
    Edmund.   'T was my duty, sir.
    Gloster. He did bewray his practice, and receiv'd
This hurt you see, striving to apprehend him.   110
    Cornwall. Is he pursued ?
    Gloster.   Ay, my good lord.
    Cornwall. If he be taken, he shall never more
Be fear'd of doing harm ; make your own purpose,
How in my strength you please.— For you, Edmund,
Whose virtue and obedience doth this instant
So much commend itself, you shall be ours.
Natures of such deep trust we shall much need ;
You we first seize on.
    Edmund.   I shall serve you, sir,
Truly, however else.
    Gloster.   For him I thank your grace.
    Cornwall. You know not why we came to visit you ?
    Regan. Thus, out of season, threading dark-eyed
            night ;   121
Occasions, noble Gloster, of some poise,

Wherein we must have use of your advice.
Our father he hath writ, so hath our sister,
Of differences which I best thought it fit
To answer from our home ; the several messengers
From hence attend dispatch. Our good old friend,
Lay comforts to your bosom, and bestow
Your needful counsel to our businesses,
Which craves the instant use.

    Gloster.   I serve you, madam. —
Your graces are right welcome.   [*Flourish. Exeunt*

Scene II. *Before Gloster's Castle*

Enter Kent *and* Oswald, *severally*

Oswald. Good dawning to thee, friend ; art of this
house ?

    Kent. Ay.

    Oswald. Where may we set our horses ?

    Kent. I' the mire.

    Oswald. Prithee, if thou lov'st me, tell me.

    Kent. I love thee not.

    Oswald. Why then I care not for thee

    Kent. If I had thee in Lipsbury pinfold, I would
make thee care for me.   10

    Oswald. Why dost thou use me thus ? I know
thee not.

    Kent. Fellow, I know thee.

    Oswald. What dost thou know me for ?

    Kent. A knave ; a rascal ; an eater of broken

meats; a base, proud, shallow, beggarly, three-suited, hundred-pound, filthy, worsted-stocking knave; a lily-livered action-taking, whoreson, glass-gazing, super-serviceable, finical rogue; one-trunk-inheriting slave; one that wouldst be a bawd in way of good service, 20 and art nothing but the composition of a knave, beggar, coward, pandar, and the son and heir of a mongrel bitch; one whom I will beat into clamorous whining, if thou deniest the least syllable of thy addition.

Oswald. Why, what a monstrous fellow art thou, thus to rail on one that is neither known of thee nor knows thee

Kent. What a brazen-faced varlet art thou, to deny thou knowest me! Is it two days ago since I tripped 30 up thy heels, and beat thee before the king? Draw, you rogue! for, though it be night, yet the moon shines. I 'll make a sop o' the moonshine of you; you whoreson cullionly barber-monger, draw.

Oswald. Away! I have nothing to do with thee.

Kent. Draw, you rascal! You come with letters against the king, and take Vanity the puppet's part against the royalty of her father. Draw, you rogue, or I 'll so carbonado your shanks! draw, you rascal! come your ways!   40

Oswald. Help, ho! murther! help!

Kent. Strike, you slave! stand, rogue, stand! you neat slave, strike!   [*Beating him*

Oswald. Help, ho! murther! murther!

Enter EDMUND, *with his rapier drawn*

Edmund. How now! What 's the matter?
[*Parting them.*
Kent. With you, goodman boy, if you please ;
come, I 'll flesh ye! Come on, young master!

Enter CORNWALL, REGAN, GLOSTER, *and* Servants

Gloster. Weapons ; arms! What 's the matter here?
Cornwall. Keep peace, upon your lives!
He dies that strikes again! What is the matter? 50
Regan. The messengers from our sister and the king?
Cornwall. What is your difference? speak.
Oswald. I am scarce in breath, my lord.
Kent. No marvel, you have so bestirred your valour.
You cowardly rascal, nature disclaims in thee ; a
tailor made thee.
Cornwall. Thou art a strange fellow; a tailor make
a man?
Kent. Ay, a tailor, sir ; a stone-cutter or a painter
could not have made him so ill, though they had 60
been but two hours o' the trade.
Cornwall. Speak yet, how grew your quarrel?
Oswald. This ancient ruffian, sir, whose life I
have spared at suit of his grey beard, —
Kent. Thou whoreson zed! thou unnecessary letter! — My lord, if you will give me leave, I will tread
this unbolted villain into mortar, and daub the wall

of a jakes with him. — Spare my grey beard, you
wagtail?

Cornwall. Peace, sirrah! —   70
You beastly knave, know you no reverence?

Kent. Yes, sir; but anger hath a privilege.

Cornwall. Why art thou angry?

Kent. That such a slave as this should wear a sword,
Who wears no honesty.   Such smiling rogues as these,
Like rats, oft bite the holy cords a-twain
Which are too intrinse t' unloose; smooth every passion
That in the natures of their lords rebel,
Being oil to fire, snow to the colder moods;
Renege, affirm, and turn their halcyon beaks   80
With every gale and vary of their masters,
Knowing nought, like dogs, but following. —
A plague upon your epileptic visage!
Smile you my speeches, as I were a fool?
Goose, if I had you upon Sarum plain,
I 'd drive ye cackling home to Camelot.

Cornwall. What, art thou mad, old fellow?

Gloster. How fell you out? say that.

Kent. No contraries hold more antipathy
Than I and such a knave.   90

Cornwall. Why dost thou call him knave?   What
    is his fault?

Kent. His countenance likes me not.

Cornwall. No more, perchance, does mine, nor his,
    nor hers.

Kent. Sir, 't is my occupation to be plain;

KING LEAR — 5

I have seen better faces in my time
Than stands on any shoulder that I see
Before me at this instant.
    Cornwall.   This is some fellow
Who, having been prais'd for bluntness, doth affect
A saucy roughness, and constrains the garb
Quite from his nature; he cannot flatter, he, —   100
An honest mind and plain, — he must speak truth !
An they will take it, so; if not, he 's plain.
These kind of knaves I know, which in this plain-
        ness
Harbour more craft and more corrupter ends
Than twenty silly-ducking observants
That stretch their duties nicely.
    Kent. Sir, in good sooth, in sincere verity,
Under the allowance of your great aspect,
Whose influence, like the wreath of radiant fire
On flickering Phœbus' front, —
    Cornwall.   What mean'st by this ?
    Kent. To go out of my dialect, which you discom- 111
mend so much. I know, sir, I am no flatterer; he
that beguiled you in a plain accent was a plain knave,
which for my part I will not be, though I should win
your displeasure to entreat me to 't.
    Cornwall. What was the offence you gave him ?
    Oswald. I never gave him any.
It pleas'd the king his master very late
To strike at me, upon his misconstruction ;
When he, compact, and flattering his displeasure, 120

Tripp'd me behind ; being down, insulted, rail'd,
And put upon him such a deal of man
That worthied him, got praises of the king
For him attempting who was self-subdued ;
And in the fleshment of this dread exploit
Drew on me here again.
    Kent.   None of these rogues and cowards
But Ajax is their fool.
    Cornwall.   Fetch forth the stocks ! —
You stubborn ancient knave, you reverend braggart,
We 'll teach you —
    Kent.   Sir, I am too old to learn ;
Call not your stocks for me. I serve the king,   130
On whose employment I was sent to you.
You shall do small respect, show too bold malice
Against the grace and person of my master,
Stocking his messenger.
    Cornwall. Fetch forth the stocks ! As I have life
        and honour,
There shall he sit till noon.
    Regan. Till noon ! till night, my lord ; and all
        night too.
    Kent. Why, madam, if I were your father's dog,
You should not use me so.
    Regan.   Sir, being his knave, I will.
    Cornwall. This is a fellow of the self-same colour 140
Our sister speaks of. — Come, bring away the stocks !
                        [*Stocks brought out.*
    Gloster. Let me beseech your grace not to do so.

His fault is much, and the good king his master
Will check him for 't; your purpos'd low correction
Is such as basest and contemned'st wretches
For pilferings and most common trespasses
Are punish'd with.   The king must take it ill
That he, so slightly valued in his messenger,
Should have him thus restrain'd.

    Cornwall.   I 'll answer that.

    Regan. My sister may receive it much more worse 150
To have her gentleman abus'd, assaulted,
For following her affairs. — Put in his legs. —

                     [Kent is put in the stocks.
Come, my lord, away. *[Exeunt all but Gloster and Kent.*

    Gloster. I am sorry for thee, friend; 't is the duke's
        pleasure,
Whose disposition, all the world well knows,
Will not be rubb'd nor stopp'd.   I 'll entreat for thee.

    Kent. Pray, do not, sir.   I have watch'd and
        travell'd hard;
Some time I shall sleep out, the rest I 'll whistle.
A good man's fortune may grow out at heels.
Give you good morrow!   160

    Gloster. [*Aside*] The duke 's to blame in this; 't will
        be ill taken.   *[Exit.*

    Kent. Good king, that must approve the common
        saw,
Thou out of heaven's benediction comest
To the warm sun! —
Approach, thou beacon to this under globe,

That by thy comfortable beams I may
Peruse this letter ! Nothing almost sees miracles
But misery.   I know 't is from Cordelia,
Who hath most fortunately been inform'd
Of my obscured course ; and shall find time   170
From this enormous state, seeking to give
Losses their remedies.   All weary and o'er-watch'd,
Take vantage, heavy eyes, not to behold
This shameful lodging.
Fortune, good night ; smile once more, turn thy wheel !
                                        [*Sleeps.*

SCENE III.   *A Part of the Heath*

Enter EDGAR

Edgar.   I heard myself proclaim'd,
And by the happy hollow of a tree
Escap'd the hunt.   No port is free ; no place,
That guard and most unusual vigilance
Does not attend my taking.   Whiles I may scape
I will preserve myself, and am bethought
To take the basest and most poorest shape
That ever penury, in contempt of man,
Brought near to beast ; my face I 'll grime with filth,
Blanket my loins, elf all my hair in knots,   10
And with presented nakedness outface
The winds and persecutions of the sky.
The country gives me proof and precedent
Of Bedlam beggars, who with roaring voices

Strike in their numb'd and mortified bare arms
Pins, wooden pricks, nails, sprigs of rosemary;
And with this horrible object, from low farms,
Poor pelting villages, sheepcotes and mills,
Sometime with lunatic bans, sometime with prayers,
Enforce their charity. Poor Turlygod! poor Tom! 20
That 's something yet; Edgar I nothing am. [*Exit.*

SCENE IV. *Before Gloster's Castle*

KENT *in the Stocks. Enter* LEAR, Fool, *and* Gentleman

    Lear. 'T is strange that they should so depart from
        home,
And not send back my messenger.
    Gentleman.   As I learn'd,
The night before there was no purpose in them
Of this remove.
    Kent.   Hail to thee, noble master!
    Lear. Ha!
Mak'st thou this shame thy pastime?
    Kent.   No, my lord.
    Fool. Ha, ha! he wears cruel garters. Horses
are tied by the heads, dogs and bears by the neck,
monkeys by the loins, and men by the legs; when a
man 's over-lusty at legs, then he wears wooden 10
nether-stocks.
    Lear. What 's he that hath so much thy place mis-
        took
To set thee here?

Kent.   It is both he and she,
Your son and daughter.
   Lear. No.
   Kent. Yes.
   Lear. No, I say.
   Kent. I say, yea.
   Lear. No, no, they would not.
   Kent. Yes, they have.   20
   Lear. By Jupiter, I swear, no !
   Kent. By Juno, I swear, ay !
   Lear.   They durst not do 't ;
They could not, would not do 't ; 't is worse than
      murther
To do upon respect such violent outrage.
Resolve me with all modest haste which way
Thou mightst deserve, or they impose, this usage,
Coming from us.
   Kent.   My lord, when at their home
I did commend your highness' letters to them,
Ere I was risen from the place that show'd
My duty kneeling, came there a reeking post,   30
Stew'd in his haste, half breathless, panting forth
From Goneril his mistress salutations,
Deliver'd letters, spite of intermission,
Which presently they read ; on whose contents
They summon'd up their meiny, straight took horse,
Commanded me to follow and attend
The leisure of their answer, gave me cold looks ;
And meeting here the other messenger,

Whose welcome I perceiv'd had poison'd mine —
Being the very fellow which of late   40
Display'd so saucily against your highness —
Having more man than wit about me, drew ;
He rais'd the house with loud and coward cries.
Your son and daughter found this trespass worth
The shame which here it suffers.

Fool. Winter 's not gone yet, if the wild geese
fly that way.

        Fathers that wear rags
          Do make their children blind ;
        But fathers that bear bags   50
          Shall see their children kind. —

But, for all this, thou shalt have as many dolours for
thy daughters as thou canst tell in a year.

Lear. O, how this mother swells up toward my heart !
Hysterica passio, down, thou climbing sorrow,
Thy element 's below ! — Where is this daughter ?

Kent. With the earl, sir, here within.

Lear. Follow me not ; stay here.   [*Exit.*

Gentleman. Made you no more offence but what you
    speak of ?

Kent. None. —   60
How chance the king comes with so small a number ?

Fool. An thou hadst been set i' the stocks for that
question, thou 'dst well deserved it.

Kent. Why, fool ?

Fool. We 'll set thee to school to an ant, to teach
thee there 's no labouring i' the winter. All that

follow their noses are led by their eyes but blind
men ; and there 's not a nose among twenty but can
smell him that 's stinking. Let go thy hold when a
great wheel runs down a hill, lest it break thy neck 70
with following it ; but the great one that goes upward,
let him draw thee after. When a wise man gives the
better counsel, give me mine again ; I would have
none but knaves follow it, since a fool gives it.

       That sir which serves and seeks for gain,
          And follows but for form,
       Will pack when it begins to rain,
          And leave thee in the storm.
       But I will tarry ; the fool will stay,
          And let the wise man fly.   80
       The knave turns fool that runs away ;
          The fool no knave, perdy.
  Kent. Where learned you this, fool ?
  Fool. Not i' the stocks, fool !

       Re-enter LEAR, *with* GLOSTER

  Lear. Deny to speak with me ?   They are sick ? they
      are weary ?
They have travell'd all the night ?   Mere fetches,
The images of revolt and flying off.
Fetch me a better answer.
    Gloster.   My dear lord,
You know the fiery quality of the duke,
How unremovable and fix'd he is   90
In his own course.

Lear. Vengeance ! plague ! death ! confusion !
Fiery ? what quality ? Why, Gloster, Gloster,
I'd speak with the Duke of Cornwall and his wife.
    Gloster. Well, my good lord, I have inform'd them so.
    Lear. Inform'd them ! Dost thou understand me,
      man ?
    Gloster. Ay, my good lord.
    Lear. The king would speak with Cornwall; the
      dear father
Would with his daughter speak, commands her service.
Are they inform'd of this ? My breath and blood !   100
Fiery ? the fiery duke ? Tell the hot duke that —
No, but not yet ; may be he is not well.
Infirmity doth still neglect all office
Whereto our health is bound ; we are not ourselves
When nature being oppress'd commands the mind
To suffer with the body. I 'll forbear,
And am fallen out with my more headier will,
To take the indispos'd and sickly fit
For the sound man. — Death on my state ! wherefore
Should he sit here ? This act persuades me   110
That this remotion of the duke and her
Is practice only. Give me my servant forth.
Go tell the duke and 's wife I 'd speak with them,
Now, presently ; bid them come forth and hear me,
Or at their chamber-door I 'll beat the drum
Till it cry sleep to death.
    Gloster. I would have all well betwixt you.   [*Exit.*
    Lear. O me, my heart, my rising heart ! But, down !

Fool. Cry to it, nuncle, as the cockney did to the
eels when she put 'em i' the paste alive ; she knapped 120
'em o' the coxcombs with a stick, and cried ' Down,
wantons, down !' 'T was her brother that, in pure
kindness to his horse, buttered his hay.

Re-enter GLOSTER, *with* CORNWALL, REGAN, *and*
Servants.

Lear. Good morrow to you both.
Cornwall.   Hail to your grace !
                              [*Kent is set at liberty.*
Regan. I am glad to see your highness.
Lear. Regan, I think you are ; I know what reason
I have to think so.   If thou shouldst not be glad,
I would divorce me from thy mother's tomb,
Sepulchring an adulteress. — [*To Kent*] O, are you
      free ?
Some other time for that. — Beloved Regan,   130
Thy sister 's naught.   O Regan, she hath tied
Sharp-tooth'd unkindness, like a vulture, here !
                              [*Points to his heart.*
I can scarce speak to thee ; thou 'lt not believe
With how deprav'd a quality — O Regan !
Regan. I pray you, sir, take patience ; I have hope
You less know how to value her desert
Than she to scant her duty.
Lear.   Say, how is that ?
Regan. I cannot think my sister in the least

Would fail her obligation; if, sir, perchance
She have restrain'd the riots of your followers,   140
'T is on such ground and to such wholesome end
As clears her from all blame.

Lear. My curses on her !

Regan.   O, sir, you are old;
Nature in you stands on the very verge
Of her confine : you should be rul'd and led
By some discretion that discerns your state
Better than you yourself.   Therefore I pray you
That to our sister you do make return ;
Say you have wrong'd her, sir.

Lear.   Ask her forgiveness ?
Do you but mark how this becomes the house :   150
' Dear daughter, I confess that I am old ;
Age is unnecessary : on my knees I beg
That you 'll vouchsafe me raiment, bed, and food.'

Regan. Good sir, no more ; these are unsightly tricks.
Return you to my sister.

Lear.   Never, Regan !
She hath abated me of half my train,
Look'd black upon me, strook me with her tongue,
Most serpent-like, upon the very heart.
All the stor'd vengeances of heaven fall
On her ingrateful top !   Strike her young bones,   160
You taking airs, with lameness !

Cornwall.   Fie, sir, fie !

Lear. You nimble lightnings, dart your blinding
      flames

Into her scornful eyes !   Infect her beauty,
You fen-suck'd fogs, drawn by the powerful sun,
To fall and blast her pride !
    Regan. O the blest gods ! so will you wish on me,
When the rash mood is on.
    Lear. No, Regan, thou shalt never have my curse ;
Thy tender-hefted nature shall not give
Thee o'er to harshness.   Her eyes are fierce, but thine
Do comfort and not burn.   'T is not in thee   171
To grudge my pleasures, to cut off my train,
To bandy hasty words, to scant my sizes,
And in conclusion to oppose the bolt
Against my coming in.   Thou better know'st
The offices of nature, bond of childhood,
Effects of courtesy, dues of gratitude ;
Thy half o' the kingdom hast thou not forgot,
Wherein I thee endow'd.
    Regan.   Good sir, to the purpose.
    Lear. Who put my man i' the stocks ? [*Tucket within.*
    Cornwall.   What trumpet 's that ?
    Regan. I know 't, — my sister's ; this approves her
        letter,   181
That she would soon be here. —

                Enter OSWALD

                        Is your lady come ?
    Lear. This is a slave, whose easy-borrow'd pride
Dwells in the fickle grace of her he follows. —
Out, varlet, from my sight !

Cornwall.   What means your grace ?
Lear. Who stock'd my servant ? — Regan, I have
     good hope
Thou didst not know on 't. — Who comes here ? —

Enter GONERIL

                                   O heavens,
If you do love old men, if your sweet sway
Allow obedience, if yourselves are old,
Make it your cause ; send down, and take my part ! —
Art not asham'd to look upon this beard ? —   191
O Regan, will you take her by the hand ?
     Goneril. Why not by the hand, sir ?   How have I
          offended ?
All 's not offence that indiscretion finds
And dotage terms so.
     Lear.   O sides, you are too tough ;
Will you yet hold ? — How came my man i' the
     stocks ?
     Cornwall. I set him there, sir ; but his own disorders
Deserv'd much less advancement.
     Lear.   You ! did you ?
     Regan. I pray you, father, being weak, seem so.
If, till the expiration of your month,   200
You will return and sojourn with my sister,
Dismissing half your train, come then to me ;
I am now from home, and out of that provision
Which shall be needful for your entertainment.
     Lear. Return to her, and fifty men dismiss'd ?

No, rather I abjure all roofs, and choose
To wage against the enmity o' the air,
To be a comrade with the wolf and owl. —
Necessity's sharp pinch! — Return with her?
Why, the hot-blooded France, that dowerless took   210
Our youngest born, — I could as well be brought
To knee his throne, and, squire-like, pension beg
To keep base life afoot.   Return with her?
Persuade me rather to be slave and sumpter
To this detested groom.   [*Pointing at Oswald.*
      Goneril.   At your choice, sir.
      Lear.   I prithee, daughter, do not make me mad.
I will not trouble thee, my child ; farewell.
We 'll no more meet, no more see one another.
But yet thou art my flesh, my blood, my daughter,
Or rather a disease that 's in my flesh,   220
Which I must needs call mine ; thou art a boil,
A plague-sore, an embossed carbuncle,
In my corrupted blood.   But I 'll not chide thee ;
Let shame come when it will, I do not call it ;
I do not bid the thunder-bearer shoot,
Nor tell tales of thee to high-judging Jove.
Mend when thou canst ; be better at thy leisure.
I can be patient ; I can stay with Regan,
I and my hundred knights.
      Regan.   Not altogether so ;
I look'd not for you yet, nor am provided   230
For your fit welcome.   Give ear, sir, to my sister ;
For those that mingle reason with your passion

Must be content to think you old, and so —
But she knows what she does.
   Lear.   Is this well spoken?
   Regan. I dare avouch it, sir. What, fifty followers?
Is it not well? What should you need of more?
Yea, or so many, sith that both charge and danger
Speak 'gainst so great a number? { How, in one house,
Should many people under two commands
Hold amity? 'T is hard, almost impossible. }   240
   Goneril. Why might not you, my lord, receive at-
       tendance
From those that she calls servants or from mine?
   Regan. Why not, my lord? If then they chanc'd to
       slack ye,
We could control them. If you will come to me, —
For now I spy a danger, — I entreat you
To bring but five and twenty ; to no more
Will I give place or notice.
   Lear. I gave you all —
   Regan.   And in good time you gave it.
   Lear. Made you my guardians, my depositaries,
But kept a reservation to be follow'd   250
With such a number. What, must I come to you
With five and twenty, Regan ? said you so ?
   Regan. And speak 't again, my lord ; no more with
      me.
   Lear. Those wicked creatures yet do look well-
      favour'd
When others are more wicked ; not being the worst

Stands in some rank of praise.—[*To Goneril*] I 'll go
    with thee ;
Thy fifty yet doth double five and twenty,
And thou art twice her love.
    Goneril.   Hear me, my lord ;
What need you five and twenty, ten, or five,
To follow in a house where twice so many   260
Have a command to tend you ?
    Regan.   What need one ?
    Lear. O, reason not the need ; our basest beggars
Are in the poorest thing superfluous.
Allow not nature more than nature needs,
Man's life is cheap as beast's.   Thou art a lady ;
If only to go warm were gorgeous,
Why, nature needs not what thou gorgeous wear'st,
Which scarcely keeps thee warm.   But for true need —
You heavens, give me that patience, patience I need !
You see me here, you gods, a poor old man,   270
As full of grief as age ; wretched in both.
If it be you that stirs these daughters' hearts
Against their father, fool me not so much
To bear it tamely ; touch me with noble anger,
And let not women's weapons, water-drops,
Stain my man's cheeks ! — No, you unnatural hags,
I will have such revenges on you both,
That all the world shall — I will do such things —
What they are, yet I know not ; but they shall be
The terrors of the earth.   You think I 'll weep ;   280
No, I 'll not weep.
            KING LEAR — 6

I have full cause of weeping, but this heart
Shall break into a hundred thousand flaws
Or ere I 'll weep. ⊢ O fool, I shall go mad !
     [*Exeunt Lear,Gloster, Kent, and Fool.*
     Storm and tempest.

 Cornwall. Let us withdraw ; 't will be a storm.

 Regan. This house is little ; the old man and 's
  people
Cannot be well bestow'd.

 Goneril. 'T is his own blame ; hath put himself from
  rest
And must needs taste his folly.

 Regan. For his particular, I 'll receive him gladly, ₂₉₀
But not one follower.

 Goneril.   So am I purpos'd.
Where is my lord of Gloster ?

 Cornwall. Follow'd the old man forth ; he is return'd.

Re-enter GLOSTER

 Gloster. The king is in high rage.

 Cornwall.   Whither is he going ?

 Gloster. He calls to horse, but will I know not
  whither.

 Cornwall. 'T is best to give him way ; he leads himself.

 Goneril. My lord, entreat him by no means to stay.

 Gloster. Alack ! the night comes on, and the high
  winds

Do sorely ruffle ; for many miles about
There 's scarce a bush.
  Regan.   O, sir, to wilful men, 300
The injuries that they themselves procure
Must be their schoolmasters.   Shut up your doors.
He is attended with a desperate train ;
And what they may incense him to, being apt
To have his ear abus'd, wisdom bids fear.
  Cornwall. Shut up your doors, my lord, 't is a wild
    night ;
My Regan counsels well.   Come out o' the storm.
              [Exeunt.

ACT III

SCENE I. *A Heath*

Storm still. Enter KENT *and a* Gentleman, *meeting*

Kent. Who 's there, besides foul weather ?

Gentleman. One minded like the weather, most un-
quietly.

Kent. I know you. Where 's the king ?

Gentleman. Contending with the fretful elements ;
Bids the wind blow the earth into the sea,

Or swell the curled waters 'bove the main,
That things might change or cease; tears his white
    hair,
Which the impetuous blasts, with eyeless rage,
Catch in their fury, and make nothing of;
Strives in his little world of man to out-scorn   10
The to-and-fro-conflicting wind and rain.
This night, wherein the cub-drawn bear would couch,
The lion and the belly-pinched wolf
Keep their fur dry, unbonneted he runs,
And bids what will take all.
    Kent.   But who is with him?
    Gentleman. None but the fool, who labours to out-
    jest
His heart-strook injuries.
    Kent.   Sir, I do know you,
And dare, upon the warrant of my note,
Commend a dear thing to you. There is division,
Although as yet the face of it is cover'd   20
With mutual cunning, 'twixt Albany and Cornwall,
Who have — as who have not that their great stars
Thron'd and set high? — servants, who seem   no
    less,
Which are to France the spies and speculations
Intelligent of our state. What hath been seen,
Either in snuffs and packings of the dukes,
Or the hard rein which both of them have borne
Against the old kind king, or something deeper,
Whereof perchance these are but furnishings, —

But, true it is, from France there comes a power ₃₀
Into this scatter'd kingdom, who already,
Wise in our negligence, have secret feet
In some of our best ports, and are at point
To show their open banner.   Now to you:
If on my credit you dare build so far
To make your speed to Dover, you shall find
Some that will thank you, making just report
Of how unnatural and bemadding sorrow
The king hath cause to plain.
I am a gentleman of blood and breeding, ₄₀
And from some knowledge and assurance offer
This office to you.
 Gentleman.   I will talk further with you.
 Kent.   No, do not.
For confirmation that I am much more
Than my out-wall, open this purse and take
What it contains.   If you shall see Cordelia, —
As fear not but you shall, — show her this ring;
And she will tell you who that fellow is
That yet you do not know.   Fie on this storm !
I will go seek the king.
 Gentleman.   Give me your hand; ₅₀
Have you no more to say?
 Kent.   Few words, but, to effect, more than all yet:
That, when we have found the king, — in which your
   pain
That way, I 'll this, — he that first lights on him
Holla the other.   *[Exeunt severally.*

SCENE II. *Another Part of the Heath. Storm still*

Enter LEAR *and* Fool

Lear. Blow, winds, and crack your cheeks! rage!
    blow!
You cataracts and hurricanoes, spout
Till you have drench'd our steeples, drown'd the cocks!
You sulphurous and thought-executing fires,
Vaunt-couriers of oak-cleaving thunderbolts,
Singe my white head! And thou, all-shaking thunder,
Strike flat the thick rotundity o' the world!
Crack nature's moulds, all germens spill at once
That make ingrateful man!

Fool. O nuncle, court holy-water in a dry house 10
is better than this rain-water out o' door. Good
nuncle, in; ask thy daughters' blessing; here 's a
night pities neither wise men nor fools.

Lear. Rumble thy bellyful! Spit, fire! spout, rain!
Nor rain, wind, thunder, fire, are my daughters.
I tax not you, you elements, with unkindness;
I never gave you kingdom, call'd you children,
You owe me no subscription. Then let fall
Your horrible pleasure; here I stand, your slave,
A poor, infirm, weak, and despis'd old man.   20
But yet I call you servile ministers,
That will with two pernicious daughters join
Your high-engender'd battles 'gainst a head
So old and white as this. O! O! 't is foul!

Fool. He that has a house to put 's head in has a good head-piece.

> The man that makes his toe
>> What he his heart should make
> Shall of a corn cry woe,
>> And turn his sleep to wake. 30

For there was never yet fair woman but she made mouths in a glass.

Lear. No, I will be the pattern of all patience; I will say nothing.

Enter KENT

Kent. Who 's there?

Fool. Marry, here 's a wise man and a fool.

Kent. Alas, sir, are you here? Things that love night Love not such nights as these; the wrathful skies Gallow the very wanderers of the dark, And make them keep their caves. Since I was man, 40 Such sheets of fire, such bursts of horrid thunder, Such groans of roaring wind and rain, I never Remember to have heard; man's nature cannot carry The affliction nor the fear.

Lear. Let the great gods, That keep this dreadful pudder o'er our heads, Find out their enemies now. — Tremble, thou wretch, That hast within thee undivulged crimes, Unwhipp'd of justice. — Hide thee, thou bloody hand, Thou perjur'd, and thou simular of virtue That art incestuous. — Caitiff, to pieces shake, 50 That under covert and convenient seeming

Has practis'd on man's life. — Close pent-up guilts,
Rive your concealing continents and cry
These dreadful summoners grace.   I am a man
More sinn'd against than sinning.
  Kent.   Alack, bare-headed !
Gracious my lord, hard by here is a hovel ;
Some friendship will it lend you 'gainst the tempest.
Repose you there, while I to this hard house —
More harder than the stones whereof 't is rais'd,
Which even but now, demanding after you,   60
Denied me to come in — return, and force
Their scanted courtesy.
  Lear.   My wits begin to turn. —
Come on, my boy ; how dost, my boy ? art cold ?
I am cold myself. — Where is this straw, my fellow ? —
The art of our necessities is strange,
That can make vile things precious. — Come, your
   hovel. —
Poor fool and knave, I have one part in my heart
That 's sorry yet for thee.
  Fool. [Sings] *He that has and a little tiny wit,*
    With hey, ho, the wind and the rain, 70
     Must make content with his fortunes fit,
    For the rain it raineth every day.
  Lear. True, boy. — Come, bring us to this hovel.
        [*Exeunt Lear and Kent.*
  Fool. I 'll speak a prophecy ere I go :
   When priests are more in word than matter ;
   When brewers mar their malt with water ;

When nobles are their tailors' tutors;
No heretics burn'd, but wenches' suitors;
When every case in law is right;
No squire in debt, nor no poor knight;   80
When slanders do not live in tongues,
Nor cutpurses come not to throngs;
Then shall the realm of Albion
Come to great confusion.
Then comes the time, who lives to see 't,
That going shall be us'd with feet.
This prophecy Merlin shall make; for I live before
his time.   [*Exit.*

SCENE III.   *Gloster's Castle*

Enter GLOSTER *and* EDMUND

Gloster. Alack, alack, Edmund, I like not this unnatural dealing.   When I desired their leave that I
might pity him, they took from me the use of mine
own house; charged me, on pain of perpetual displeasure, neither to speak of him, entreat for him,
or any way sustain him.

Edmund. Most savage and unnatural !

Gloster. Go to; say you nothing.   There 's a
division between the dukes, and a worse matter than
that.   I have received a letter this night; 't is dan- 10
gerous to be spoken; I have locked the letter in my
closet.   These injuries the king now bears will be
revenged home; there is part of a power already

footed; we must incline to the king. I will look
him, and privily relieve him; go you and maintain
talk with the duke, that my charity be not of him perceived. If he ask for me, I am ill and gone to bed.
If I die for it, as no less is threatened me, the king
my old master must be relieved. There is strange
things toward, Edmund; pray you, be careful.   [*Exit.*

Edmund. This courtesy, forbid thee, shall the duke
Instantly know, and of that letter too.   22
This seems a fair deserving, and must draw me
That which my father loses, — no less than all.
The younger rises when the old doth fall.   [*Exit.*

SCENE IV. *The Heath. Before a Hovel*

Enter LEAR, KENT, *and* Fool

Kent. Here is the place, my lord; good my lord,
     enter.
The tyranny of the open night 's too rough
For nature to endure.   [*Storm still.*
     Lear.   Let me alone.
     Kent. Good my lord, enter here.
     Lear.   Wilt break my heart?
     Kent. I had rather break mine own. Good my
          lord, enter.
     Lear. Thou think'st 't is much that this conten-
          tious storm
Invades us to the skin; so 't is to thee,
But where the greater malady is fix'd,

The lesser is scarce felt. Thou 'dst shun a bear;
But if thy flight lay toward the roaring sea,   10
Thou 'dst meet the bear i' the mouth. When the
    mind 's free
The body 's delicate; the tempest in my mind
Doth from my senses take all feeling else
Save what beats there. Filial ingratitude!
Is it not as this mouth should tear this hand
For lifting food to 't? But I will punish home.
No, I will weep no more. In such a night
To shut me out! Pour on; I will endure.
In such a night as this! O Regan, Goneril!
Your old kind father, whose frank heart gave all, — 20
O, that way madness lies! let me shun that;
No more of that!
    Kent.   Good my lord, enter here.
    Lear. Prithee, go in thyself; seek thine own ease.
This tempest will not give me leave to ponder
On things would hurt me more. But I 'll go in. —
In, boy; go first. — You houseless poverty, —
Nay, get thee in. I 'll pray, and then I 'll sleep. —
                       [*Fool goes in.*
Poor naked wretches, wheresoe'er you are,
That bide the pelting of this pitiless storm,
How shall your houseless heads and unfed sides,   30
Your loop'd and window'd raggedness, defend you
From seasons such as these? — O, I have ta'en
Too little care of this! — Take physic, pomp;
Expose thyself to feel what wretches feel,

That thou mayst shake the superflux to them
And show the heavens more just.

Edgar. [*Within*] Fathom and half, fathom and
half! Poor Tom!   [*The Fool runs out from the hovel.*

Fool. Come not in here, nuncle, here 's a spirit.
Help me, help me!   40

Kent. Give me thy hand. — Who 's there?

Fool. A spirit, a spirit! he says his name 's poor
Tom.

Kent. What art thou that dost grumble there i'
the straw?   Come forth.

Enter EDGAR *disguised as a madman*

Edgar. Away! the foul fiend follows me! Through
the sharp hawthorn blow the winds. Hum! go to
thy bed, and warm thee.

Lear. Didst thou give all to thy daughters?   And
art thou come to this?   50

Edgar. Who gives any thing to poor Tom? whom
the foul fiend hath led through fire and through
flame, through ford and whirlpool, o'er bog and
quagmire; that hath laid knives under his pillow,
and halters in his pew; set ratsbane by his por-
ridge; made him proud of heart, to ride on a bay
trotting-horse over four-inched bridges, to course his
own shadow for a traitor.   Bless thy five wits! Tom 's
a-cold.   O, do de, do de, do de!   Bless thee from
whirlwinds, star-blasting, and taking!   Do poor 60
Tom some charity, whom the foul fiend vexes.

There could I have him now, and there, and there
again, and there.   [*Storm still.*

    Lear. What, have his daughters brought him to this
        pass ? —
Couldst thou save nothing? Wouldst thou give 'em all?
    Fool. Nay, he reserved a blanket, else we had been
all shamed.
    Lear. Now, all the plagues that in the pendulous air
Hang fated o'er men's faults light on thy daughters !
    Kent. He hath no daughters, sir.   70
    Lear. Death, traitor ! nothing could have subdued
        nature
To such a lowness but his unkind daughters.
Is it the fashion that discarded fathers
Should have thus little mercy on their flesh ?
Judicious punishment ! 't was this flesh begot
Those pelican daughters.
    Edgar. Pillicock sat on Pillicock-hill ;
Halloo, halloo, loo, loo !
    Fool. This cold night will turn us all to fools and
madmen.   80
    Edgar. Take heed o' the foul fiend ; obey thy
parents ; keep thy word justly ; swear not ; commit
not with man's sworn spouse ; set not thy sweet
heart on proud array. Tom 's a-cold.
    Lear. What hast thou been ?
    Edgar. A serving-man, proud in heart and mind ;
that curled my hair, wore gloves in my cap, swore
as many oaths as I spake words, and broke them in

the sweet face of heaven; one that slept in the con-
triving of lust and waked to do it. Wine loved I 90
deeply, dice dearly, and in woman out-paramoured
the Turk; false of heart, light of ear, bloody of
hand; hog in sloth, fox in stealth, wolf in greediness,
dog in madness, lion in prey. Let not the creaking
of shoes nor the rustling of silks betray thy poor
heart to woman. Keep thy foot out of brothels, thy
pen from lenders' books, and defy the foul fiend. —
Still through the hawthorn blows the cold wind;
says suum, mun, nonny. Dolphin my boy, my boy,
sessa! let him trot by.   [*Storm still.*

  Lear. Thou wert better in thy grave than to an- 101
swer with thy uncovered body this extremity of the
skies. Is man no more than this? Consider him
well. Thou owest the worm no silk, the beast no
hide, the sheep no wool, the cat no perfume. Ha!
here 's three on 's are sophisticated! Thou art the
thing itself; unaccommodated man is no more but
such a poor, bare, forked animal as thou art. — Off,
off, you lendings! come, unbutton here.

  Fool. Prithee, nuncle, be contented; 't is a 110
naughty night to swim in. Now a little fire in a
wide field were like an old lecher's heart, a small
spark, all the rest on 's body cold. — Look, here
comes a walking fire.

  Edgar. This is the foul Flibbertigibbet. He begins at curfew and walks at first cock; he gives the
web and the pin, squints the eye, and makes the

hare-lip ; mildews the white wheat and hurts the poor creature of earth.

Saint Withold footed thrice the old ;   12c

He met the nightmare and her nine-fold ;

Bid her alight,

And her troth plight,

And, aroint thee, witch, aroint thee !

Enter GLOSTER, *with a torch.*

Kent. How fares your grace ?

Lear. What 's he ?

Kent. Who 's there ? What is 't you seek ?

Gloster. What are you there ? Your names ?

Edgar. Poor Tom, that eats the swimming frog, the toad, the tadpole, the wall-newt and the water ; 13o that in the fury of his heart, when the foul fiend rages, eats cow-dung for sallets; swallows the old rat and the ditch-dog ; drinks the green mantle of the standing pool ; who is whipped from tithing to tithing, and stocked, punished, and imprisoned ; who hath three suits to his back, six shirts to his body ;

Horse to ride, and weapon to wear ;

But mice and rats and such small deer

Have been Tom's food for seven long year.

Beware my follower. — Peace, Smulkin ! peace, thou 140 fiend !

Gloster. What, hath your grace no better company ?

Edgar. The prince of darkness is a gentleman ; Modo he 's called, and Mahu.

Gloster. Our flesh and blood, my lord, is grown so vile
That it doth hate what gets it.

Edgar. Poor Tom 's a-cold.

Gloster. Go in with me ; my duty cannot suffer
To obey in all your daughters' hard commands.
Though their injunction be to bar my doors　　　150
And let this tyrannous night take hold upon you,
Yet have I ventur'd to come seek you out,
And bring you where both fire and food is ready.

Lear. First let me talk with this philosopher. —
What is the cause of thunder ?

Kent. Good my lord, take his offer ; go into the
　　　house.

Lear. I 'll talk a word with this same learned
　　　Theban. —
What is your study ?

Edgar. How to prevent the fiend and to kill vermin.

Lear. Let me ask you one word in private.　　　160

Kent. Importune him once more to go, my lord ;
His wits begin to unsettle.

Gloster.　　　　　　　Canst thou blame him ?
　　　　　　　　　　　[*Storm still.*
His daughters seek his death. Ah, that good Kent !
He said it would be thus, poor banish'd man !
Thou say'st the king grows mad ; I 'll tell thee, friend,
I am almost mad myself. I had a son,
Now outlaw'd from my blood ; he sought my life,
But lately, very late. I lov'd him, friend,
No father his son dearer ; true to tell thee,

KING LEAR — 7

The grief hath craz'd my wits. What a night 's this!—
I do beseech your grace,—
  Lear.   O, cry you mercy, sir.— 171
Noble philosopher, your company.
  Edgar. Tom 's a-cold.
  Gloster. In, fellow, there, into the hovel; keep thee
   warm.
  Lear. Come, let 's in all.
  Kent.   This way, my lord.
  Lear.   With him;
I will keep still with my philosopher.
  Kent. Good my lord, soothe him; let him take the
   fellow.
  Gloster. Take him you on.
  Kent. Sirrah, come on ; go along with us.
  Lear. Come, good Athenian.   180
  Gloster. No words, no words; hush!
  Edgar. *Child Rowland to the dark tower came ;*
    His word was still,— Fie, foh, and fum,
    I smell the blood of a British man. [*Exeunt.*

SCENE V. *Gloster's Castle*

Enter CORNWALL *and* EDMUND

 Cornwall. I will have my revenge ere I depart his
house.
 Edmund. How, my lord, I may be censured, that
nature thus gives way to loyalty, something fears me
to think of.

Cornwall. I now perceive it was not altogether your brother's evil disposition made him seek his death, but a provoking merit, set a-work by a reprovable badness in himself.

Edmund. How malicious is my fortune, that I 10 must repent to be just ! This is the letter he spoke of, which approves him an intelligent party to the advantages of France. O heavens ! that this treason were not, or not I the detector !

Cornwall. Go with me to the duchess.

Edmund. If the matter of this paper be certain, you have mighty business in hand.

Cornwall. True or false, it hath made thee earl of Gloster. Seek out where thy father is, that he may be ready for our apprehension.   20

Edmund. [*Aside*] If I find him comforting the king, it will stuff his suspicion more fully. — I will persever in my course of loyalty, though the conflict be sore between that and my blood.

Cornwall. I will lay trust upon thee, and thou shalt find a dearer father in my love.   [*Exeunt.*

SCENE VI. *A Chamber in a Farmhouse adjoining the Castle*

Enter GLOSTER, LEAR, KENT, Fool, *and* EDGAR

Gloster. Here is better than the open air ; take it thankfully. I will piece out the comfort with what addition I can. I will not be long from you.

Kent. All the power of his wits have given way to his impatience. The gods reward your kindness!

[*Exit Gloster.*

Edgar. Frateretto calls me, and tells me Nero is an angler in the lake of darkness. — Pray, innocent, and beware the foul fiend.

Fool. Prithee, nuncle, tell me whether a madman be a gentleman or a yeoman?   10

Lear. A king, a king!

Fool. No, he 's a yeoman that has a gentleman to his son; for he 's a mad yeoman that sees his son a gentleman before him.

Lear. To have a thousand with red burning spits Come hizzing in upon 'em, —

Edgar. The foul fiend bites my back.

Fool. He 's mad that trusts in the tameness of a wolf, a horse's health, a boy's love, or a whore's oath.

Lear. It shall be done; I will arraign them straight.— 20 [*To Edgar*] Come, sit thou here, most learned jus-
        ticer. —

[*To the Fool*] Thou, sapient sir, sit here. — Now, you
        she foxes!

Edgar. Look, where he stands and glares! — Wantest thou eyes at trial, madam?

      Come o'er the bourn, Bessy, to me.

Fool.   *Her boat hath a leak,*

        And she must not speak

       Why she dares not come over to thee.

Edgar. The foul fiend haunts poor Tom in the

voice of a nightingale. Hoppedance cries in Tom's 30
belly for two white herring. — Croak not, black
angel; I have no food for thee.

Kent. How do you, sir? Stand you not so amaz'd.
Will you lie down and rest upon the cushions?

Lear. I 'll see their trial first. — Bring in their evi-
     dence. —

[*To Edgar*] Thou robed man of justice, take thy
     place, —

[*To the Fool*] And thou, his yoke-fellow of equity,
Bench by his side. — [*To Kent*] You are o' the commis-
     sion,

Sit you too.

     Edgar. Let us deal justly.   40

         Sleepest or wakest thou, jolly shepherd?
           Thy sheep be in the corn;
           And for one blast of thy minikin mouth,
           Thy sheep shall take no harm.

Pur! the cat is gray.

Lear. Arraign her first; 't is Goneril. I here
take my oath before this honourable assembly, she
kicked the poor king her father.

Fool. Come hither, mistress. Is your name
Goneril?   50

     Lear. She cannot deny it.

     Fool. Cry you mercy, I took you for a joint-stool.

     Lear. And here 's another, whose warp'd looks pro-
     claim

What store her heart is made on. — Stop her there!

Arms, arms, sword, fire! Corruption in the place!—
False justicer, why hast thou let her scape?

Edgar. Bless thy five wits!

Kent. O pity!— Sir, where is the patience now,
That you so oft have boasted to retain?

Edgar. [*Aside*] My tears begin to take his part so
  much,   60
They mar my counterfeiting.

Lear. The little dogs and all,
Tray, Blanch, and Sweetheart, see, they bark at me.

Edgar. Tom will throw his head at them.—
Avaunt, you curs!

   Be thy mouth or black or white,
   Tooth that poisons if it bite;
   Mastiff, greyhound, mongrel grim,
   Hound or spaniel, brach or lym,
   Or bobtail tike or trundle-tail,   70
   Tom will make him weep and wail;
   For, with throwing thus my head,
   Dogs leap'd the hatch, and all are fled.
Do de, de, de! Sessa! Come, march to wakes and
fairs and market-towns. Poor Tom, thy horn is dry.

Lear. Then let them anatomize Regan; see what
breeds about her heart. Is there any cause in nature
that makes these hard hearts?—[*To Edgar*] You,
sir, I entertain for one of my hundred; only I do not
like the fashion of your garments. You will say so
they are Persian; but let them be changed.

Kent. Now, good my lord, lie here and rest awhile.

Lear. Make no noise, make no noise ; draw the
curtains ; so, so.   We 'll go to supper i' the morning.

Fool. And I 'll go to bed at noon.

Re-enter GLOSTER

Gloster. Come hither, friend ; where is the king
    my master ?

Kent. Here, sir ; but trouble him not, his wits are
    gone.

Gloster. Good friend, I prithee, take him in thy
    arms ;

I have o'erheard a plot of death upon him.

There is a litter ready ; lay him in 't,   90

And drive toward Dover, friend, where thou shalt meet

Both welcome and protection.   Take up thy master.

If thou shouldst dally half an hour, his life,

With thine, and all that offer to defend him,

Stand in assured loss.   Take up, take up ;

And follow me, that will to some provision

Give thee quick conduct.

    Kent.   Oppress'd nature sleeps.

This rest might yet have balm'd thy broken sinews,

Which, if convenience will not allow,

Stand in hard cure. — [*To the Fool*] Come, help to
    bear thy master ;   100

Thou must not stay behind.

    Gloster.   Come, come, away.

[*Exeunt all but Edgar.*

Edgar. When we our betters see bearing our woes,

We scarcely think our miseries our foes.
Who alone suffers suffers most i' the mind,
Leaving free things and happy shows behind;
But then the mind much sufferance doth o'erskip,
When grief hath mates, and bearing fellowship.
How light and portable my pain seems now,
When that which makes me bend makes the king bow,
He childed as I father'd! Tom, away!   110
Mark the high noises, and thyself bewray,
When false opinion, whose wrong thoughts defile thee,
In thy just proof repeals and reconciles thee.
What will hap more to-night, safe scape the king!
Lurk, lurk.   [*Exit.*

SCENE VII. *Gloster's Castle*

Enter CORNWALL, REGAN, GONERIL, EDMUND, *and*
Servants

Cornwall. [*To Goneril*] Post speedily to my lord
your husband; show him this letter; the army of
France is landed. — Seek out the villain Gloster.

          [*Exeunt some of the Servants.*

Regan. Hang him instantly.

Goneril. Pluck out his eyes.

Cornwall. Leave him to my displeasure — Edmund, keep you our sister company. The revenges
we are bound to take upon your traitorous father
are not fit for your beholding. Advise the duke,
where you are going, to a most festinate prepara- 10
tion; we are bound to the like. Our posts shall be

swift and intelligent betwixt us. — Farewell, dear
sister. — Farewell, my lord of Gloster. —

Enter OSWALD

How now! where 's the king?

Oswald. My lord of Gloster hath convey'd him hence.
Some five or six and thirty of his knights,
Hot questrists after him, met him at gate ;
Who, with some other of the lord's dependants,
Are gone with him toward Dover, where they boast
To have well-armed friends.

Cornwall.　　　　　　Get horses for your mistress.

Goneril. Farewell, sweet lord, and sister.　　　21

Cornwall. Edmund, farewell. —

　　　　　　[*Exeunt Goneril, Edmund, and Oswald.*
　　　　　　　Go seek the traitor Gloster.
Pinion him like a thief, bring him before us. —

　　　　　　　　　　[*Exeunt other Servants.*
Though well we may not pass upon his life
Without the form of justice, yet our power
Shall do a courtesy to our wrath, which men
May blame but not control. — Who 's there? the traitor?

Enter GLOSTER, *brought in by two or three*

Regan. Ingrateful fox! 't is he.

Cornwall. Bind fast his corky arms.

Gloster. What means your graces? — Good my
　　　friends, consider　　　　　　　　　30
You are my guests ; do me no foul play, friends.

Cornwall. Bind him, I say.

Regan.   Hard, hard. — O filthy traitor !

Gloster. Unmerciful lady as you are, I 'm none.

Cornwall. To this chair bind him. — Villain, thou
     shalt find —   [*Regan plucks his beard.*

Gloster. By the kind gods, 't is most ignobly done
To pluck me by the beard.

Regan. So white, and such a traitor !

Gloster.   Naughty lady,
These hairs which thou dost ravish from my chin
Will quicken and accuse thee.   I am your host ;
With robbers' hands my hospitable favours   40
You should not ruffle thus.   What will you do ?

Cornwall. Come, sir, what letters had you late from
     France ?

Regan. Be simple-answer'd, for we know the truth.

Cornwall. And what confederacy have you with the
     traitors
Late footed in the kingdom ?

Regan. To whose hands have you sent the lunatic
     king ?
Speak.

Gloster. I have a letter guessingly set down,
Which came from one that 's of a neutral heart,
And not from one oppos'd.

Cornwall.   Cunning.

Regan.   And false.   50

Cornwall. Where hast thou sent the king ?

Gloster.   To Dover.

Regan. Wherefore to Dover. Wast thou not charg'd
    at peril —
Cornwall. Wherefore to Dover ? — Let him first
    answer that.
Gloster. I am tied to the stake, and I must stand
    the course.
Regan. Wherefore to Dover?
Gloster. Because I would not see thy cruel nails
Pluck out his poor old eyes, nor thy fierce sister
In his anointed flesh stick boarish fangs.
The sea, with such a storm as his bare head
In hell-black night endur'd, would have buoy'd up   60
And quench'd the stelled fires ;
Yet, poor old heart, he holp the heavens to rain.
If wolves had at thy gate howl'd that stern time,
Thou shouldst have said, ' Good porter, turn the
    key,
All cruels else subscribe.' But I shall see
The winged vengeance overtake such children.
    Cornwall. See 't shalt thou never. — Fellows, hold
    the chair. —
Upon these eyes of thine I 'll set my foot.
    Gloster. He that will think to live till he be old,
Give me some help ! — O cruel ! O you gods !   70
    Regan. One side will mock another ; the other
    too.
    Cornwall. If you see vengeance —
    1 *Servant.*   Hold your hand, my lord !
I have serv'd you ever since I was a child ;

But better service have I never done you
Than now to bid you hold.

    Regan.   How now, you dog !

    1 *Servant.* If you did wear a beard upon your chin,
I 'd shake it on this quarrel.   What do you mean ?

    Cornwall. My villain !   [*They draw and fight.*

    1 *Servant.* Nay, then, come on, and take the chance
      of anger.   79

    Regan. Give me thy sword. — A peasant stand up
      thus !   [*Takes a sword, and runs at him behind.*

    1 *Servant.* O, I am slain !—My lord, you have
      one eye left
To see some mischief on him. — O !   [*Dies.*

    Cornwall. Lest it see more, prevent it. — Out, vile
      jelly !
Where is thy lustre now ?

    Gloster. All dark and comfortless. — Where 's my
      son Edmund ? —
Edmund, enkindle all the sparks of nature,
To quit this horrid act.

    Regan.   Out, treacherous villain !
Thou call'st on him that hates thee ; it was he
That made the overture of thy treasons to us,
Who is too good to pity thee.   90

    Gloster. O my follies ! then Edgar was abus'd. —
Kind gods, forgive me that, and prosper him !

    Regan. Go thrust him out at gates, and let him smell
His way to Dover. — [*Exit one with Gloster.*]   How
      is 't, my lord ? how look you ?

Cornwall. I have receiv'd a hurt; follow me, lady. —
Turn out that eyeless villain; throw this slave
Upon the dunghill. — Regan, I bleed apace;
Untimely comes this hurt. Give me your arm.
　　　　　　　　　[Exit Cornwall, led by Regan.
　2 *Servant.* I 'll never care what wickedness I do,
If this man come to good.
　3 *Servant.*　　　　　　If she live long,　　100
And in the end meet the old course of death,
Women will all turn monsters.
　2 *Servant.* Let 's follow the old earl, and get the
　　　Bedlam
To lead him where he would; his roguish madness
Allows itself to any thing.
　3 *Servant.* Go thou. I 'll fetch some flax and
　　　whites of eggs
To apply to his bleeding face. Now, heaven help him!
　　　　　　　　　　[Exeunt severally.

DOVER CLIFF

ACT IV

Scene I. *The Heath*

Enter Edgar

Edgar. Yet better thus, and known to be contemn'd.
Than still contemn'd and flatter'd. To be worst,
The lowest and most dejected thing of fortune,
Stands still in esperance, lives not in fear.
The lamentable change is from the best;
The worst returns to laughter. Welcome, then,
Thou unsubstantial air that I embrace!
The wretch that thou hast blown unto the worst
Owes nothing to thy blasts. — But who comes here?

Enter GLOSTER, *led by an* Old Man

My father, poorly led? — World, world, O world!   10
But that thy strange mutations make us hate thee,
Life would not yield to age.
    Old Man.   O my good lord,
I have been your tenant, and your father's tenant,
These fourscore years.
    Gloster. Away, get thee away; good friend, be gone.
Thy comforts can do me no good at all;
Thee they may hurt.
    Old Man.   You cannot see your way.
    Gloster. I have no way, and therefore want no eyes;
I stumbled when I saw.   Full oft 't is seen,
Our means secure us, and our mere defects   20
Prove our commodities. — O dear son Edgar,
The food of thy abused father's wrath!
Might I but live to see thee in my touch,
I 'd say I had eyes again!
    Old Man.   How now! Who 's there?
    Edgar. [*Aside*] O gods! Who is 't can say 'I am
        at the worst?'
I am worse than e'er I was.
    Old Man.   'T is poor mad Tom.
    Edgar. [*Aside*] And worse I may be yet; the worst
        is not
So long as we can say 'This is the worst.'
    Old Man. Fellow, where goest?
    Gloster.   Is it a beggar-man?

Old Man. Madman and beggar too.   30
Gloster. He has some reason, else he could not beg.
I' the last night's storm I such a fellow saw,
Which made me think a man a worm.   My son
Came then into my mind, and yet my mind
Was then scarce friends with him.   I have heard more
    since.
As flies to wanton boys, are we to the gods ;
They kill us for their sport.
Edgar.   [*Aside*] How should this be ?
Bad is the trade that must play fool to sorrow,
Angering itself and others. — Bless thee, master !
Gloster. Is that the naked fellow ?
Old Man.   Ay, my lord.   40
Gloster. Then, prithee, get thee gone.   If for my sake
Thou wilt o'ertake us hence a mile or twain
I' the way toward Dover, do it for ancient love ;
And bring some covering for this naked soul,
Which I 'll entreat to lead me.
Old Man.   Alack, sir, he is mad.
Gloster. 'T is the times' plague, when madmen lead
    the blind.
Do as I bid thee, or rather do thy pleasure ;
Above the rest, be gone.
Old Man. I 'll bring him the best 'parel that I have,
Come on 't what will.   [*Exit.*
Gloster. Sirrah, naked fellow, —   51
Edgar. Poor Tom 's a-cold. — [*Aside*] I cannot daub
    it further.

Gloster. Come hither, fellow.

Edgar. [*Aside*] And yet I must. — Bless thy sweet
eyes, they bleed.

Gloster. Know'st thou the way to Dover?

Edgar. Both stile and gate, horse-way and foot-
path. Poor Tom had been scared out of his good
wits. Bless thee, good man's son, from the foul
fiend! Five fiends have been in poor Tom at once;
of lust, as Obidicut; Hobbididence, prince of dumb- 60
ness; Mahu, of stealing; Modo, of murther; Flibbertigibbet, of mopping and mowing, who since
possesses chambermaids and waiting-women. So,
bless thee, master!

    Gloster. Here, take this purse, thou whom the
        heaven's plagues
Have humbled to all strokes; that I am wretched
Makes thee the happier. — Heavens, deal so still!
Let the superfluous and lust-dieted man,
That slaves your ordinance, that will not see
Because he does not feel, feel your power quickly; 70
So distribution should undo excess,
And each man have enough. — Dost thou know Dover?

    Edgar. Ay, master.

    Gloster. There is a cliff whose high and bending head
Looks fearfully in the confined deep:
Bring me but to the very brim of it,
And I 'll repair the misery thou dost bear
With something rich about me; from that place
I shall no leading need.

Edgar.   Give me thy arm ;
Poor Tom shall lead thee.   [*Exeunt.*

SCENE II. *Before the Duke of Albany's Palace*

Enter GONERIL *and* EDMUND

Goneril. Welcome, my lord ; I marvel our mild husband
Not met us on the way. —

Enter OSWALD

                    Now, where 's your master ?
Oswald. Madam, within ; but never man so chang'd.
I told him of the army that was landed ;
He smil'd at it. I told him you were coming ;
His answer was, ' The worse.' Of Gloster's treachery,
And of the loyal service of his son,
When I inform'd him, then he call'd me sot,
And told me I had turn'd the wrong side out.
What most he should dislike seems pleasant to him ; 10
What like, offensive.
    Goneril. [*To Edmund*] Then shall you go no further.
It is the cowish terror of his spirit,
That dares not undertake ; he 'll not feel wrongs
Which tie him to an answer. Our wishes on the way
May prove effects. Back, Edmund, to my brother ;
Hasten his musters and conduct his powers.
I must change arms at home, and give the distaff
Into my husband's hands. This trusty servant

Shall pass between us ; ere long you are like to hear,
If you dare venture in your own behalf, 　　　　20
A mistress's command. Wear this ; spare speech.
　　　　　　　　　　　　　　　　[*Giving a favour.*
Decline your head ; this kiss, if it durst speak,
Would stretch thy spirits up into the air.
Conceive, and fare thee well.

　　Edmund. Yours in the ranks of death.
　　Goneril. 　　　　　　　My most dear Gloster !
　　　　　　　　　　　　　　　　　[*Exit Edmund.*
O, the difference of man and man !
To thee a woman's services are due ;
My fool usurps my body.

　　Oswald. 　　　　　Madam, here comes my lord.
　　　　　　　　　　　　　　　　　　　[*Exit.*

　　　　　　　　Enter ALBANY

　　Goneril. I have been worth the whistle.
　　Albany. 　　　　　　　　　O Goneril !
You are not worth the dust which the rude wind 　30
Blows in your face. I fear your disposition.
That nature which contemns it origin
Cannot be border'd certain in itself ;
She that herself will sliver and disbranch
From her material sap perforce must wither
And come to deadly use.

　　Goneril. No more ; the text is foolish.
　　Albany. Wisdom and goodness to the vile seem vile ;
Filths savour but themselves. What have you done ?
Tigers, not daughters, what have you perform'd ? 　40

A father, and a gracious aged man,
Whose reverence even the head-lugg'd bear would lick
Most barbarous, most degenerate ! have you madded.
Could my good brother suffer you to do it ?
A man, a prince, by him so benefited !
If that the heavens do not their visible spirits
Send quickly down to tame these vile offences,
It will come,
Humanity must perforce prey on itself,
Like monsters of the deep.
  Goneril.   Milk-liver'd man ! 50
That bear'st a cheek for blows, a head for wrongs ;
Who hast not in thy brows an eye discerning
Thine honour from thy suffering ; that not know'st
Fools do those villains pity who are punish'd
Ere they have done their mischief, — where 's thy
   drum ?
France spreads his banners in our noiseless land,
With plumed helm thy state begins to threat,
Whilst thou, a moral fool, sit'st still and criest
' Alack, why does he so ? '
  Albany.   See thyself, devil !
Proper deformity seems not in the fiend 60
So horrid as in woman.
  Goneril.   O vain fool !
  Albany. Thou changed and self-cover'd thing, for
  shame,
Be-monster not thy feature. Were 't my fitness
To let these hands obey my blood,

They are apt enough to dislocate and tear
Thy flesh and bones. Howe'er thou art a fiend,
A woman's shape doth shield thee.
  Goneril. Marry, your manhood now ! —

Enter a Messenger

  Albany. What news ?
  Messenger. O, my good lord, the Duke of Corn-
        wall 's dead ;   70
Slain by his servant, going to put out
The other eye of Gloster.
  Albany.   Gloster's eyes !
  Messenger. A servant that he bred, thrill'd with re-
        morse,
Oppos'd against the act, bending his sword
To his great master, who thereat enrag'd
Flew on him and amongst them fell'd him dead,
But not without that harmful stroke which since
Hath pluck'd him after.
  Albany.   This shows you are above,
You justicers, that these our nether crimes
So speedily can venge ! — But, O poor Gloster !   80
Lost he his other eye ?
  Messenger.   Both, both, my lord. —
This letter, madam, craves a speedy answer ;
'T is from your sister.
  Goneril.   [*Aside*] One way I like this well ;
But being widow, and my Gloster with her,
May all the building in my fancy pluck

Upon my hateful life : another way,
The news is not so tart. — I 'll read and answer. [*Exit.*

    Albany. Where was his son when they did take his
        eyes ?

    Messenger. Come with my lady hither.

    Albany.   He is not here.

    Messenger. No, my good lord; I met him back
        again.   90

    Albany. Knows he the wickedness ?

    Messenger. Ay, my good lord; 't was he inform'd
        against him,

And quit the house on purpose, that their punishment
Might have the freer course.

    Albany.   Gloster, I live

To thank thee for the love thou show'dst the king,
And to revenge thine eyes. — Come hither, friend ;
Tell me what more thou know'st.   [*Exeunt.*

    SCENE III.   *The French Camp near Dover*

      Enter KENT *and a* Gentleman

  Kent. Why the King of France is so suddenly
gone back, know you the reason ?

  Gentleman. Something he left imperfect in the
state which since his coming forth is thought of,
which imports to the kingdom so much fear and danger that his personal return was most required and
necessary.

  Kent. Who hath he left behind him general ?

Gentleman. The Marshal of France, Monsieur La
Far.   10

Kent. Did your letters pierce the queen to any
demonstration of grief ?

Gentleman. Ay, sir ; she took them, read them in
    my presence,
And now and then an ample tear trill'd down
Her delicate cheek.   It seem'd she was a queen
Over her passion, who most rebel-like
Sought to be king o'er her.

Kent.   O, then it mov'd her.

Gentleman. Not to a rage ; patience and sorrow
    strove
Who should express her goodliest.   You have seen
Sunshine and rain at once : her smiles and tears   20
Were like a better way ; those happy smilets
That play'd on her ripe lip seem'd not to know
What guests were in her eyes, which parted thence
As pearls from diamonds dropp'd.   In brief,
Sorrow would be a rarity most belov'd,
If all could so become it.

Kent.   Made she no verbal question ?

Gentleman. Faith, once or twice she heav'd the name
    of father
Pantingly forth, as if it press'd her heart ;
Cried ' Sisters ! sisters !   Shame of ladies ! sisters !
Kent ! father ! sisters !   What, i' the storm ? i' the
    night ?   30
Let pity not be believ'd ! '   There she shook

The holy water from her heavenly eyes,
And, clamour-moisten'd, then away she started
To deal with grief alone.
    Kent.   It is the stars,
The stars above us, govern our conditions;
Else one self maïe and mate could not beget
Such different issues. — You spoke not with her since?
    Gentleman. No.
    Kent. Was this before the king return'd?
    Gentleman.   No, since.
    Kent. Well, sir, the poor distressed Lear 's i' the
        town,   40
Who sometime in his better tune remembers
What we are come about, and by no means
Will yield to see his daughter.
    Gentleman.   Why, good sir?
    Kent. A sovereign shame so elbows him; his own
        unkindness,
That stripp'd her from his benediction, turn'd her
To foreign casualties, gave her dear rights
To his dog-hearted daughters, — these things sting
His mind so venomously that burning shame
Detains him from Cordelia.
    Gentleman.   Alack, poor gentleman!
    Kent. Of Albany's and Cornwall's powers you heard
        not?   50
    Gentleman. 'T is so, they are afoot.
    Kent. Well, sir, I 'll bring you to our master Lear,
And leave you to attend him. Some dear cause

Will in concealment wrap me up awhile ;
When I am known aright, you shall not grieve
Lending me this acquaintance.   I pray you, go
Along with me.   [*Exeunt.*

SCENE IV. *The Same. A Tent*

Enter, with drum and colours, CORDELIA, Doctor, *and*
Soldiers

   Cordelia. Alack, 't is he I   Why, he was met even
     now
As mad as the vex'd sea ; singing aloud,
Crown'd with rank fumiter and furrow-weeds,
With burdocks, hemlock, nettles, cuckoo-flowers,
Darnel, and all the idle weeds that grow
In our sustaining corn. — A century send forth ;
Search every acre in the high-grown field,
And bring him to our eye. — [*Exit an Officer.*] — What
     can man's wisdom
In the restoring his bereaved sense ?
He that helps him take all my outward worth.   10
   Doctor. There is means, madam.
Our foster-nurse of nature is repose,
The which he lacks ; that to provoke in him,
Are many simples operative whose power
Will close the eye of anguish.
   Cordelia.   All blest secrets,
All you unpublish'd virtues of the earth,
Spring with my tears ! be aidant and remediate

In the good man's distress ! — Seek, seek for him,
Lest his ungovern'd rage dissolve the life
That wants the means to lead it.

Enter a Messenger

Messenger.   News, madam ;   20
The British powers are marching hitherward.
      Cordelia. 'T is known before ; our preparation stands
In expectation of them. — O dear father,
It is thy business that I go about ;
Therefore great France
My mourning and important tears hath pitied.
No blown ambition doth our arms incite,
But love, dear love, and our aged father's right ;
Soon may I hear and see him !   [*Exeunt.*

SCENE V. *Gloster's Castle*

Enter REGAN *and* OSWALD

Regan. But are my brother's powers set forth ?
Oswald.   Ay, madam.
Regan. Himself in person there ?
Oswald.   Madam, with much ado ;
Your sister is the better soldier.
Regan. Lord Edmund spake not with your lord at
      home ?
Oswald. No, madam.
Regan. What might import my sister's letter to him ?
Oswald. I know not, lady.

Regan. Faith, he is posted hence on serious matter.
It was great ignorance, Gloster's eyes being out,
To let him live ; where he arrives he moves   10
All hearts against us.   Edmund, I think, is gone,
In pity of his misery, to dispatch
His nighted life ; moreover, to descry
The strength o' the enemy.
    Oswald. I must needs after him, madam, with my
        letter.
    Regan. Our troops set forth to-morrow ; stay with us.
The ways are dangerous.
    Oswald.   I may not, madam ;
My lady charg'd my duty in this business.
    Regan. Why should she write to Edmund ?   Might
        not you
Transport her purposes by word ?   Belike,   20
Some things — I know not what.   I 'll love thee much, —
Let me unseal the letter.
    Oswald.   Madam, I had rather —
    Regan. I know your lady does not love her husband,
I am sure of that ; and at her late being here
She gave strange œillades and most speaking looks
To noble Edmund.   I know you are of her bosom.
    Oswald. I, madam ?
    Regan. I speak in understanding ; you are, I know 't.
Therefore I do advise you, take this note.
My lord is dead ; Edmund and I have talk'd,   30
And more convenient is he for my hand
Than for your lady's ; you may gather more.

If you do find him, pray you, give him this;
And when your mistress hears thus much from you,
I pray, desire her call her wisdom to her.
So, fare you well.
If you do chance to hear of that blind traitor,
Preferment falls on him that cuts him off.

   Oswald. Would I could meet him, madam! I should
      show   39
What party I do follow.

   Regan.   Fare thee well.   [*Exeunt.*

         Scene VI. *Fields near Dover*

   Enter Gloster, *and* Edgar *dressed like a peasant*

   Gloster. When shall I come to the top of that same
      hill?

   Edgar. You do climb up it now; look, how we labour.

   Gloster. Methinks the ground is even.

   Edgar.   Horrible steep.
Hark, do you hear the sea?

   Gloster.   No, truly.

   Edgar. Why, then, your other senses grow imperfect
By your eyes' anguish.

   Gloster.   So may it be indeed;
Methinks thy voice is alter'd, and thou speak'st
In better phrase and matter than thou didst.

   Edgar. You 're much deceiv'd; in nothing am I
      chang'd
But in my garments.

Gloster.   Methinks you 're better-spoken.   10
Edgar. Come on, sir; here 's the place.   Stand still.
    How fearful
And dizzy 't is to cast one's eyes so low!
The crows and choughs that wing the midway air
Show scarce so gross as beetles.   Half way down
Hangs one that gathers sampire, dreadful trade!
Methinks he seems no bigger than his head.
The fishermen that walk upon the beach
Appear like mice; and yond tall anchoring bark
Diminish'd to her cock; her cock, a buoy
Almost too small for sight.   The murmuring surge,   20
That on the unnumber'd idle pebble chafes,
Cannot be heard so high.   I 'll look no more,
Lest my brain turn and the deficient sight
Topple down headlong.
    Gloster.   Set me where you stand.
    Edgar. Give me your hand.   You are now within a foot
Of the extreme verge.   For all beneath the moon
Would I not leap upright.
    Gloster.   Let go my hand.
Here, friend, 's another purse; in it a jewel
Well worth a poor man's taking; fairies and gods
Prosper it with thee!   Go thou further off;   30
Bid me farewell, and let me hear thee going.
    Edgar. Now fare ye well, good sir.
    Gloster.   With all my heart.
    Edgar. [*Aside*] Why I do trifle thus with his despair
Is done to cure it.

Gloster. [*Kneeling*] O you mighty gods!
This world I do renounce, and in your sights
Shake patiently my great affliction off.
If I could bear it longer, and not fall
To quarrel with your great opposeless wills,
My snuff and loathed part of nature should
Burn itself out. If Edgar live, O bless him! —   40
Now, fellow, fare thee well.
    Edgar.   Gone, sir; farewell. —
                        [*He falls forward.*
[*Aside*] And yet I know not how conceit may rob
The treasury of life, when life itself
Yields to the theft. Had he been where he thought,
By this had thought been past. Alive or dead? —
Ho, you sir! friend! Hear you, sir! speak! —
[*Aside*] Thus might he pass indeed; yet he revives. —
What are you, sir?
    Gloster.   Away, and let me die.
    Edgar. Hadst thou been aught but gossamer,
        feathers, air,
So many fathom down precipitating,   50
Thou 'dst shiver'd like an egg; but thou dost breathe,
Hast heavy substance, bleed'st not, speak'st, art sound.
Ten masts at each make not the altitude
Which thou hast perpendicularly fell;
Thy life 's a miracle. Speak yet again.
    Gloster. But have I fallen, or no?
    Edgar. From the dread summit of this chalky
        bourn.

Look up a-height; the shrill-gorg'd lark so far
Cannot be seen or heard.   Do but look up.
   Gloster.   Alack, I have no eyes.   60
Is wretchedness depriv'd that benefit,
To end itself by death?   'T was yet some comfort,
When misery could beguile the tyrant's rage,
And frustrate his proud will.
   Edgar.   Give me your arm.
Up; so.   How is 't?   Feel you your legs?   You
     stand.
   Gloster.   Too well, too well.
   Edgar.   This is above all strangeness.
Upon the crown o' the cliff, what thing was that
Which parted from you?
   Gloster.   A poor unfortunate beggar.
   Edgar. As I stood here below, methought his
     eyes
Were two full moons; he had a thousand noses,   70
Horns whelk'd and wav'd like the enridged sea.
It was some fiend; therefore, thou happy father,
Think that the clearest gods, who make them honours
Of men's impossibilities, have preserv'd thee.
   Gloster.   I do remember now.   Henceforth I 'll
     bear
Affliction till it do cry out itself
'Enough, enough,' and die.   That thing you speak
     of,
I took it for a man; often 't would say
'The fiend, the fiend:' he led me to that place.

Edgar. Bear free and patient thoughts. — But who
comes here ?   80

Enter LEAR, *fantastically dressed with wild flowers*

The safer sense will ne'er accommodate
His master thus.

Lear. No, they cannot touch me for coining ; I
am the king himself.

Edgar. O thou side-piercing sight l

Lear. Nature 's above art in that respect. —
There's your press-money. — That fellow handles his
bow like a crow-keeper. — Draw me a clothier's
yard. — Look, look, a mouse l   Peace, peace ; this
piece of toasted cheese will do 't. — There 's my 90
gauntlet ; I 'll prove it on a giant. — Bring up the
brown bills. — O, well flown, bird l i' the clout, i' the
clout l hewgh l — Give the word.

Edgar. Sweet marjoram.

Lear. Pass.

Gloster. I know that voice.

Lear. Ha l Goneril, — with a white beard l — They
flattered me like a dog ; and told me I had white hairs
in my beard ere the black ones were there.   To say
ay and no to every thing that I said l   Ay and no 100
too was no good divinity.   When the rain came to
wet me once and the wind to make me chatter, when
the thunder would not peace at my bidding, there I
found 'em, there I smelt 'em out.   Go to, they are

not men o' their words: they told me I was every
thing; 't is a lie, I am not ague-proof.

Gloster. The trick of that voice I do well remember.
Is 't not the king?

Lear.   Ay, every inch a king.
When I do stare, see how the subject quakes. —
I pardon that man's life. — What was thy cause?   110
Adultery?
Thou shalt not die. Die for adultery? No;
For Gloster's bastard son
Was kinder to his father than my daughters. —
Give me an ounce of civet, good apothecary, to
sweeten my imagination; there 's money for thee.

Gloster. O, let me kiss that hand!

Lear. Let me wipe it first; it smells of mortality.

Gloster. O ruin'd piece of nature! This great world
Shall so wear out to nought. Dost thou know me?   120

Lear. I remember thine eyes well enough. Dost
thou squiny at me? No, do thy worst, blind Cupid;
I 'll not love. Read thou this challenge; mark but
the penning of it.

Gloster. Were all thy letters suns, I could not see.

Edgar. [*Aside*] I would not take this from report;
        it is,
And my heart breaks at it.

Lear. Read.

Gloster. What, with the case of eyes?

Lear. Oh, ho, are you there with me? No eyes   130
in your head, nor no money in your purse? Your

eyes are in a heavy case, your purse in a light; yet
you see how this world goes.

Gloster. I see it feelingly.

Lear. What, art mad? A man may see how this
world goes with no eyes. Look with thine ears; see
how yond justice rails upon yond simple thief. Hark,
in thine ear; change places, and, handy-dandy, which
is the justice, which is the thief? Thou hast seen
a farmer's dog bark at a beggar?   140

Gloster. Ay, sir.

Lear. And the creature run from the cur? There
thou mightst behold the great image of authority; a
dog 's obeyed in office. —
The usurer hangs the cozener.
Through tatter'd clothes great vices do appear;
Robes and furr'd gowns hide all. Plate sin with gold,
And the strong lance of justice hurtless breaks;
Arm it in rags, a pigmy's straw does pierce it.
None does offend, none, I say, none; I 'll able 'em. 150
Take that of me, my friend, who have the power
To seal the accuser's lips. Get thee glass eyes;
And, like a scurvy politician, seem
To see the things thou dost not. —
Now, now, now, now; pull off my boots. Harder,
        harder: so.

Edgar. [*Aside*] O, matter and impertinency mix'd!
Reason in madness!

Lear. If thou wilt weep my fortunes, take my eyes.
I know thee well enough; thy name is Gloster.

Thou must be patient; we came crying hither.   160
Thou know'st, the first time that we smell the air,
We wawl and cry.   I will preach to thee ; mark.
    Gloster.   Alack, alack the day !
    Lear.   When we are born, we cry that we are come
To this great stage of fools.   This' a good block ;
It were a delicate stratagem, to shoe
A troop of horse with felt.   I 'll put 't in proof ;
And when I have stolen upon these sons-in-law,
Then, kill, kill, kill, kill, kill, kill !

Enter a Gentleman, *with* Attendants

    Gentleman.   O, here he is ; lay hand upon him. — Sir,
Your most dear daughter —   171
    Lear.   No rescue ?   What, a prisoner ?   I am even
The natural fool of fortune.   Use me well ;
You shall have ransom.   Let me have a surgeon ;
I am cut to the brains.
    Gentleman.   You shall have any thing.
    Lear.   No seconds ? all myself ?
Why, this would make a man a man of salt,
To use his eyes for garden water-pots,
Ay, and laying autumn's dust.
    Gentleman.   Good sir, —   180
    Lear.   I will die bravely, like a smug bridegroom.
        What !
I will be jovial.   Come, come ; I am a king,
My masters, know you that ?
    Gentleman.   You are a royal one, and we obey you.

Lear. Then there 's life in 't.   Come, an you get
it, you shall get it by running.   Sa, sa, sa, sa.
                    [*Exit running; Attendants follow.*
    Gentleman. A sight most pitiful in the meanest wretch,
Past speaking of in a king !   Thou hast one daughter,
Who redeems nature from the general curse
Which twain have brought her to.   190
    Edgar. Hail, gentle sir.
    Gentleman.   Sir, speed you ; what 's your will ?
    Edgar. Do you hear aught, sir, of a battle toward ?
    Gentleman. Most sure and vulgar ; every one hears
        that,
Which can distinguish sound.
    Edgar.   But, by your favour,
How near 's the other army ?
    Gentleman. Near and on speedy foot; the main
        descry
Stands on the hourly thought.
    Edgar.   I thank you, sir ; that 's all.
    Gentleman. Though that the queen on special cause
        is here,
Her army is mov'd on.
    Edgar.   I thank you, sir.   [*Exit Gentleman.*
    Gloster. You ever-gentle gods, take my breath from
        me ;   200
Let not my worser spirit tempt me again
To die before you please !
    Edgar.   Well pray you, father.
    Gloster. Now, good sir, what are you ?

Edgar. A most poor man, made tame to fortune's
        blows,
Who, by the art of known and feeling sorrows,
Am pregnant to good pity.   Give me your hand,
I 'll lead you to some biding.
    Gloster.   Hearty thanks;
The bounty and the benison of heaven
To boot, and boot !

                Enter OSWALD

    Oswald.   A proclaim'd prize !   Most happy !
That eyeless head of thine was first fram'd flesh   210
To raise my fortunes. — Thou old unhappy traitor,
Briefly thyself remember ; the sword is out
That must destroy thee.
    Gloster.   Now let thy friendly hand
Put strength enough to 't.   [*Edgar interposes,*
    Oswald.   Wherefore, bold peasant,
Darest thou support a publish'd traitor ?   Hence !
Lest that the infection of his fortune take
Like hold on thee.   Let go his arm.
    Edgar. Chill not let go, zir, without vurther 'casion.
    Oswald. Let go, slave, or thou diest !
    Edgar. Good gentleman, go your gait, and let poor 220
volk pass.   An chud ha' bin zwaggered out of my
life, 't would not ha' bin zo long as 't is by a vort-
night.   Nay, come not near th' old man ; keep out,
che vor ye, or ise try whether your costard or my
ballow be the harder ; chill be plain with you.
    Oswald. Out, dunghill !   [*They fight*

Edgar. Chill pick your teeth, zir.   Come ; no
matter vor your foins.   [*Oswald falls*.

  Oswald. Slave, thou hast slain me.   Villain, take my
     purse :
If ever thou wilt thrive, bury my body,   230
And give the letters which thou find'st about me
To Edmund Earl of Gloster ; seek him out
Upon the English party. — O, untimely death !
Death !   [*Dies*.

  Edgar. I know thee well ; a serviceable villain,
As duteous to the vices of thy mistress
As badness would desire.

  Gloster.   What, is he dead ?

  Edgar. Sit you down, father ; rest you. —
Let's see these pockets ; the letters that he speaks of
May be my friends.   He 's dead ; I am only sorry   240
He had no other deathsman.   Let us see :
Leave, gentle wax ; and, manners, blame us not.
To know our enemies' minds, we 'd rip their hearts ;
Their papers, is more lawful.

  [Reads] ' *Let our reciprocal vows be remembered.*
You have many opportunities to cut him off ; if your
will want not, time and place will be fruitfully offered.
There is nothing done, if he return the conqueror ; then
am I the prisoner, and his bed my gaol, from the loathed
warmth whereof deliver me and supply the place for 250
your labour.

  ' *Your — wife, so I would say — affectionate servant,*
                                    ' GONERIL.'

O indistinguish'd space of woman's will!
A plot upon her virtuous husband's life!
And the exchange my brother! — Here, in the sands,
Thee I 'll rake up, the post unsanctified
Of murtherous lechers, and in the mature time
With this ungracious paper strike the sight
Of the death-practis'd duke.   For him 't is well   260
That of thy death and business I can tell.
     Gloster. The king is mad.   How stiff is my vile
          sense,
That I stand up and have ingenious feeling
Of my huge sorrows!   Better I were distract;
So should my thoughts be sever'd from my griefs,
And woes by wrong imaginations lose
The knowledge of themselves.   [*Drum afar off*.
     Edgar.   Give me your hand;
Far off, methinks, I hear the beaten drum.
Come, father, I 'll bestow you with a friend.   [*Exeunt*.

SCENE VII. *A Tent in the French Camp*. LEAR *on a
     bed asleep, soft music playing;* Gentleman *and others
     attending*

          Enter CORDELIA, KENT, *and* Doctor

Cordelia. O thou good Kent, how shall I live and
          work,
To match thy goodness?   My life will be too short,
And every measure fail me.
     Kent. To be acknowledg'd, madam, is o'er-paid.

All my reports go with the modest truth,
Nor more nor clipp'd, but so.
  Cordelia.   Be better suited;
These weeds are memories of those worser hours.
I prithee, put them off.
  Kent.   Pardon, dear madam;
Yet to be known shortens my made intent.
My boon I make it, that you know me not   10
Till time and I think meet.
  Cordelia. Then be 't so, my good lord. — How does
   the king?
  Doctor. Madam, sleeps still.
  Cordelia. O you kind gods,
Cure this great breach in his abused nature!
The untun'd and jarring senses, O wind up
Of this child-changed father!
  Doctor.   So please your majesty
That we may wake the king? he hath slept long.
  Cordelia. Be govern'd by your knowledge, and pro-
   ceed
I' the sway of your own will. — Is he array'd? 20
  Gentleman. Ay, madam; in the heaviness of sleep
We put fresh garments on him.
  Doctor. Be by, good madam, when we do awake him;
I doubt not of his temperance.
  Cordelia.   Very well.
  Doctor. Please you, draw near. — Louder the music
   there!
  Cordelia. O my dear father! Restoration hang

Thy medicine on my lips, and let this kiss
Repair those violent harms that my two sisters
Have in thy reverence made !
    Kent.   Kind and dear princess !
    Cordelia. Had you not been their father, these white
        flakes   30
Did challenge pity of them. Was this a face
To be oppos'd against the warring winds ?
To stand against the deep dread-bolted thunder ?
In the most terrible and nimble stroke
Of quick, cross lightning ? to watch — poor perdu ! —
With this thin helm ? Mine enemy's dog,
Though he had bit me, should have stood that night
Against my fire ; and wast thou fain, poor father,
To hovel thee with swine and rogues forlorn.
In short and musty straw ? Alack, alack !   40
'T is wonder that thy life and wits at once
Had not concluded all. — He wakes ; speak to him.
    Doctor. Madam, do you ; 't is fittest.
    Cordelia. How does my royal lord ? How fares your
        majesty ?
    Lear. You do me wrong to take me out o' the grave.
Thou art a soul in bliss ; but I am bound
Upon a wheel of fire, that mine own tears
Do scald like molten lead.
    Cordelia.   Sir, do you know me ?
    Lear. You are a spirit, I know ; when did you die ?
    Cordelia. Still, still, far wide !   50
    Doctor. He 's scarce awake ; let him alone awhile.

Lear. Where have I been? Where am I? Fair
    daylight?
I am mightily abus'd. I should e'en die with pity,
To see another thus. I know not what to say.
I will not swear these are my hands. Let 's see;
I feel this pin prick. Would I were assur'd
Of my condition!
    Cordelia.   O, look upon me, sir,
And hold your hands in benediction o'er me.
No, sir, you must not kneel.
    Lear.   Pray, do not mock me.
I am a very foolish fond old man,
Fourscore and upward, not an hour more nor less;
And, to deal plainly,
I fear I am not in my perfect mind.
Methinks I should know you and know this man;
Yet I am doubtful: for I am mainly ignorant
What place this is, and all the skill I have
Remembers not these garments, nor I know not
Where I did lodge last night. Do not laugh at me;
For, as I am a man, I think this lady
To be my child Cordelia.
    Cordelia.   And so I am, I am!   70
    Lear. Be your tears wet? yes, faith. I pray, weep
    not.
If you have poison for me, I will drink it.
I know you do not love me, for your sisters
Have, as I do remember, done me wrong;
You have some cause, they have not.

Cordelia.   No cause, no cause !

Lear. Am I in France ?

Kent.   In your own kingdom, sir.

Lear. Do not abuse me.

Doctor. Be comforted, good madam : the great rage,
You see, is kill'd in him ; and yet 't is danger
To make him even o'er the time he has lost.   80
Desire him to go in ; trouble him no more
Till further settling.

Cordelia. Will 't please your highness walk ?

Lear. You must bear with me. Pray you now,
forget and forgive ; I am old and foolish.

                    [*Exeunt all but Kent and Gentleman.*

Gentleman. Holds it true, sir, that the Duke of
Cornwall was so slain ?

Kent. Most certain, sir.

Gentleman. Who is conductor of his people ?

Kent. As 't is said, the bastard son of Gloster.   90

Gentleman. They say Edgar, his banished son, is
with the Earl of Kent in Germany.

Kent. Report is changeable. 'T is time to look
about ; the powers of the kingdom approach apace.

Gentleman. The arbitrement is like to be bloody.
Fare you well, sir.   [*Exit.*

Kent. My point and period will be throughly
          wrought,
Or well or ill, as this day's battle 's fought.   [*Exit.*

DOVER CASTLE

ACT V

SCENE I. *The British Camp, near Dover*

Enter, with drum and colours, EDMUND, REGAN, Gentlemen, *and* Soldiers

  Edmund. Know of the duke if his last purpose hold,
Or whether since he is advis'd by aught
To change the course.   He 's full of alteration
And self-reproving.   Bring his constant pleasure.
                    [*To a Gentleman, who goes out.*
  Regan. Our sister's man is certainly miscarried.
  Edmund. 'T is to be doubted, madam.

Regan.   Now, sweet lord,
You know the goodness I intend upon you;
Tell me — but truly — but then speak the truth,
Do you not love my sister?
　　Edmund.   In honour'd love.
　　Regan. But have you never found my brother's
　　　　way   10
To the forfended place?
　　Edmund.   That thought abuses you.
　　Regan. I am doubtful that you have been conjunct
And bosom'd with her, as far as we call hers.
　　Edmund. No, by mine honour, madam.
　　Regan. I never shall endure her. Dear my lord,
Be not familiar with her.
　　Edmund.   Fear me not. —
She and the duke her husband!

Enter, with drum and colours, ALBANY, GONERIL, *and*
　　　　　　　　Soldiers

　　Goneril. [*Aside*] I had rather lose the battle than
　　　　that sister
Should loosen him and me.
　　Albany. Our very loving sister, well be-met. —   20
Sir, this I hear: the king is come to his daughter,
With others whom the rigour of our state
Forc'd to cry out. Where I could not be honest,
I never yet was valiant; for this business,
It toucheth us, as France invades our land,

Not bolds the king, with others, whom, I fear,
Most just and heavy causes make oppose.
 Edmund. Sir, you speak nobly.
 Regan.   Why is this reason'd ?
 Goneril. Combine together 'gainst the enemy ;
For these domestic and particular broils   30
Are not the question here.
 Albany.   Let 's then determine
With the ancient of war on our proceeding.
 Edmund. I shall attend you presently at your
   tent.
 Regan. Sister, you 'll go with us ?
 Goneril. No.
 Regan. 'T is most convenient ; pray you, go with
   us.
 Goneril. [*Aside*] O, ho, I know the riddle ! — I will
   go.

  As they are going out, enter EDGAR *disguised*

 Edgar. If e'er your grace had speech with man so
   poor,
Hear me one word.
 Albany.   I 'll overtake you. — Speak.
       [*Exeunt all but Albany and Edgar.*
 Edgar. Before you fight the battle, ope this letter. 40
If you have victory, let the trumpet sound
For him that brought it ; wretched though I seem,
I can produce a champion that will prove
What is avouched there.   If you miscarry,

Your business of the world hath so an end,
And machination ceases.   Fortune love you!
   Albany. Stay till I have read the letter.
   Edgar.   I was forbid it.
When time shall serve, let but the herald cry,
And I 'll appear again.   49
   Albany. Why, fare thee well; I will o'erlook thy
     paper.   [*Exit Edgar.*

Re-enter EDMUND

   Edmund. The enemy 's in view; draw up your
     powers.
Here is the guess of their true strength and forces
By diligent discovery; but your haste
Is now urg'd on you.
   Albany.   We will greet the time.   [*Exit.*
   Edmund. To both these sisters have I sworn my
     love;
Each jealous of the other, as the stung
Are of the adder.   Which of them shall I take?
Both? one? or neither?   Neither can be enjoy'd,
If both remain alive.   To take the widow
Exasperates, makes mad her sister Goneril;   60
And hardly shall I carry out my side,
Her husband being alive.   Now then we 'll use
His countenance for the battle; which being done,
Let her who would be rid of him devise
His speedy taking-off.   As for the mercy
Which he intends to Lear and to Cordelia, —

The battle done, and they within our power,
Shall never see his pardon ; for my state
Stands on me to defend, not to debate.   *[Exit.*

SCENE II. *A Field between the two Camps*

Alarum within.   Enter, with drum and colours, LEAR,
CORDELIA, *and* Soldiers, *over the stage ; and exeunt*

Enter EDGAR *and* GLOSTER

Edgar. Here, father, take the shadow of this tree
For your good host ; pray that the right may thrive.
If ever I return to you again,
I 'll bring you comfort.
 Gloster.   Grace go with you, sir !
           [Exit Edgar.

Alarum and retreat within.   Re-enter EDGAR

Edgar. Away, old man, give me thy hand ; away !
King Lear hath lost, he and his daughter ta'en.
Give me thy hand ; come on.
 Gloster. No further, sir ; a man may rot even here.
 Edgar. What, in ill thoughts again ?   Men must en-
   dure
Their going hence, even as their coming hither ; 10
Ripeness is all.   Come on.
 Gloster.   And that 's true too.
           [Exeunt.

SCENE III. *The British Camp near Dover*

Enter, in conquest, with drum and colours, EDMUND ;
LEAR *and* CORDELIA, *prisoners;* Captain, Soldiers,
etc.

Edmund. Some officers take them away ; good guard,
Until their greater pleasures first be known
That are to censure them.
 Cordelia.   We are not the first
Who, with best meaning, have incurr'd the worst.
For thee, oppressed king, I am cast down ;
Myself could else out-frown false fortune's frown.
Shall we not see these daughters and these sisters ?
 Lear. No, no, no, no ! Come, let 's away to
  prison ;
We two alone will sing like birds i' the cage.
When thou dost ask me blessing, I 'll kneel down 10
And ask of thee forgiveness. So we 'll live,
And pray, and sing, and tell old tales, and laugh
At gilded butterflies, and hear poor rogues
Talk of court news ; and we 'll talk with them too,
Who loses and who wins, who 's in, who 's out,
And take upon 's the mystery of things,
As if we were God's spies ; and we 'll wear out,
In a wall'd prison, packs and sects of great ones
That ebb and flow by the moon.
 Edmund.   Take them away.
 Lear. Upon such sacrifices, my Cordelia, 20
  KING LEAR — 10

The gods themselves throw incense.　Have I caught
　　thee ?
He that parts us shall bring a brand from heaven,
And fire us hence like foxes.　Wipe thine eyes ;
The good-years shall devour them, flesh and fell,
Ere they shall make us weep : we 'll see 'em starv'd first.
Come.　　　　　　[*Exeunt Lear and Cordelia, guarded.*
　Edmund. Come hither, captain ; hark.
Take thou this note [*giving a paper*]; go follow them
　　to prison.
One step I have advanc'd thee ; if thou dost
As this instructs thee, thou dost make thy way　　30
To noble fortunes.　Know thou this, that men
Are as the time is ; to be tender-minded
Does not become a sword.　Thy great employment
Will not bear question ; either say thou 'lt do 't
Or thrive by other means.
　Captain.　　　　　　　I 'll do 't, my lord.
　Edmund. About it ; and write happy when thou hast
　　done.
Mark, — I say, instantly, and carry it so
As I have set it down.
　Captain. I cannot draw a cart, nor eat dried oats ;　39
If 't be man's work, I 'll do 't.　　　　　　[*Exit.*

Flourish. Enter ALBANY, GONERIL, REGAN, *another*
　　Captain, *and* Soldiers

　Albany. Sir, you have show'd to-day your valiant
　　strain,

And fortune led you well; you have the captives
That were the opposites of this day's strife.
I do require them of you, so to use them
As we shall find their merits and our safety
May equally determine.
  Edmund.   Sir, I thought it fit
To send the old and miserable king
To some retention and appointed guard;
Whose age had charms in it, whose title more,
To pluck the common bosom on his side,   50
And turn our impress'd lances in our eyes
Which do command them. With him I sent the queen;
My reason all the same: and they are ready
To-morrow, or at further space, to appear
Where you shall hold your session. At this time
We sweat and bleed; the friend hath lost his friend,
And the best quarrels, in the heat, are curs'd
By those that feel their sharpness.
The question of Cordelia and her father
Requires a fitter place.
  Albany.   Sir, by your patience, 60
I hold you but a subject of this war,
Not as a brother.
  Regan.   That 's as we list to grace him.
Methinks our pleasure might have been demanded
Ere you had spoke so far. He led our powers,
Bore the commission of my place and person;
The which immediacy may well stand up,
And call itself your brother.

Goneril.   Not so hot;
In his own grace he doth exalt himself
More than in your addition.
     Regan.   In my rights,
By me invested, he compeers the best.   7c
     Albany. That were the most, if he should husband
          you.
     Regan. Jesters do oft prove prophets.
     Goneril.   Holla, holla !
That eye that told you so look'd but a-squint.
     Regan. Lady, I am not well; else I should answer
From a full-flowing stomach. — General,
Take thou my soldiers, prisoners, patrimony :
Dispose of them, of me ; the walls are thine.
Witness the world, that I create thee here
My lord and master.
     Goneril.   Mean you to enjoy him ?
     Albany. The let-alone lies not in your good will.   8o
     Edmund. Nor in thine, lord.
     Albany.   Half-blooded fellow, yes.
     Regan. [*To Edmund*] Let the drum strike, and prove
          my title thine.
     Albany. Stay yet ; hear reason. — Edmund, I arrest
          thee
On capital treason ; and, in thy arrest,
This gilded serpent [*pointing to Goneril*]. — For your
          claim, fair sister,
I bar it in the interest of my wife ;
'T is she is sub-contracted to this lord,

And I, her husband, contradict your bans.
If you will marry, make your loves to me ;
My lady is bespoke.
   Goneril.   An interlude !   90
   Albany. Thou art arm'd, Gloster ; let the trumpet
      sound.
If none appear to prove upon thy person
Thy heinous, manifest, and many treasons,
There is my pledge [*throwing down a glove*]. I 'll prove
      it on thy heart,
Ere I taste bread, thou art in nothing less
Than I have here proclaim'd thee.
   Regan.   Sick, O, sick !
   Goneril. [*Aside*] If not, I 'll ne'er trust medicine.
   Edmund. [*Throwing down a glove*] There 's my ex-
      change. What in the world he is
That names me traitor, villain-like he lies.
Call by thy trumpet ; he that dares approach,   100
On him, on you, — who not ? — I will maintain
My truth and honour firmly.
   Albany. A herald, ho !
   Edmund.   A herald, ho, a herald !
   Albany. Trust to thy single virtue ; for thy sol-
      diers,
All levied in my name, have in my name
Took their discharge.
   Regan.   My sickness grows upon me.
   Albany. She is not well. — Convey her to my tent. —
                  [*Exit Regan, led.*

Enter a Herald

Come hither, herald. — Let the trumpet sound, —
And read out this.   109
   Captain. Sound, trumpet !   [*A trumpet sounds.*
   Herald. [Reads] ' *If any man of quality or degree
within the lists of the army will maintain upon Ed-
mund, supposed Earl of Gloster, that he is a manifold
traitor, let him appear by the third sound of the trum-
pet ; he is bold in his defence.*'
   Edmund. Sound !   [*First trumpet.*
   Herald. Again !   [*Second trumpet.*
   Herald. Again !   [*Third trumpet.*
                       [*Trumpet answers within.*

Enter EDGAR, *at the third sound, armed, with a trumpet
before him*

   Albany. Ask him his purposes, why he appears
Upon this call o' the trumpet.
   Herald.   What are you ?   120
Your name, your quality? and why you answer
This present summons ?
   Edgar.   Know, my name is lost,
By treason's tooth bare-gnawn and canker-bit ;
Yet am I noble as the adversary
I come to cope.
   Albany.   Which is that adversary?
   Edgar. What 's he that speaks for Edmund Earl of
    Gloster ?

Edmund. Himself; what say'st thou to him?
  Edgar.   Draw thy sword,
That, if my speech offend a noble heart,
Thy arm may do thee justice ; here is mine.
Behold, it is the privilege of mine honours,   130
My oath, and my profession.   I protest, —
Maugre thy strength, place, youth, and eminence,
Despite thy victor sword and fire-new fortune,
Thy valour and thy heart, — thou art a traitor,
False to thy gods, thy brother, and thy father,
Conspirant 'gainst this high illustrious prince,
And, from the extremest upward of thy head
To the descent and dust below thy foot,
A most toad-spotted traitor.   Say thou ' No,'
This sword, this arm, and my best spirits are bent 140
To prove upon thy heart, whereto I speak,
Thou liest.
  Edmund. In wisdom I should ask thy name ;
But, since thy outside looks so fair and warlike,
And that thy tongue some say of breeding breathes,
What safe and nicely I might well delay
By rule of knighthood, I disdain and spurn.
Back do I toss these treasons to thy head,
With the hell-hated lie o'erwhelm thy heart ;
Which, for they yet glance by and scarcely bruise, 150
This sword of mine shall give them instant way,
Where they shall rest for ever. — Trumpets, speak !
     [*Alarums.   They fight.   Edmund falls.*
  Albany. Save him, save him !

Goneril.   This is practice, Gloster;
By the law of arms thou wast not bound to answer
An unknown opposite : thou art not vanquish'd,
But cozen'd and beguil'd.
    Albany.   Shut your mouth, dame,
Or with this paper shall I stop it. — Hold, sir ;
Thou worse than any name, read thine own evil. —
No tearing, lady ; I perceive you know it.
                        [*Gives the letter to Edmund.*
    Goneril. Say, if I do, the laws are mine, not thine.
Who can arraign me for 't ?   [*Exit.*
    Albany.   Most monstrous ! O ! — 161
Know'st thou this paper ?
    Edmund.   Ask me not what I know.
    Albany. Go after her : she 's desperate ; govern her.
    Edmund. What you have charg'd me with, that have
        I done ;
And more, much more : the time will bring it out.
'T is past, and so am I. — But what art thou
That hast this fortune on me ? If thou 'rt noble,
I do forgive thee.
    Edgar.   Let 's exchange charity.
I am no less in blood than thou art, Edmund ;
If more, the more thou hast wrong'd me.   170
My name is Edgar, and thy father's son.
The gods are just, and of our pleasant vices
Make instruments to plague us.
The dark and vicious place where thee he got
Cost him his eyes.

Edmund.   Thou hast spoken right, 't is true :
The wheel is come full circle ; I am here.
    Albany. Methought thy very gait did prophesy
A royal nobleness.   I must embrace thee ;
Let sorrow split my heart if ever I
Did hate thee or thy father !
    Edgar.   Worthy prince, I know 't.
    Albany. Where have you hid yourself ?   181
How have you known the miseries of your father ?
    Edgar. By nursing them, my lord.   List a brief tale ;
And when 't is told, O that my heart would burst !
The bloody proclamation to escape,
That follow'd me so near, — O, our lives' sweetness !
That we the pain of death would hourly die
Rather than die at once ! — taught me to shift
Into a madman's rags, to assume a semblance
That very dogs disdain'd ; and in this habit   190
Met I my father with his bleeding rings,
Their precious stones new lost, became his guide,
Led him, begg'd for him, sav'd him from despair ;
Never, — O fault ! — reveal'd myself unto him,
Until some half-hour past, when I was arm'd.
Not sure, though hoping, of this good success,
I ask'd his blessing, and from first to last
Told him my pilgrimage ; but his flaw'd heart, —
Alack, too weak the conflict to support ! —
'Twixt two extremes of passion, joy and grief,   200
Burst smilingly.
    Edmund.   This speech of yours hath mov'd me,

And shall perchance do good. But speak you on;
You look as you had something more to say.
   Albany. If there be more, more woful, hold it in;
For I am almost ready to dissolve,
Hearing of this.
   Edgar.   This would have seem'd a period
To such as love not sorrow; but another,
To amplify too much, would make much more,
And top extremity.
Whilst I was big in clamour there came in a man   210
Who, having seen me in my worst estate,
Shunn'd my abhorr'd society; but then, finding
Who 't was that so endur'd, with his strong arms
He fasten'd on my neck, and bellow'd out
As he 'd burst heaven, threw him on my father,
Told the most piteous tale of Lear and him
That ever ear receiv'd; which in recounting
His grief grew puissant, and the strings of life
Began to crack. Twice then the trumpets sounded,
And there I left him tranc'd.
   Albany.   But who was this?   220
   Edgar. Kent, sir, the banish'd Kent; who in disguise
Follow'd his enemy king, and did him service
Improper for a slave.

     Enter a Gentleman *with a bloody knife*

   Gentleman. Help, help, O, help!
   Edgar.   What kind of help?
   Albany.   Speak, man.

Edgar. What means that bloody knife?

Gentleman.   'T is hot, it smokes!
It came even from the heart of — O, she's dead!

Albany. Who dead? speak, man.

Gentleman. Your lady, sir, your lady! and her sister
By her is poison'd; she confesses it.

Edmund. I was contracted to them both; all three
Now marry in an instant.

Edgar.   Here comes Kent.   231

Albany. Produce the bodies, be they alive or dead.
This judgment of the heavens, that makes us tremble,
Touches us not with pity. —   [*Exit Gentleman.*

Enter KENT

                              O, is this he?
The time will not allow the compliment
Which very manners urges.

Kent.   I am come
To bid my king and master aye good night.
Is he not here?

Albany.   Great thing of us forgot! —
Speak, Edmund, where 's the king? and where 's Cor-
         delia? —
See'st thou this object, Kent?   240
         [*The bodies of Goneril and Regan are brought in.*

Kent. Alack, why thus?

Edmund.   Yet Edmund was belov'd.
The one the other poison'd for my sake,
And after slew herself.

Albany. Even so. — Cover their faces.

Edmund. I pant for life ; some good I mean to do,
Despite of mine own nature. — Quickly send,
Be brief in it, to the castle ! for my writ
Is on the life of Lear and on Cordelia.
Nay, send in time !

Albany.   Run, run, O, run !

Edgar. To who, my lord ? — Who has the office ?
          send   250
Thy token of reprieve.

Edmund. Well thought on ; take my sword,
Give it the captain.

Albany.   Haste thee, for thy life !
                              [*Exit Edgar.*

Edmund. He hath commission from thy wife and me
To hang Cordelia in the prison, and
To lay the blame upon her own despair,
That she fordid herself.

Albany. The gods defend her ! — Bear him hence
          awhile.   [*Edmund is borne off.*

Re-enter LEAR, *with* CORDELIA *dead in his arms ;*
     EDGAR, Captain, *and others following*

Lear. Howl, howl, howl, howl ! O, you are men of
          stones !
Had I your tongues and eyes, I 'd use them so   260
That heaven's vault should crack. She 's gone for
          ever !
I know when one is dead, and when one lives.

She 's dead as earth.   Lend me a looking-glass ;
If that her breath will mist or stain the stone,
Why, then she lives.
    Kent.   Is this the promis'd end ?
    Edgar. Or image of that horror ?
    Albany.   Fall and cease !
    Lear. This feather stirs ! she lives ! if it be so,
It is a chance which does redeem all sorrows
That ever I have felt.
    Kent.   O my good master !
    Lear. Prithee, away !
    Edgar.   'T is noble Kent, your friend.
    Lear. A plague upon you, murtherers, traitors, all ! 271
I might have sav'd her ! now she 's gone for ever ! —
Cordelia, Cordelia ! stay a little. Ha !
What is 't thou say'st ? — Her voice was ever soft,
Gentle and low, an excellent thing in woman. —
I kill'd the slave that was a-hanging thee.
    Captain. 'T is true, my lords, he did.
    Lear.   Did I not, fellow?
I have seen the day, with my good biting falchion
I would have made them skip. I am old now,
And these same crosses spoil me. — Who are you ?   280
Mine eyes are not o' the best; I 'll tell you straight.
    Kent. If Fortune brag of two she lov'd and hated,
One of them ye behold.
    Lear. This is a dull sight. — Are you not Kent ?
    Kent.   The same,
Your servant Kent. Where is your servant Caius ?

Lear. He 's a good fellow, I can tell you that;
He 'll strike, and quickly too. He 's dead and rotten.
    Kent. No, my good lord; I am the very man —
    Lear. I 'll see that straight.
    Kent. That from your first of difference and decay
Have follow'd your sad steps —
    Lear.   You are welcome hither.
    Kent. Nor no man else; all 's cheerless, dark, and
        deadly.   292
Your eldest daughters have fordone themselves,
And desperately are dead.
    Lear.   Ay, so I think.
    Albany. He knows not what he says, and vain it is
That we present us to him.
    Edgar.   Very bootless.

Enter a Captain

    Captain. Edmund is dead, my lord.
    Albany.   That 's but a trifle here. —
You lords and noble friends, know our intent.
What comfort to this great decay may come
Shall be applied: for us, we will resign,   300
During the life of this old majesty,
To him our absolute power; — [*To Edgar and Kent*]
        you, to your rights,
With boot, and such addition as your honours
Have more than merited. All friends shall taste
The wages of their virtue, and all foes
The cup of their deservings. — O, see, see!

Lear. And my poor fool is hang'd !   No, no, no life !
Why should a dog, a horse, a rat, have life,
And thou no breath at all ?   Thou 'lt come no more,
Never, never, never, never, never ! —   310
Pray you, undo this button ; thank you, sir. —
Do you see this ?   Look on her, — look, — her lips, —
Look there, look there !   [*Dies.*
    Edgar.   He faints ! — My lord, my lord !
    Kent. Break, heart ; I prithee, break !
    Edgar.   Look up, my lord.
    Kent. Vex not his ghost.   O, let him pass ! he hates
        him
That would upon the rack of this tough world
Stretch him out longer.
    Edgar.   He is gone, indeed.
    Kent. The wonder is he hath endur'd so long ;
He but usurp'd his life.
    Albany. Bear them from hence. — Our present busi-
        ness   320
Is general woe. — [*To Kent and Edgar*] Friends of my
        soul, you twain
Rule in this realm, and the gor'd state sustain.
    Kent. I have a journey, sir, shortly to go ;
My master calls me, I must not say no.
    Albany. The weight of this sad time we must obey,
Speak what we feel, not what we ought to say.
The oldest hath borne most ; we that are young
Shall never see so much, nor live so long.
                        [*Exeunt, with a dead march.*

NOTES

NORMAN GATEWAY — DOVER CASTLE

NOTES

INTRODUCTION

THE METRE OF THE PLAY. — It should be understood at the outset that *metre*, or the mechanism of verse, is something altogether distinct from the *music* of verse. The one is matter of rule, the other of taste and feeling. Music is not an absolute necessity of verse; the metrical form is a necessity, being that which constitutes the verse.

The plays of Shakespeare (with the exception of rhymed passages, and of occasional songs and interludes) are all in unrhymed or *blank* verse ; and the normal form of this blank verse is illustrated by i. 1. 54 of the present play : " As much as child e'er lov'd or father found."

This line, it will be seen, consists of ten syllables, with the even syllables (2d, 4th, 6th, 8th, and 10th) accented, the odd syllables (1st, 3d, etc.) being unaccented. Theoretically, it is made up of

five *feet* of two syllables each, with the accent on the second syllable. Such a foot is called an *iambus* (plural, *iambuses*, or the Latin
iambi), and the form of verse is called *iambic*.

This fundamental law of Shakespeare's verse is subject to certain
modifications, the most important of which are as follows: —

1. After the tenth syllable an unaccented syllable (or even two
such syllables) may be added, forming what is sometimes called a
female line; as in i. 1. 55: "A love that makes breath poor and
speech unable." The rhythm is complete with the second syllable
of *unable*, the third being an extra eleventh syllable. In i. 1. 37
("And you, our no less loving son of Albany") we have two extra
syllables, the rhythm being complete with the first syllable of *Albany*.

2. The accent in any part of the verse may be shifted from an
even to an odd syllable; as in i. 1. 46: "Which of you shall we
say doth love us most?" and 51 · "Dearer than eyesight, space,
and liberty." In both lines the accent is shifted from the second to
the first syllable. This change occurs very rarely in the tenth syllable, and seldom in the fourth; and it is not allowable in two suc-
cessive accented syllables.

3. An extra unaccented syllable may occur in any part of the
line; as in i. 1. 39, 59, and 60. In 39 the second syllable of *several*
is superfluous; in 59 the second syllable of *shadowy;* and in 60
that of *plenteous*. In line 64 (a female line) the word *am* is superfluous.

4. Any unaccented syllable, occurring in an even place immediately before or after an even syllable which is properly accented, is
reckoned as accented for the purposes of the verse ; as, for instance,
in lines 51 and 70. In 51 the last syllable of *liberty*, and in 70 that
of *felicitate*, are metrically equivalent to accented syllables ; and so
with the fourth syllable of *hereditary* in 74 and of *validity* in 76
(both being female lines), and the third of *Burgundy* in 79.

5. In many instances in Shakespeare words must be *lengthened*
in order to fill out the rhythm: —

(*a*) In a large class of words in which *e* or *i* is followed by another vowel, the *e* or *i* is made a separate syllable; as *ocean, opinion, soldier, patience, partial, marriage,* etc. For instance, in this play, iv. 5. 3 ("Your sister is the better soldier") appears to have only nine syllables, but *soldier* is a trisyllable; and the same is true of *gorgeous* in ii. 4. 266: "If only to go warm were gorgeous." This lengthening occurs most frequently at the end of the line, but there are few instances of it in *Lear.*

(*b*) Many monosyllables ending in *r, re, rs, res,* preceded by a long vowel or diphthong, are often made dissyllables; as *fare, fear, dear, fire, hair, hour, more* (see on i. 4. 347 and v. 3. 170), *your,* etc. In iii. 2. 15 ("Nor rain, wind, thunder, fire, are my daughters") *fire* is a dissyllable. If the word is repeated in a verse it is often both monosyllable and dissyllable; as in *M. of V.* iii. 2. 20: "And so, though yours, not yours. Prove it so," where either *yours* (preferably the first) is a dissyllable, the other being a monosyllable. In *J. C.* iii. 1. 172: "As fire drives out fire, so pity, pity," the first *fire* is a dissyllable.

(*c*) Words containing *l* or *r*, preceded by another consonant, are often pronounced as if a vowel came between the consonants; as in *T. of S.* ii. 1. 158: "While she did call me rascal fiddler" [fidd(e)ler]; *All 's Well,* iii. 5. 43: "If you will tarry, holy pilgrim" [pilg(e)rim]; *C. of E.* v. 1. 360: "These are the parents of these children" (childeren, the original form of the word); *W. T.* iv. 4. 76: "Grace and remembrance [rememb(e)rance] be to you both!" etc.

(*d*) Monosyllabic exclamations (*ay, O, yea, nay, hail,* etc.) and monosyllables otherwise emphasized are similarly lengthened; also certain longer words; as *commandement* in the *M. of V.* (iv. 1. 444); *safety* (trisyllable) in *Ham.* i. 3. 21; *business* (trisyllable, as originally pronounced) in *J. C.* iv. 1. 22: "To groan and sweat under the business" (so in several other passages); and other words mentioned in the notes to the plays in which they occur.

6. Words are also *contracted* for metrical reasons, like plurals and possessives ending in a sibilant, as *balance, horse* (for *horses*

and *horse's*), *princess, sense, marriage* (plural and possessive), *image* (see note on ii. 4. 87), etc. So with many adjectives in the super-lative (like *cold'st* in i. 1. 249, *stern'st, kind'st, secret'st*, etc.), and certain other words.

7. The *accent* of words is also varied in many instances for met-rical reasons. Thus we find both *révenue* and *revénue* in the first scene of the *M. N. D.* (lines 6 and 158), *cónfine* (noun) and *con-fíne* (see note on ii. 4. 145), *mátúre* (see on iv. 6. 258) and *ma-túre, púrsue* and *pursúe, dístinct* and *distínct*, etc.

These instances of variable accent must not be confounded with those in which words were uniformly accented differently in the time of Shakespeare; like *aspéct* (see on ii. 2. 108), *impórtune, sepúlchre* (verb; see on ii. 4. 129), *perséver* (never *persevére*), *perséverance, rheúmatic*, etc.

8. *Alexandrines*, or verses of twelve syllables, with six accents, occur here and there in the plays. They must not be confounded with female lines with two extra syllables (see on 1 above) or with other lines in which two extra unaccented syllables may occur.

9. *Incomplete* verses, of one or more syllables, are scattered through the plays. See i. 1. 49, 99, 101, 102, etc.

10. *Doggerel* measure is used in the very earliest comedies (*L. L. L.* and *C. of E.* in particular) in the mouths of comic characters, but nowhere else in those plays, and never anywhere in plays written after 1598.

11. *Rhyme* occurs frequently in the early plays, but diminishes with comparative regularity from that period until the latest. Thus, in *L. L. L.* there are about 1100 rhyming verses (about one-third of the whole number), in the *M. N. D.* about 900, in *Richard II.* and *R. and J.* about 500 each, while in *Cor.* and *A. and C.* there are only about 40 each, in the *Temp.* only two, and in the *W. T.* none at all, except in the chorus introducing act iv. Songs, interludes, and other matter not in ten-syllable measure are not included in this enumeration. In the present play, out of some 2200 ten-syllable verses, only about seventy are in rhyme.

Alternate rhymes are found only in the plays written before 1599 or 1600. In the *M. of V.* there are only four lines at the end of iii. 2. In *Much Ado* and *A. Y. L.*, we also find a few lines, but none at all in this and subsequent plays.

Rhymed couplets, or "rhyme-tags" are often found at the end of scenes; as in 9 of the 26 scenes of the present play. In *Ham.*, 14 out of 20 scenes, and in *Macb.*, 21 out of 28, have such "tags;" but in the latest plays they are not so frequent. The *Temp.*, for instance, has but one, and the *W. T.* none.

12. In this edition of Shakespeare, the final *-ed* of past tenses and participles *in verse* is printed *-'d* when the word is to be pronounced in the ordinary way; as in *answer'd*, line 43, and *lov'd*, line 54, of the first scene. But when the metre requires that the *-ed* be made a separate syllable, the *e* is retained; as in *not-to-be-endured*, i. 4. 209, where *endured* is a trisyllable. The only variation from this rule is in verbs like *cry, die, sue*, etc., the *-ed* of which is very rarely, if ever, made a separate syllable.

SHAKESPEARE'S USE OF VERSE AND PROSE IN THE PLAYS. — This is a subject to which the critics have given very little attention, but it is an interesting study. In *Lear* we find scenes entirely in verse or in prose, and others in which the two are mixed. In general, we may say that verse is used for what is distinctly poetical, and prose for what is not poetical. The distinction, however, is not so clearly marked in the earlier as in the later plays. The second scene of the *M. of V.*, for instance, is in prose, because Portia and Nerissa are talking about the suitors in a familiar and playful way; but in the *T. G. of V.*, where Julia and Lucetta are discussing the suitors of the former in much the same fashion, the scene is in verse. Dowden, commenting on *Rich. II.*, remarks: " Had Shakespeare written the play a few years later, we may be certain that the gardener and his servants (iii. 4) would not have uttered stately speeches in verse, but would have spoken homely prose, and that humour would have mingled with the pathos of the scene. The same remark may be made with reference to the subsequent scene (v. 5) in which his groom visits the dethroned king in the Tower." Comic characters and those in low life generally speak in prose in the later plays, as Dowden intimates, but in the very earliest ones doggerel verse is much used instead. See on 11 above.

The change from prose to verse is well illustrated in the third scene of the *M. of V.* It begins with plain prosaic talk about a business matter; but when Antonio enters, it rises at once to the higher level of poetry. The sight of Antonio reminds Shylock of his hatred of the Merchant, and the passion expresses itself in verse, the vernacular tongue of poetry. We have a similar change in the first scene of *J. C.*, where, after the quibbling "chaff" of the mechanics about their trades, the mention of Pompey reminds the Tribune of their plebeian fickleness, and his scorn and indignation flame out in most eloquent verse.

The reasons for the choice of prose or verse are not always so clear as in these instances. We are seldom puzzled to explain the prose, but not unfrequently we meet with verse where we might expect prose. As Professor Corson remarks (*Introduction to Shakespeare*, 1889), "Shakespeare adopted verse as the general tenor of his language, and therefore expressed much in verse that is within the capabilities of prose; in other words, his verse constantly encroaches upon the domain of prose, but his prose can never be said to encroach upon the domain of verse." If in rare instances we think we find exceptions to this latter statement, and prose actually seems to usurp the place of verse, I believe that careful study of the passage will prove the supposed exception to be apparent rather than real.

SOME BOOKS FOR TEACHERS AND STUDENTS. — A few out of the many books that might be commended to the teacher and the critical student are the following: Halliwell-Phillipps's *Outlines of the Life of Shakespeare* (7th ed. 1887); Sidney Lee's *Life of Shakespeare* (1898; for ordinary students the abridged ed. of 1899 is preferable); Schmidt's *Shakespeare Lexicon* (3d ed. 1902); Littledale's ed. of Dyce's *Glossary* (1902); Bartlett's *Concordance to Shakespeare* (1895); Abbott's *Shakespearian Grammar* (1873); Furness's "New Variorum" ed. of *Lear* (1880; encyclopædic and exhaustive); Dowden's *Shakspere : His Mind and Art* (American ed. 1881); Hudson's *Life, Art, and Characters of Shakespeare* (revised ed. 1882); Mrs. Jameson's *Characteristics of Women* (several eds.; some with the title, *Shakespeare Heroines*); Ten Brink's *Five Lectures on Shakespeare* (1895); Boas's *Shakespeare and His Predecessors* (1895); Dyer's *Folk-lore of Shakespeare* (American ed. 1884); Gervinus's *Shakespeare Commentaries* (Bunnett's translation, 1875); Wordsworth's *Shakespeare's Knowledge of the Bible* (3d ed. 1880); Elson's *Shakespeare in Music* (1901).

Some of the above books will be useful to all readers who are interested in special subjects or in general criticism of Shakespeare. Among those which are better suited to the needs of ordinary readers and students, the following may be mentioned: Mabie's *William Shakespeare : Poet, Dramatist, and Man* (1900); Phin's *Cyclopædia and Glossary of Shakespeare* (1902; more compact and cheaper than Dyce); Dowden's *Shakspere Primer* (1877; small but invaluable); Rolfe's *Shakespeare the Boy* (1896 ; treating of the home and school life, the games and sports, the manners, customs, and folk-lore of the poet's time); Guerber's *Myths of Greece and Rome* (for young students who may need information on mythological allusions not explained in the notes).

Black's *Judith Shakespeare* (1884; a novel, but a careful study of the scene and the time) is a book that I always commend to young people, and their elders will also enjoy it. The Lambs' *Tales from Shakespeare* is a classic for beginners in the study of the dramatist ; and in Rolfe's ed. the plan of the authors is carried out in the Notes by copious illustrative quotations from the plays. Mrs. Cowden-Clarke's *Girlhood of Shakespeare's Heroines* (several eds.) will particularly interest girls; and both girls and boys will find Bennett's *Master Skylark* (1897) and Imogen Clark's *Will Shakespeare's Little Lad* (1897) equally entertaining and instructive.

H. Snowden Ward's *Shakespeare's Town and Times* (1896) and John Leyland's *Shakespeare Country* (1900) are copiously illustrated books (yet inexpensive) which may be particularly commended for school libraries.

ABBREVIATIONS IN THE NOTES. — The abbreviations of the names of Shakespeare's plays will be readily understood ; as *T. N.* for *Twelfth Night, Cor.* for *Coriolanus,* 3 *Hen. VI.* for *The Third Part of King Henry the Sixth,* etc. *P. P.* refers to *The Passionate Pilgrim ; V. and A.* to *Venus and Adonis ; L. C.* to *Lover's Complaint ;* and *Sonn.* to the *Sonnets.*

Other abbreviations that hardly need explanation are *Cf.* (*confer,* compare), *Fol.* (following), *Id.* (*idem,* the same), and *Prol.* (prologue). The numbers of the lines in the references (except for the present play) are those of the "Globe" edition (the cheapest and best edition of *Shakespeare* in one compact volume), which is now generally accepted as the standard for line-numbers in works of reference (Schmidt's *Lexicon,* Abbott's *Grammar,* Dowden's *Primer,* the publications of the New Shakspere Society, etc.).

THE STORIES OF THE PLAY AS TOLD BY HOLINSHED AND SIDNEY. — The story of Lear and his daughters as told by Holinshed (ed. 1574) is as follows : [1] —

" Leir the sonne of Baldud, was admitted ruler ouer the Britaines, in the yeere of the world 3105, at what time Ioas raigned as yet in Iuda. This Leir was a prince of right noble demeanor, gouerning his land and subiects in great wealth. He made the towne of Caerlier nowe called Leicester, which standeth vpon the riuer of Sore. It is written that he had by his wife three daughters without other issue, whose names were Gonorilla, Regan, and Cordeilla, which daughters he greatly loued, but specially Cordeilla the yoongest farre aboue the two elder. When this Leir therefore was come to great yeeres, & began to waxe vnweldie through age, he thought to vnderstand the affections of his daughters towards

[1] See Furness, p. 384 fol.

him, and preferre hir whome he best loued, to the succession ouer the kingdome. Whervpon he first asked Gonorilla the eldest, how well shee loued him: who calling hir gods to record, protested, that she loued him more than hir owne life, which by right and reason shoulde be most deere vnto hir. With which answer the father being well pleased, turned to the second, and demanded of hir how well she loued him: who answered (confirming hir saiengs with great othes) that she loued him more than toung could expresse, and farre aboue all other creatures of the world.

"Then called he his yoongest daughter Cordeilla before him, and asked of hir what account she made of him: vnto whome she made this answer as followeth: Knowing the great loue and fatherlie zeale that you haue always borne towards me, (for the which I maie not answere you otherwise than I thinke, and as my conscience leadeth me) I protest vnto you, that I haue loued you euer, and will continuallie (while I liue) loue you as my naturall father. And if you would more vnderstand of the loue that I beare you, assertaine your selfe, that so much as you haue, so much you are worth, and so much I loue you, and no more. The father being nothing content with this answer, married his two eldest daughters, the one vnto Henninus, the Duke of Cornewal, and the other vnto Maglanus, the Duke of Albania, betwixt whome he willed and ordeined that his land should be deuided after his death, and the one halfe thereof immediatelie should be assigned to them in hand : but for the third daughter Cordeilla he reserued nothing.

"Neuertheless it fortuned that one of the princes of Gallia (which now is called France) whose name was Aganippus, hearing of the beautie, womanhood, and good conditions of the said Cordeilla, desired to haue hir in mariage, and sent ouer to hir father, requiring that he mighte haue hir to wife: to whome answere was made, that he might haue his daughter, but as for anie dower he could haue none, for all was promised and assured to hir other sisters alreadie. Aganippus notwithstanding this answer of deniall to receiue anie thing by way of dower with Cordeilla, tooke hir to wife, onlie moued thereto (I saie) for respect of hir person and amiable vertues. This Aganippus was one of the twelue kings that ruled Gallia in those daies, as in the Brittish historie it is recorded. But to proceed.

"After that Leir was fallen into age, the two dukes that had married his two eldest daughters, thinking long yer the gouernment of 'the land did come to their hands, arose against him in armour, and reft from him the gouernance of the land, vpon conditions to be continued for terme of life: by the which he was put to his portion, that is, to liue after a rate assigned to him for the maintenance of his estate, which in processe of time was diminished as well by Maglanus as by Henninus. But the greatest griefe that Leir tooke, was to see the vnkindnesse of his daughters, which seemed to thinke that all was too much which their father had, the same being neuer so little: in so much, that going from the one to the other, he was brought to that miserie, that scarslie they would allow him one seruaunt to waite vpon him.

"In the end, such was the vnkindnesse, or (as I maie saie) the vnnaturalnesse which he found in his two daughters, notwithstanding their faire and pleasant words vttered in time past, that being constreined of necessitie, he fled the land, and sailed into Gallia, there to seeke some comfort of his youngest daughter Cordeilla whom before time he hated. The ladie Cordeilla hearing that he was arriued in poore estate, she first sent to him priuilie a certeine summe of monie to apparell himselfe withall, and to reteine a certein number of seruants that might attende vpon him in honorable wise, as apperteined to the estate which he had borne: and then so accompanied, she appointed him to come to the court, which he did, and was so ioifullie, honorablie, and louinglie receiued, both by his sonne in law Aganippus, and also by his daughter Cordeilla, that his hart was greatlie comforted; for he was no lesse honored, than if he had beene king of the whole countrie himselfe.

"Now when he had informed his son in law and his daughter in what sort he had beene vsed by his other daughters, Aganippus caused a mightie armie to be put in readinesse, and likewise a greate nauie of ships to be rigged, to passe ouer into Britaine with Leir his father in law, to see him againe restored to his kingdome. It was accorded, that Cordeilla should also go with him to take possession of the land, the which he promised to leaue vnto hir, as the rightfull inheritour after his decesse, notwithstanding any former grant made to hir sisters or to their husbands in anie maner of wise.

"Herevpon, when this armie and nauie of ships were readie, Leir and his daughter Cordeilla with hir husband tooke the sea, and arriuing in Britaine, fought with their enimies, and discomfited them in battell, in which Maglanus and Henninus were slaine : and then was Leir restored to his kingdome, which he ruled after this by the space of two yeeres, and then died, fortie yeeres after he first began to reigne. His bodie was buried at Leicester in a vaut vnder the chanell of the riuer of Sore beneath the towne.

"Cordeilla the yoongest daughter of Leir was admitted Q. and supreme gouernesse of Britaine, in the yeere of the world 3155, before the bylding of Rome 54, Uzia was then reigning in Juda, and Jeroboam ouer Israell. This Cordeilla after hir father's deceasse ruled the land of Britaine right worthilie during the space of fiue yeeres, in which meane time her husband died, and then about the end of those fiue yeeres, hir two nephewes Margan and Cunedag, sonnes to hir aforesaid sisters, disdaining to be vnder the gouernment of a woman, leuied warre against hir, and destroied a great part of the land, and finallie tooke hir prisoner, and laid hir fast in ward, wherewith she tooke suche griefe, being a woman of a manlie courage, and despairing to recouer libertie, there she slue hirselfe."

The following extract from Sir Philip Sidney's *Arcadia* (lib. ii. pp. 133–138, ed. 1598) contains the story, referred to on page 11 above, from which Shakespeare derived the incidents of his plot in which Gloster figures. It is entitled, in the ed. of 1590, "The pitifull state, and story of the Paphlagonian vnkinde king, and his kind sonne, first related by the son, then by the blind father: " —

"It was in the kingdome of *Galacia*, the season being (as in the depth of winter) verie cold, and as then sodainlie growne to so extreame and foule a storme, that neuer any winter (I thinke) brought forth a fowler child : so that the Princes were euen cōpelled by the haile, that the pride of the winde blew into their faces, to seeke some shrowding place which a certain hollow rocke offering vnto them, they made it their shield against the tempests furie. And so staying there, till the violence there of was passed, they heard the speach of a couple, who not perceiuing them, being hid within that rude canapie, held a straunge and pitifull disputation, which made them step out, yet in such sort, as they might see vnseene. There they perceiued an aged man, and a young, scarcelie come to the age of a man, both poorely arrayed, extreamely weather-beaten; the olde man blind, the young man leading him : and yet through all those miseries in both there seemed to appeare a kind of noble- nesse, not sutable to that affliction. But the first words they heard, were these of the old man. Well *Leonatus* (said he) since I can- not perswade thee to leade me to that which should end my griefe, and thy trouble, let me now intreat thee to leaue me : feare not, my miserie cannot be greater then it is, and nothing doth become me but miserie : feare not the daunger of my blind steps, I cannot fall worse then I am: and do not I pray thee, do not obstinately continue to infect thee with my wretchednesse : but flie, flie from this region only worthie of me. Deare father (answered he) do not take away from me the only remnant of my happinesse : while I haue power to do you seruice, I am not whollie miserable. Ah my sonne (said he, and with that he groned, as if sorrow straue to breake his heart) how euill fits it me to haue such a sonne, and how much doth thy kindnesse vpbraid my wickednesse ? These dole- full speeches, and some others to like purpose (well shewing they had not bene borne to the fortune they were in,) moued the Princes to go out vnto them, and aske the younger what they were ?

Sirs (answered he with a good grace, and made the more agreeable by a certaine noble kind of piteousnesse) I see well you are straungers, that know not our miserie, so well here knowne, that no man dare know, but that we must be miserable. Indeed our state is such, as though nothing is so needfull vnto vs as pitie, yet nothing is more dangerous vnto vs, then to make our selues so knowne as may stirre pitie; but your presence promiseth that crueltie shall not ouer-runne hate : and if it did, in truth our state is sunke below the degree of feare.

" This old man (whom I leade) was lately rightfull Prince of this countrie of *Paphlagonia*, by the hard-hearted vngratefulnesse of a sonne of his, depriued, not onely of his kingdome (whereof no forraine forces were euer able to spoyle him) but of his sight, the riches which Nature graunts to the poorest creatures. Whereby, and by other his vnnaturall dealings, he hath bene driuen to such griefe, as euen now he would haue had me to haue led him to the top of this rocke, thence to cast himselfe headlong to death : and so would haue made me, who receiued my life of him, to be the worker of his destruction. But noble Gentlemen, said he, if either of you haue a father, and feele what dutifull affection is engraffed in a sonnes heart, let me intreat you to conueigh this afflicted Prince to some place of rest and securitie : amongst your worthie acts it shall be none of the least, that a king of such might and fame, & so vniustlie oppressed, is in any sort by you relieued.

" But before they could make him answere, his father beganne to speake. Ah my sonne, said he, how euill an Historian are you, that leaue out the chiefe knot of all the discourse? my wickednesse, my wickednesse : and if thou doest it to spare my eares, (the only sense now left me proper for knowledge) assure thy selfe thou doest mistake me : and I take witnesse of that Sunne which you see (with that he cast vp his blind eyes, as if he would hunt for light) and wish my selfe in worse case then I do wish my selfe, which is as euill as may be, if I speake vntrulie, that nothing is so welcome to my thoughts, as the publishing of my shame. Therefore know you

Gentlemen (to whom from my heart I wish that it may not proue some ominous foretoken of misfortune to haue met with such a miser as I am) that whatsoeuer my son (ô God, that truth binds me to reproch him with the name of my son) hath said is true. But besides those truthes, this also is true, that hauing had in lawfull mariage, of a mother fit to beare royall children, this sonne (such a one as partly you see, and better shall know by my short declaration) and so enioyed the expectations in the world of him, till he was growne to iustifie their expectations (so as I needed enuie no father for the chiefe comfort of mortalitie, to leaue another onesselfe after me) I was caried by a bastard sonne of mine (if at least I be bound to beleeue the words of that base woman my concubine, his mother) first to mislike, then to hate, lastlie to destroy, or to do my best to destroy this sonne (I thinke you thinke) vndeseruing destruction. What wayes he vsed to bring me to it, if I should tell you, I should tediouslie trouble you with as much poisonous hypocrisie, desperate fraud, smooth malice, hidden ambition, and smiling enuie, as in anie liuing person could be harboured : but I list it not; no remembrance of naughtinesse delights me but mine owne ; and me thinks, the accusing his traps might in some maner excuse my fault, which certainlie I lothe to do. But the conclusion is, that I gaue orders to some seruants of mine, whom I thought as apt for such charities as my selfe, to leade him out into a forrest, and there to kill him.

"But those theeues (better natured to my sonne then myselfe) spared his life, letting him go to learne to liue poorely : which he did, giuing himselfe to be a priuate souldier in a countrey here by : but as he was ready to be greatly aduanced for some noble peeces of seruice which he did, he heard newes of me: who (drunke in my affection to that vnlawfull and vnnaturall sonne of mine) suffered my selfe so to be gouerned by him, that all fauours and punishments passed by him, all offices, and places of importance distributed to his fauorites ; so that ere I was aware, I had left my selfe nothing but the name of a King : which he shortly wearie of too, with many indignities (if any thing may be called an indignitie, which was laid vpon me) threw me out of my seat, and put out my eyes; and then (proud in his tyrannie) let me go, neither imprisoning, nor killing me ; but rather delighting to make me feele my miserie ; miserie indeed, if euer there were anie ; full of wretchedness, fuller of disgrace, and fullest of guiltinesse. And as he came to the crowne by so vniust means, as vniustlie he kept it, by force of straunger souldiers in *Cittadels*, the neasts of tyrannie, and murderers of libertie ; disarming all his owne countrimen, that no man durst shew himself a wel-willer of mine: to say the truth (I thinke) few of them being so (considering my cruell follie to my good sonne, and foolish kindnesse to my vnkind bastard :) but if there were any who felt a pitie of so great a fall, and had yet any sparkes of vnslaine dutie left in them towards me ; yet durst they not shew it, scarcelie with giuing me almes at their doores ; which yet was the onlie sustenance of my distressed life, no bodie daring to shew so much charitie, as to lend me a hand to guide my darke steps: till this sonne of mine (God knowes, worthy of a more vertuous, and more fortunate father) forgetting my abhominable wrongs, not recking daunger, and neglecting the present good way hee was in of doing himselfe good, came hither to do this kind office you see him performe towards me, to my vnspeakeable griefe ; not onlie because his kindnesse is a glasse euen to my blind eyes of my naughtiness, but that aboue all griefes, it grieues me he should desperatelie aduenture the losse of his well-deseruing life for mine, that yet owe more to Fortune for my deserts, as if he would carie mudde in a chest of Chrystall: for well I know, he that now raigneth, how much so euer (and with good reason) he despiseth me, of all men despised ; yet he will not let slip any aduantage to make away him, whose iust title (ennobled by courage & goodnesse) may one day shake the seat of a neuer secure tyrannie. And for this cause I craued of him to leade me to the top of this rocke, indeed I must confesse, with meaning to free him from so serpentine a companion as I am. But he finding what I purposed, onely therein since he was borne, shewed himselfe disobedient vnto me. And now Gentlemen, you haue the true storie, which I pray you publish to the world, that my mischieuous proceedings may be the glorie of his filial pietie, the onlie reward now left for so great a merite. And if it may be, let me obtaine that of you, which my sonne denies me : for neuer was there more pity in sauing any, then in ending me, both because therin my agonie shall end, & so you shal preserue this excellent young man, who else wilfully followes his owne ruine."

ACT I

SCENE I. — *Enter* . . . GLOSTER. In the 1st folio the name is here spelt " *Gloucester*," but in many places in the play (as in *Rich. III.*) it is " *Gloster* " or " *Glouster*," and the abbreviations used are " *Glo.*," " *Glou.*," " *Glost.*," etc. The 1st quarto has " *Gloster*," as have the majority of the modern eds.

1. *Had more affected.* Had been more partial to. The verb is intransitive in *A. and C.* i. 3. 71 : " As thou affect'st " (= likest, pleasest).

2. *Albany.* Holinshed derives the name from Albanacte, or Albanactus, the youngest son of Brute. He gave the name *Albania* to that portion of Britain left him by his father, including all the territory north of the Humber.

5. *Qualities.* The folio reading; the quartos have " equalities," which some editors prefer. *Curiosity* = careful scrutiny. Cf. i. 2. 4 and i. 4. 71. S. uses the word nowhere else except in *T. of A.* iv. 3. 303, where it has a similar sense (= nicety).

7. *Moiety.* Often used for a fraction other than a half. Cf. 1 *Hen. IV.* iii. 1. 96, etc. The meaning of the passage is : the *qualities* or values are so balanced that the nicest discrimination cannot *make choice* among them.

11. *Brazed.* Cf. *Ham.* iii. 4. 37 : " If damned custom have not braz'd it so," etc.

13. *Proper.* Comely; as often. Cf. *Oth.* iv. 3. 35 : " a proper man," etc.

16. *Something.* The adverbial use is very common in S.

27. *Out.* Seeking his fortune abroad. Cf. *T. G. of V.* i. 3. 7 : —

> " He wonder'd that your lordship
> Would suffer him to spend his youth at home,
> While other men, of slender reputation,
> Put forth their sons to seek preferment out; "

that is, in foreign countries.

28. *Sennet.* A succession of notes on the trumpet or cornet.

31. *Darker.* More secret; or " what has not been told before " (Johnson).

33. *In three.* We still say " cut in two," " break in two," etc. *Fast* = fixed, settled; like *constant* in 38 below.

40. *France and Burgundy.* King Lear lived, as the chronicle says, " in the times of Joash, King of Judah." S. appears to imagine Lear as king in the rough times following Charlemagne, when France and Burgundy had become separate nations (Moberly).

44, 45. For *both* with more than two nouns, cf. *V. and A.* 747 : " Both favour, savour, hue, and qualities; " *W. T.* iv. 4. 56 : " She was both pantler, butler, cook; " 1 *Hen. IV.* v. 1. 107 : " Both he and they and you," etc.

48. *Where nature,* etc. Where your natural affection deservedly claims it as due. For *challenge,* cf. *Oth.* i. 3. 188, ii. 1. 213, *Rich II.* ii. 3. 134, etc. See also iv. 7. 31 below.

50. *Word.* The folio reading. The quartos have " words," which some prefer. *Wield* = manage, express.

51. *Space.* Space in general, the world; as *liberty* is the freedom to enjoy it (Schmidt).

56. *Beyond all manner,* etc. " Beyond all assignable quantity :

I love you beyond limits, and cannot say it is *so much*, for how much soever I should name, it would yet be more" (Johnson). But *so much* may refer to the comparisons just made.

57. *What shall Cordelia speak?* The folio reading, retained by Furness and others; the quarto, which is generally followed, has "do" for *speak*. As Furness remarks, the choice of readings, apart from authority, depends on whether we take *Love and be silent* as imperative or not.

59. *Shadowy.* "Shady" (the quarto reading). Cf. *T. G. of V.* v. 4. 2: "This shadowy desert, unfrequented woods." For *champaigns* = plains, cf. *T. N.* ii. 5. 174: "Daylight and champaign discovers not more." *Rich'd* (= enriched) is used by S. nowhere else.

63. *Cornwall.* The quartos add "speake," which most editors adopt.

64. *Self.* Cf. iv. 3. 36 below: "one self mate." See also *C. of E.* v. 1. 10: "that self chain," etc.

65. *And prize me*, etc. And I reckon myself equal to her in affection.

66. *Names my very deed of love.* Describes my love in very deed, or just as it is.

67. *That.* In that, because.

69. *Which the most precious square of sense professes.* The folio reading; the quartos have "possesses." The choice between the two depends on the meaning of *square of sense*, which it is not easy to make out. Johnson says: "Perhaps *square* means only *compass, comprehension.*" Edwards makes it "the full complement of all the senses;" Moberly, "the choicest estimate of sense;" Wright, "the most delicately sensitive part of my nature." If S. wrote the word, it must have one of these meanings — rule, estimate, compass, or range; but there may be some corruption. For a fuller discussion of the enigma the reader may consult Furness, who has a full page of fine print upon it. He reads *professes*, and remarks: "Whatever meaning or no-meaning we may attach to *square of*

sense, it seems clear to me that Regan refers to the joys which that square *professes* to bestow."

70. *Felicitate.* Made happy; the only instance of the word in S. For the form, cf. *degenerate, consecrate, suffocate,* and the like, used as participles or adjectives.

73. *More ponderous.* The quartos have " more richer," which some editors adopt. Schmidt remarks: " *Light* was the usual term applied to a wanton, frivolous, and fickle love; 'light o' love' was a proverbial expression. But the opposite of this, *heavy,* could not be here employed, because that means uniformly, in a moral sense, melancholy, sad; nor is *weighty* any better; therefore S. chose *ponderous.*"

76. *Validity.* Value. In *A. W.* v. 3. 192, the word is used with reference to a ring.

78. *Our last and least.* The folio reading, adopted by Furness and other editors; but many follow the quartos, which have " the last, not least in our deere love." Cf. *J. C.* iii. 1. 189: " Though last, not least in love." Malone quotes *The Spanish Tragedy,* written before 1593: " The third and last, not least, in our account." The expression also occurs in Peele, Middleton, Beaumont and Fletcher, etc. White says: " Plainly this passage was rewritten before the folio was printed. The last part of 82, as it appears in the quartos, shows that the figurative allusion to the King of France and the Duke of Burgundy could have formed no part of the passage when that text was printed. And in the rewriting there was a happy change made from the commonplace of 'last not least' to an allusion to the personal traits and family position of Cordelia. The impression produced by all the passages in which she appears or is referred to is, that she was her father's little pet, while her sisters were big, bold, brazen beauties. Afterward, in this very scene, Lear says of her to Burgundy: 'If aught within that *little* seeming substance, or all of it, *with our displeasure pieced,*' etc. When she is dead, too, her father, although an infirm old man, 'fourscore and upward,' carries her body in his arms. Cordelia

was evidently the least, as well as the youngest and best beloved, of the old king's daughters; and therefore he says to her, 'Now our joy, what can you say to justify my intention of giving you the richest third of the kingdom, although you are the youngest born and the least royal in your presence ?' The poet's every touch upon the figure of Cordelia paints her as, with all her firmness of character, a creature to nestle in a man's bosom, — her father's or her husband's, — and to be cherished almost like a little child; and this happy after-thought brings the picture into perfect keeping, and at the very commencement of the drama impresses upon the mind a characteristic trait of a personage who plays an important part in it, although she is little seen." As Furness says, " *If last, not least* was a hackneyed phrase in Shakespeare's time, it is all the more reason why it should not be used here."

79. *Milk.* A metonymy for pastures. Moberly remarks : " In ascribing vines to France, and not to Burgundy, S. may have thought of the pastoral countries of Southern Belgium as forming part of Burgundy, as they did till the death of Charles the Bold, 1477."

80. *Interess'd.* Theobald's reading, adopted by the editors generally. The folio has " interest," which Schmidt retains, considering it a contracted form of *interested.* Steevens quotes Drayton's *Polyolbion,* preface : " he is someway or other by his blood interessed therein; " and Ben Jonson, *Sejanus,* iii. 1 : —

> " but that the dear republic,
> Our sacred laws, and just authority
> Are interess'd therein, I should be silent."

Wright adds examples of *interessed* from Massinger, Florio, and Minsheu.

82. *Nothing, my lord.* Coleridge remarks : " There is something of disgust at the ruthless hypocrisy of her sisters, and some little faulty admixture of pride and sullenness in Cordelia's ' Nothing; ' and her tone is well contrived, indeed, to lessen the

glaring absurdity of Lear's conduct, but answers the yet more important purpose of forcing away the attention from the nursery-tale the moment it has served its end, that of supplying the canvas for the picture. This is also materially furthered by Kent's opposition, which displays Lear's moral incapability of resigning the sovereign power in the very act of disposing of it. Kent is, perhaps, the nearest to perfect goodness in all Shakespeare's characters, and yet the most individualized. There is an extraordinary charm in his bluntness, which is that only of a nobleman, arising from a contempt of overstrained courtesy, and combined with easy placability where goodness of heart is apparent. His passionate affection for, and fidelity to, Lear act on our feelings in Lear's own favour; virtue seems to be in company with him."

85. *Nothing will come of nothing.* An allusion to the old maxim, *Ex nihilo nihil fit.* Cf. i. 4. 124 below.

88. *According to my bond.* According to my duty, as I am bound by filial obligation. Cf. *A. W.* i. 3. 194: —

> " *Countess.* Love you my son?
> *Helena.*   Do not you love him, madam?
> *Countess.* Go not about; my love hath in 't a bond
> Whereof the world takes note."

89. *Mend.* For the antithesis of *mend* and *mar*, cf. *V. and A.* 478, *R. of L.* 578, and *Sonn.* 103. 10. For *make* and *mar*, cf. *R. and J.* i. 2. 13, *A. Y. L.* i. 1. 34, etc.

92. *As are right fit.* Some make this = " as (they) are right fit (to be returned); " but, as Furness suggests, it may be an instance of the relative use of *as.* Cf. i. 4. 60 below.

95. *Love you all.* Give you all their love. For the adverbial use of *all* (= altogether), cf. *T. of A.* i. 1. 139: " I will dispossess her all," etc. See also iv. 7. 42 below.

96. *Plight.* Pledge, troth; the only instance of the noun in this sense in S., though the verb (see iii. 4. 123 below) occurs several times.

105. *Hecate.* A dissyllable; as regularly in S. except in 1 *Hen. VI.* iii. 2. 64. Wright remarks that this is "a significant fact as regards Shakespeare's share in that play." It would not of itself, however, settle the question; for Milton uses *Hecate* both as a dissyllable (*Comus*, 135) and as a trisyllable (*Id.* 535).

106. *Operation of the orbs.* An astrological allusion.

107. *Whom.* For *which;* as often.

111. *The barbarous Scythian.* Wright cites Purchas, *Pilgrimage,* ed. 1614, p. 396: "These customes were generall to the Scythians in Europe and Asia (for which cause *Scytharum facinora patrare,* grew into a prouerbe of immane crueltie, and their Land was iustly called Barbarous): others were more speciall and peculiar to particular Nations Scythian." Cf. *T. A.* i. 1. 131: "Was ever Scythia half so barbarous?"

112. *Makes his generation messes.* Devours his children. For *generation* = progeny, cf. *W. T.* ii. 1. 148, *Rich. II.* v. 5. 8, *T. and C.* iii. 1. 146 (cf. *Matthew* iii. 7), etc. As Herodotus tells us that the Scythians ate their aged relatives, Craig suggests that *generation* may mean *parents,* but that is improbable.

115. *Sometime.* For the adjective use (= former, whilom), cf. *Rich. II.* v. 1. 37, *Ham.* i. 2. 8, etc. *Sometimes* was similarly used; as in *Rich. II.* i. 2. 54, v. 5. 75, etc.

117. *Dragon.* Moberly remarks: "A natural trope for Lear to use, as, like Arthur, he would wear a helmet, —

> "'On which for crest the golden dragon clung
> For Britain.'"

Wrath is put by metonymy for the object of the wrath.

118. *To set my rest.* The expression is evidently suggested by the card-playing phrase *set up my rest,* though with a reference also to the sense of *rest* = repose. For a similar instance see *R. and J.* v. 3. 110: —

> "O, here
> Will I set up my everlasting rest."

Set up my rest was the usual phrase in the game of primero, and, as Furness notes, the one elsewhere used by S.; but we find *set my rest* in Minsheu's *Dialogues*, 1599. The following extract from a dialogue illustrating the game shows that some of its technicalities were much like those of certain games still in vogue: " *O*. Let the cardes come to me, for I deale them; one, two, three, fower, one, two, three, fower. *M*. Passe. *R*. Passe. *L*. Passe. *O*. I set so much. *M*. I will none. *R*. Ile none. *L*. I must of force see it; deale the cards. *M*. Giue me fower cards; Ile see as much as he sets. *R*. See heere my rest; let euery one be in. *M*. I am come to passe againe. *R*. And I too. *L*. I do the selfe same. *O*. I set my rest. *M*. Ile see it. *R*. I also. *L*. I cannot giue it ouer. *M*. I was a small prime. *L*. I am flush."

119. *Hence, and avoid my sight!* It has been disputed whether this is addressed to Cordelia or Kent. The only reason given for the former view is that Cordelia does not go out, as, it is said, she would be likely to do upon such a command; but neither does Kent obey the order, and Cordelia would perhaps be no more likely to leave at the first impatient word of her father. Before she has fairly time to go, the order is given to call in France to take her if he will.

121. *Who stirs?* Delius takes this to be a threat, to frighten the by-standers from any chance opposition. Moberly says: " The courtiers seem unwilling to obey a command so reckless." Furness, with a finer insight, asks: " May it not be that the circle of courtiers are so horror-struck at Lear's outburst of fury, and at Cordelia's sudden and impending doom, that they stand motionless and forget to move? "

123. *Digest.* Metaphorically = amalgamate, combine.

124. *Marry her.* Get her a husband.

126. *Effects.* Attributes, accompaniments.

130. *Only.* For the transposition, cf. *Much Ado*, iii. 1. 23, iv. 1. 323, *A. Y. L.* i. 2. 204, etc.

131. *Addition.* Titular honour. Many editors adopt the " addi-

tions" of the quartos, but cf. ii. 2. 25 below, where the singular, as the context shows, refers to a multiplicity of titles. See also v. 3. 69.

132. *Revenue.* Accented by S. on the first or second syllable, as suits the measure. *Of the rest* is antithetical to *The name*, etc., and includes all powers and attributes not thus reserved.

138. *Make from.* Go from, get away from. Cf. *make to* (*V. and A.* 5, *C. of E.* i. 1. 93), *make for* (*W. T.* iv. 4. 554), etc.

139. *The fork.* That is, the barbed arrowhead. Cf. *A. Y. L.* ii. 1. 24: "forked heads" (of arrows). For *invade*, cf. iii. 4. 7 below. The only other instances of the word in S. are v. 1. 25 below and *Hen. V.* i. 2. 136.

141. *What wouldst thou do ?* "This is spoke on seeing his master put his hand to his sword" (Capell).

144. *Reserve thy state.* The quartos have "Reuerse thy doome," which most of the editors follow; but Furness ably defends the folio reading: "Kent is such a noble fellow that we who know Cordelia's truthfulness and honesty, and have heard her words spoken aside, cannot but think that he is here pleading her cause. But I am afraid we are too hasty. Kent is pleading, not for Cordelia, but for Lear himself; he has not as yet made the slightest allusion to Cordelia. When Lear denounces her, Kent, who sees that Lear is crushing the only chance of future happiness, starts forward with 'Good my liege;' but before he can utter another word Lear interrupts him, and interprets his exclamation as an intercession for Cordelia; and we fall into the same error, so that when Kent speaks again we keep up the same illusion, whereas all that he now says breathes devotion to the king, and to no one else. The folly to which majesty falls is not the casting off of a daughter, — that is no more foolish in a king than in a subject, — but it is the surrendering of revenue, of sway, and of the crown itself, — this is hideous rashness, this is power bowing to flattery. Hence, Kent entreats Lear 'to reserve his state.' And to show still more conclusively that Lear, and not Cordelia, is chiefly in his thoughts, in his very next speech he says that the motive for which he now risks his life is the safety

of the king. Furthermore, when Lear has been turned out of doors and his daughters have usurped all his powers, Gloucester (iii. 4. 163) says, 'Ah, that good Kent! He said it would be thus,' which cannot well refer to any other passage than the present. Moreover, had Kent been so devoted to Cordelia as to suffer banishment for her sake, would he not have followed her to France rather than followed as a servant his great patron whom he had thought on in his prayers? It need scarcely be added that ' reserve thy state ' means 'retain thy royal dignity and power.' "

146. *Answer my life,* etc. That is, let my life be answerable for my judgment.

149. *Reverbs.* Probably the poet's own contraction of *reverberates,* as no other instance of the word has been found.

151. *Wage.* Stake, set as a *wager.* Cf. *Cymb.* i. 4. 144: " I will wage against your gold, gold to it."

154. *Blank.* The *white* or centre of a target. " See better," says Kent, " and keep me always in your view " (Johnson).

156. *Swear'st.* Elsewhere S. has *swear by* in this sense; but such omission of prepositions after other verbs is common enough.

159. *Revoke thy gift.* Here the quartos and some editors read "doom" for *gift.*

164. *Strain'd.* Exaggerated, excessive; as in 2 *Hen. IV.* i. I. 161 : " This strained passion doth you wrong, my lord."

166. *Nor . . . nor.* Often used by S. for *neither . . . nor.* We sometimes find three or more parts thus joined; as in *R. and J.* ii. 2. 40, *Oth.* iii. 4. 116, etc.

167. *Our potency made good,* etc. " As a proof that I am not a mere threatener, that I have power as well as will to punish, take the due reward of thy demerits; hear thy sentence " (Malone).

169. *Diseases.* Dis-eases, discomforts. Cf. I *Hen. VI.* ii. 5. 44: " And in that ease I 'll tell thee my disease; " *T. of A.* iii. I. 56: "Thou disease of a friend, and not himself! " Cf. also the verb (= make uneasy, disturb) in *Cor.* i. 3. 117: "she will but disease our better mirth."

173. *Away!* etc. Dr. Bucknill says: "Lear's treatment of Kent; his ready threat in reply to Kent's deferential address; his passionate interruptions and reproaches; his attempted violence, checked by Albany and Cornwall; and, finally, the cruel sentence of banishment, cruelly expressed, — all these are the acts of a man in whom passion has become disease."

175. *Sith.* Since; as in ii. 4. 237 below.

179. *And your large speeches,* etc. "And may your acts substantiate your ample protestations" (Clarke).

183. *Here 's.* The singular verb is often thus used before a plural subject.

185. *Address toward.* Address ourselves to. We find *toward* with *address* = direct, in *L. L. L.* v. 2. 92 : —

> "Toward that shade I might behold address'd
> The king and his companions."

186. *Hath rivall'd.* Hath been a rival or competitor; the only instance of the verb in S. *In the least* = at the least. In ii. 4. 138 below it is used as now = in the smallest degree.

191. *So.* That is, worthy of such a dowry. There is a kind of play on *dear,* as the next line shows: when she was dear in love we held her dear in price.

193. *Little-seeming.* Little in appearance. See on 78 above.

194. *Piec'd.* That is, pieced out. Cf. iii. 6. 2 below.

195. *Like.* Please. Cf. ii. 2. 92 below : "His countenance likes me not."

197. *Owes.* Owns, possesses; as often. Cf. i. 4. 126 below.

199. *Stranger'd.* Estranged, alienated; the only instance of the verb in S.

201. *Makes not up.* Comes to no decision.

204. *Make such a stray.* Go so far astray. For the ellipsis of *as,* cf. 212 just below.

206. *Avert.* Turn; the only instance of the verb in S. *Aversion* he does not use at all. The double comparative, as in *more*

worthier, is common in S. We have at least six examples in this play; and the double superlative in "most poorest" (ii. 3. 7).

210. *Argument.* Theme, subject; as in ii. 1. 9 below.

211. *In this trice of time.* We still use the expression "in a trice " (*T. N.* iv. 2. 123, etc.). "On a trice " occurs in *Temp.* v. 1. 238.

212. *Dismantle.* Elsewhere in S. the object of the verb is that from which anything is stripped, as in modern usage. Cf. *W. T.* iv. 4. 66 and *Ham.* iii. 2. 293.

214. *Such . . . that.* Cf. ii. 2. 122 below: "such a deal of man that worthied him."

215. *Monsters.* Makes monstrous; as in *Cor.* ii. 2. 81 : "To hear my nothings monster'd."

216. *Fallen. Must be* is understood. *Fallen into taint* = become tainted. Malone paraphrases the passage thus : " Either her offence *must be* monstrous, or, if she has not committed any such offence, the affection which you always professed to have for her *must be* tainted and decayed." Craig suggests that *or* = ere, as not unfrequently. The latter clause would then mean " ere the warm affection you always professed for her should thus suddenly have changed to hate."

219. *For.* Because; as in i. 2. 5 below. Cf. *M. of V.* i. 3. 43, *M. for M.* ii. 1. 27, etc.

222. *Nor other foulness.* The quartos have "murder or " or " murder, or," and the folios "murther, or." Collier suggested the emendation. Moberly remarks : "The gradation, ' vicious blot, murder, foulness,' would not be happy. Moreover, from the parallel expression, ' vicious mole of nature,' in *Ham.* i. 4. 24, we may conclude that in this line Cordelia refers to natural defects, which Lear might be supposed to have just discovered; but in the next line to evil actions from all suspicions of which she wishes to be cleared." Furness agrees with Moberly as to the gradation, and adds : " This alone is so un-Shakespearian that of itself it would taint the line. . . . And mark how admirably the lines are bal-

anced: 'vicious blot or other foulness,' 'unchaste action or dishonour'd step.' "

225. *But even for want*, etc. We should have expected " even the want," as Hanmer reads, but the sense is clear, and such " confusion of construction " is not uncommon in S.

226. *Still-soliciting*. Ever-begging. Cf. *still-vexed* in *Temp.* i. 2. 229, and *still-closing* in *Id.* iii. 3. 64.

227. *That*. See on 214 above.

228. *Hath lost me*. Hath caused me to *lose*. Cf. i. 2. 118 below: " It shall lose thee nothing." *In* = in respect to.

231. *Unspoke*. The only instance of the form in S. *Unspoken* occurs only in *Cymb.* v. 5. 139.

233. *Love's not love*, etc. Cf. *Sonn.* 116.

234. *Regards*. Considerations; as in *Ham.* ii. 2. 79, iii. 1. 87, etc. The relative often takes a singular verb, though the antecedent is plural. Cf. ii. 4. 272 below: " If it be you that stirs," etc.

235. *Entire point*. Main point.

243. *Respects of*. Considerations of. Cf. *Ham.* iii. 2. 193: " base respects of thrift," etc.

249. *Cold'st*. Such harsh contracted superlatives are common.

253. *Waterish*. Used contemptuously. Burgundy was the best-watered district of France. There is a play on the other sense of " weak, poor," which we have in *Oth.* iii. 3. 15: " waterish diet." S. uses the word only twice.

254. *Unpriz'd*. Not prized by others, unappreciated; used nowhere else by S.

255. *Unkind*. Unnatural; or combining that sense with the more familiar one. Cf. iii. 4. 72 below: " his unkind daughters."

256. " *Here* and *where* have the power of nouns: Thou losest this residence to find a better residence in another place " (Johnson).

260. *Benison*. Blessing; as in *Macb.* ii. 4. 40 and iv. 6. 208 below.

263. *Ye jewels*. The early eds. have " The jewels," which may

possibly be what S. wrote ; but *The* and *Ye,* being constantly written alike in that day, were liable to be confounded by the printer.
Rowe's emendation is generally adopted. *Wash'd* is often applied
to tears ; as in *Much Ado,* i. 1. 27, iv. 1. 156, *R.* and *J.* ii. 3. 70,
iii. 2. 130, etc.

267. *Professed bosoms.* Professed love. Pope changed *professed*
to " professing ; " but *bosoms* = love ; as in v. 3. 50 below. Cf. *M.
for M.* iv. 3. 139 : " And you shall have your bosom on this
wretch " (that is, your heart's desire). See also *W. T.* iv. 4. 574
and *Oth.* iii. 1. 58.

269. *Prefer.* Commend. Cf. *J. C.* v. 5. 62 : " Ay, if Messala
will prefer me to you," etc.

271. *Prescribe not us.* Elsewhere in S. we have *prescribe to,* but
here *us* may be a dative, as often.

273. *At fortune's alms.* At the charity of fortune. The expression *fortune's alms* occurs again in *Oth.* iii. 4. 122.

274. *And well are worth the want,* etc. And are justly denied
the natural kindness you have failed to show.

275. *Plighted.* Complicated ; literally, folded. The quartos
have " pleated " or " pleeted," and some modern eds. " plaited."
Cf. Milton, *Comus,* 301 : " the plighted clouds ; " and Spenser,
F. Q. iii. 9. 21 : " her well-plighted frock."

276. *Cover.* Henley sees an allusion to *Proverbs,* xxviii. 13.

287. *Grossly.* Palpably, evidently (Schmidt) ; as in *C. of E.* ii.
2. 171, *A. W.* i. 3. 184, etc.

290. *Of his time.* Of his life. Cf. *M. of V.* i. 1. 129: " my
time something too prodigal," etc. See also i. 2. 44 below.

292. *Long-ingraffed.* The quartos have " long ingrafted." S.
uses both *graff* and *graft. Long-ingraffed condition* = " qualities
of mind confirmed by long habit " (Malone). For *condition,* cf. iv.
3. 35 below.

296. *Unconstant.* Capricious ; used by S. several times, but *in-
constant* oftener. *Like* = likely, as often.

Moberly remarks: " These women come of themselves, and a

once, to the feeling which it requires all Iago's arts to instil into Othello ; on whom it is at length urged that Desdemona must be irregular in mind, or she would not have preferred him to the 'curled darlings' of Venice."

300. *Hit.* Agree ; the quarto reading. The folios have "sit," which some editors adopt.

302. *Offend.* Injure ; as in *M. of V.* iv. i. 140: "Thou but offend'st thy lungs to speak so loud," etc. The meaning seems to be : if the king goes on in this way, we shall be only the worse off for his surrender of the kingdom to us.

304. *I' the heat.* "While the iron is hot," as the proverb hath it.

SCENE II. — 1. *Thou, Nature,* etc. As Steevens remarks, Edmund speaks of *nature* in opposition to *custom,* and not to the existence of a God. Cf. 17 below.

3. *Stand in the plague.* Be exposed to the *plague,* or vexation.

4. *Curiosity.* "Over-nice scrupulousness" (Steevens). See on i. 1. 5 above. *Deprive* = deprive of my rights as a son, disinherit.

5. *For that.* Because that. See on i. 1. 219 above. *Moonshines* = months; like *moons* in *Oth.* i. 3. 84, *A. and C.* iii. 12. 16, etc.

6. *Lag of.* Lagging behind, later than. Cf. *Rich. III.* ii. 1. 90: "That came too lag to see him buried."

7. *Compact.* Compacted, put together. Cf. *M. N. D.* v. 1. 8, *A. Y. L.* ii. 7. 5, etc. See on i. 1. 70 above.

8. *Generous.* Noble-minded, befitting one of noble birth. Cf. *T. and C.* ii. 2. 154, etc.

9. *Honest.* Chaste; as often. Cf. *A. Y. L.* i. 2. 40, etc.

16. *Top the.* Capell's correction of the "tooth'" of the quartos and the "to' th'" or "to th'" of the folios. For *top* = overtop, rise above, see *Macb.* iv. 3. 57, etc.

19. *Subscrib'd.* Surrendered, signed away. Cf. *T. of S.* i. 1. 81, *T. and C.* iv. 5. 105, etc.

20. *Confin'd to exhibition.* Restricted to an allowance or mere maintenance. Cf. *T. G. of V.* i. 3. 69 : —

> " What maintenance he from his friends receives,
> Like exhibition shalt thou have from me."

Nares cites Ben Jonson, *Silent Woman,* iii. 1 : " Behave yourself distinctly, and with good morality; or, I protest, I 'll take away your exhibition."

21. *Upon the gad.* On the spur of the moment. *Gad* = goad, or an iron-pointed rod used in driving cattle. S. uses the word only here and in *T. A.* iv. 1. 103, where it means a *stylus,* or ancient pen.

28. *Terrible.* Affrighted ; used passively, like many adjectives in *-ble.*

33. *O'er-read.* Read over. So *o'erlooking* in next line = looking over. Cf. v. 1. 50 below.

38. *Are to blame.* Are to be blamed, are blamable. Active infinitives are often thus used passively.

42. *Essay or taste.* Trial or test. For *essay,* cf. *Sonn.* 110. 8 : " And worst essays prov'd thee my best of love." S. uses the word only twice, having elsewhere *assay,* of which it is only another form. As Steevens notes, both *essay* (or *assay*) and *taste* are terms from royal tables. For the custom of *taking the assay* (or *say*), see *K. John,* v. 6. 28 and *Rich. II.* v. 5. 99.

43. *Policy and reverence.* Policy of holding in reverence. For the construction, see on i. 4. 349 below.

44. *The best of our times.* The best portions of our lives. See on i. 1. 290 above.

45. *Oldness.* Old age ; used by S. nowhere else.

46. *Idle and fond.* Weak and foolish. For *fond,* cf. i. 4. 308 and iv. 7. 60 below. For *who,* see on i. 1. 107 above. It is true that *tyranny* implies a person or persons, but the *it* shows that it is grammatically and rhetorically neuter.

59. *Closet.* Private room, chamber ; as often. Cf. *Matthew,*

vi. 6. In iii. 3. 12 below it may have the same meaning, though Schmidt takes it to be used in the modern sense; as in *Macb.* v. 1. 6 and *Oth.* iv. 2. 22.

60. *Character.* Handwriting; as in ii. 1. 74 below. See also *T. N.* v. 1. 354, *W. T.* v. 2. 38, *Ham.* iv. 7. 53, etc.

63. *That.* That is, the *matter* or contents.

71. *Sons at perfect age.* That is, *being* of age. For *declined*, cf. *Oth.* iii. 3. 265: "Declin'd into the vale of years."

75. *Detested.* Equivalent to *detestable;* as often. Cf. i. 4. 269 and ii. 4. 215 below.

82. *Where.* Whereas; as often.

86. *Pawn down.* That is, lay down as a pledge. Cf. *Oth.* iv. 2. 13: "Lay down my soul at stake."

90. *Your honour.* The usual address to a lord in the time of S. Cf. *Rich. III.* iii. 2. 107, 110, 116, etc. *Feel* = test, sound. *Pretence of danger* = dangerous purpose. Cf. i. 4. 71 below.

92. *Auricular.* Used by S. only here.

99. *Wind me into him.* Insinuate yourself into his confidence. Cf. *Cor.* iii. 3. 64: "to wind Yourself into a power tyrannical." For the expletive *me* (like the Latin "ethical dative"), cf. *Ham.* ii. 2. 601 : "Who does me this?" etc.

100. *Unstate myself.* Give up my state, sacrifice my fortune and position. Cf. *A. and C.* iii. 13. 30 : —

> "Yes, like enough, high-battled Cæsar will
> Unstate his happiness," etc.

101. *To be in a due resolution.* To be fully *resolved* (see *J. C.* iii. 1. 131, etc.) or satisfied on this point.

102. *Convey.* Manage artfully. Cf. *Macb.* iv. 3. 71, *Hen. V.* i. 2. 74, etc.

105. *These late eclipses,* etc. Moberly remarks: "As to the current belief in astrology, we may remember that, at the time when this play was written, Dr. Dee, the celebrated adept, was grieving for his lost patroness, Queen Elizabeth; that the profli-

gate court of James I. was in 1618 frightened by the appearance
of a comet into a temporary fit of gravity; and that even Charles I.
sent £500 as a fee to William Lilly for consulting the stars as to his
flight from Hampton Court in 1647." Cf. *Sonn.* 107. 6: —

> " The mortal moon hath her eclipse endur'd,
> And the sad augurs mock their own presage!"

See also *Ham.* i. 1. 120 and *Oth.* v. 2. 99. Milton has several allusions to the ominous nature of eclipses; as in the grand image in
P. L. i. 594: —
> "as when the sun new-risen
> Looks through the horizontal misty air,
> Shorn of his beams; or from behind the moon,
> In dim eclipse, disastrous twilight sheds
> On half the nations, and with fear of change
> Perplexes monarchs."

106. *Though the wisdom of nature,* etc.   "That is, though
natural philosophy can give account of eclipses, yet we feel their
consequences" (Johnson). Moberly remarks: "This curious view
is repeated, with remarkable force of language, by Sir T. Browne,
even in the less credulous times when he wrote his *Treatise on
Vulgar Errors :* 'That two suns or moons should appear, is not
worth the wonder. But that the same should fall out at the point
of some decisive action, that these two should make but one line
in the book of fate, and stand together in the great Ephemerides
of God, besides the philosophical assignment of the cause, it may
admit a Christian apprehension in the signalty.' We learn also
from Bishop Burnet that Lord Shaftesbury believed in astrology,
and thought that the souls of men live in the stars."

108. *Sequent.* Cf. *A. W.* ii. 2. 56: "Indeed your 'O Lord,
sir!' is very sequent to your whipping."

113. *Bias of nature.* Natural tendency. The metaphor is taken
from the game of bowls, and is a favourite one with S.

115. *Hollowness.* Insincerity. For the figure, cf. i. 1. 148.

116. *Disquietly.* Causing disquiet; used by S. only here.

118. *Lose.* See on i. 1. 228 above.

121. *Foppery.* Foolishness; as in *M. of V.* ii. 5. 35.

123. *We make guilty*, etc. Cf. *J. C.* i. 2. 140: —

> "The fault, dear Brutus, is not in our stars,
> But in ourselves, that we are underlings."

Disasters is an astrological term.

125. *On necessity.* As in the folios; the quartos have " by necessity," which, according to Schmidt, is not found elsewhere in S. For *on necessity*, cf. *L. L. L.* i. 1. 149, 155. Cf. *on* (or *upon*) *compulsion* (*M. of V.* iv. 1. 183, 1 *Hen. IV.* ii. 4. 261, *T. and C.* ii. 2. 153) and *by compulsion* (here and in *K. John,* ii. 1. 218). Schmidt considers that " S. has an unmistakable preference for *on* and *upon* to express that which gives the motive or impulse to anything;" but some of the examples he gives can be readily balanced by others in which other prepositions are used. For instance, he quotes "on constraint" from *K. John,* v. 1. 28; but we find " by constraint" in *A. W.* iv. 2. 16. So against "upon instinct" in 1 *Hen. IV.* ii. 4. 331, we may put "by instinct" in *Rich. III.* ii. 3. 42, etc. "On malice" occurs in *Rich. II.* i. 1. 9, while elsewhere we have "through malice," " from malice," " out of malice," " with malice," " in malice," etc., some of these occurring several times each.

126. *Treachers.* Traitors; used by S. only here. Cf. Spenser, *F. Q.* i. 4. 41: " No knight, but treachour, full of false despight."

Spherical predominance is an astrological expression. Cf. *predominant* in *A. W.* i. 1. 211: —

> "*Helena.* The wars have so kept you under that you must needs have been born under Mars.
> *Parolles.* When he was predominant.
> *Helena.* When he was retrograde, I think, rather; "

and *W. T.* i. 2. 202: —

> " It is a bawdy planet, that will strike
> Where 't is predominant."

128. *Influence* is another astrological word, rarely used by S. except with reference, direct or indirect, to the power of the heavenly bodies. Cf. Milton, *P. L.* iv. 669 : —

> " which these soft fires
> Not only enlighten, but with kindly heat
> Of various influence foment and warm,
> Temper or nourish, or in part shed down
> Their stellar virtue on all kinds that grow
> On earth," etc.

Cf. *Job*, xxxviii. 31. *Spherical* = planetary ; the only instance of this sense in S.

131. *Like the catastrophe*, etc. "That is, just as the circumstance which decides the catastrophe of a play intervenes on the very nick of time" (Heath). It may, however, be a hit at the inartistic structure of the early comedies.

132. *Cue.* One of S.'s favourite figures drawn from stage practice. *Like Tom o' Bedlam* = like a " Bedlam beggar," such as Edgar afterward pretends to be. See ii. 3. 6–20 below.

134. *Fa, sol, la, mi.* Dr. Burney says : "S. shows by the context that he was well acquainted with the property of these syllables in solmization, which imply a series of sounds so unnatural that ancient musicians prohibited their use. Edmund, speaking of eclipses as portents and prodigies, compares the dislocation of events, the times being out of joint, to the unnatural and offensive sounds, *fa sol la mi*." Probably, however, Edmund is merely singing to himself in order not to seem to observe Edgar's approach.

141. *Succeed.* Follow, come to pass. Cf. *success* = issue, whether good or bad ; as in "bad success" (*T. and C.* ii. 2. 117), "vile success " (*Oth*. iii. 3. 322), etc.

144. *Diffidences.* Distrust, suspicions. Cf. *K. John*, i. 1. 65 : " And wound her honour with this diffidence." S. uses the word only twice.

145. *Dissipation of cohorts* would seem to mean the breaking up of military organizations; but it is very likely either spurious or corrupt.

160. *With the mischief of your person.* That is, even with harm to your person. For the intransitive use of *allay*, cf. 3 *Hen. VI.* i. 4. 146: "And when the rage allays, the rain begins."

163. *Have a continent forbearance.* "Restrain your feelings and keep away" (Craig).

166. *Fitly.* When the fit time comes.

173. *Image and horror.* Horrible reality. For the "hendiadys," cf. 43 above.

178. *Harms.* Harmful acts. For the plural, cf. *R. of L.* 28, 1694, 1 *Hen. VI.* iv. 7. 46, etc.

180. *Practices.* Plots, artifices; as often. Cf. ii. 1. 75 below.

SCENE III.— **2.** *Chiding of.* For *of* with verbals, cf. ii. 1. 40 and v. 3. 206 below.

3. Coleridge remarks of Oswald: "The steward should be placed in exact antithesis to Kent, as the only character of utter irredeemable baseness in S. Even in this the judgment and invention of the poet are very observable; for what else could the willing tool of a Goneril be? Not a vice but this of baseness was left open to him."

8. *On every trifle.* On every trifling occasion. In *Temp.* ii. 2. 8, we find "For every trifle."

15. *Distaste.* Cf. *T. and C.* ii. 2. 66: "Although my will distaste what it elected."

17. *Idle.* Weak, foolish; as in i. 2. 46 above.

18. *Authorities.* For the plural, cf. *M. for M* iv. 4. 6: "And why meet him at the gates, and redeliver our authorities there?"

21. *With checks as flatteries*, etc. This line has puzzled the critics, and various unsatisfactory emendations have been proposed. Taking it as it stands, we may accept Tyrwhitt's explanation: "with checks, as well as flatteries, when they (that is, flatteries) are seen to be abused." Craig makes *as* = " instead of, for (that is, rather than)."

SCENE IV. — 2. *Diffuse.* Disorder it, and so disguise it, as he had disguised his dress. Cf. *Hen. V.* v. 2. 61 : " diffus'd attire." There, as here and in *Rich. III.* i. 2. 78, the early eds. spell the word *defuse*, which some editors retain; but the folio has " diffused " in *M. W.* iv. 4. 54 : " some diffused song; " where the word seems to mean wild or disordered.

4. *Raz'd.* Erased. Cf. *Sonn.* 25. 11 : " from the book of honour razed quite," etc.

6. *So may it come.* It may come to pass; not a parenthetical wish, as some take it.

12. *What dost thou profess ?* What dost thou " set up for," what is thy *profession*, or calling? Cf. *T. of S.* ind. 2. 22 : " by present profession a tinker." See also *J. C.* i. 1. 5, *Ham.* v. 1. 35, etc. Kent, in his reply, plays upon the word.

16. *Converse.* Have converse with, associate with. Cf. *A. Y. L.* v. 2. 66, etc.

17. *To fear judgment* = to fear litigation, or being brought before a judge. Schmidt makes it refer to the Last Judgment.

18. *To eat no fish.* That is, to be a Protestant. To eat fish on account of religious scruples was in Queen Elizabeth's time the mark of a Papist and an enemy to the government.

25. *Who.* For *whom*, as often. Cf. iv. 3. 8 and v. 3. 250 below.

33. *Keep honest counsel.* Keep a secret when honour requires it.

34. *Curious* = elegant or elaborate. Cf. *Cymb.* v. 5. 361 : " a most curious mantle," etc.

38. *To love.* That is, *as* to love. For the ellipsis, cf. ii. 4. 12 below.

43. *Knave.* Servant; originally, boy. The modern sense was, however, coming into use in the time of S. Cf. *Temp.* ii. 1. 166, etc.

47. *Clotpoll.* Clodpole, blockhead. It is used literally (= head) in *Cymb.* iv. 2. 184 : " I have sent Cloten's clotpoll down the stream."

55. *Roundest.* Bluntest, plainest. Cf. *T. N.* ii. 3. 102, *Ham.* iii. 1. 191, etc.

60. *That . . . as.* See on i. 1. 92 above.

68. *Rememberest.* Remindest. Cf. *K. John,* iii. 4. 96: "Remembers me of all his gracious parts," etc.

69. *Most faint.* Very slight. The *neglect* has been so *faint* that he has been doubtful whether it was intentional.

71. *Curiosity.* "Scrupulous watchfulness of his own dignity" (Steevens). See on i. 1. 6 above, and cf. i. 2. 4. *Very pretence =* actual intention. See on i. 2. 88 above.

73. *This two days.* S. uses *this* or *these* interchangeably in such expressions.

76. *The fool hath much pined away.* As Clarke notes, there is much significance in this little speech and in Lear's rejoinder: "It serves . . . to mark him at once as a creation apart from all other of Shakespeare's fools; it serves to depict Cordelia's power of attaching and endearing those around her; and it serves to denote her old father's already awakened consciousness that he has done her grievous injustice."

87. *Bandy.* A metaphor from tennis. Cf. *R. and J.* ii. 5. 14: —

> "Had she affections and warm youthful blood,
> She would be as swift in motion as a ball;
> My words would bandy her to my sweet love,
> And his to me;"

L. L. L. v. 2. 29: "Well bandied both; a set of wit well play'd," etc. Furness quotes Cotgrave, *Fr. Dict.:* "*Iouër à bander & à racler contre.* To bandy against, at Tennis; and (by metaphor) to pursue with all insolencie, rigour, extremitie."

88. *Strucken.* Cf. *J. C.* ii. 2. 114: "Cæsar, 't is strucken eight."

89. *Foot-ball player.* The game was then "a somewhat vulgar recreation, practised by the London apprentices in Cheapside to the terror of respectable citizens." Cf. *C. of E.* ii. 1. 83.

98. *Earnest.* Money paid in advance to bind the bargain. Cf. *W. T.* iv. 4. 659, etc.

99. *Enter Fool.* "'Now, our joy, though last, not least,' my dearest of all Fools, Lear's Fool! Ah, what a noble heart, a gentle and a loving one, lies beneath that parti-coloured jerkin! . . . Look at him! It may be your eyes see him not as mine do, but he appears to me of a light delicate frame, every feature expressive of sensibility even to pain, with eyes lustrously intelligent, a mouth blandly beautiful, and withal a hectic flush upon his cheek. Oh that I were a painter! Oh that I could describe him as I knew him in my boyhood, when the Fool made me shed tears, while Lear did but terrify me! . . . When the Fool enters, throwing his coxcomb at Kent, and instantly follows it up with allusions to the miserable rashness of Lear, we ought to understand him from that moment to the last. Throughout this scene his wit, however varied, still aims at the same point, and in spite of threats, and regardless how his words may be construed by Goneril's creatures, with the eagerness of a filial love he prompts the old king to 'resume the shape which he had cast off.' 'This is not altogether fool, my lord.' But, alas! it is too late; and when driven from the scene by Goneril, he turns upon her with an indignation that knows no fear of the 'halter' for himself: 'A fox when one has caught her, And such a daughter, Should sure to the slaughter, If my cap would buy a halter.' That such a character should be distorted by players, printers, and commentators! Observe every word he speaks; his meaning, one would imagine, could not be misinterpreted; and when at length, finding his covert reproaches can avail nothing, he changes his discourse to simple mirth, in order to distract the sorrows of his master. When Lear is in the storm, who is with him? None — not even Kent — 'None but the Fool; who labours to out-jest His heart-struck injuries.' The tremendous agony of Lear's mind would be too painful, and even deficient in pathos, without this poor faithful servant at his side. It is he that touches our hearts with pity, while Lear fills the imagination to aching" (C. A. Brown).

After quoting this and Charles Cowden-Clarke's comments on the Fool, in which he takes the ground that he is "a youth, not a grown man," Furness remarks: "After these long and good notes by my betters I wish merely to record humbly but firmly my conviction that the Fool, one of Shakespeare's most wonderful characters, is not a boy, but a man — one of the shrewdest, tenderest of men, whom long life had made shrewd, and whom afflictions had made tender; his wisdom is too deep for any boy, and could be found only in a man, removed by not more than a score of years from the king's own age; he had been Lear's companion from the days of Lear's early manhood." For myself, I fully agree with this latter view of the Fool. Not only does much that he says show a shrewd-ness which can only be the result of long experience and observation of men and things, but his intense sympathy for Lear seems to me beyond the capacity of boyish years. On the other hand, Lear's addressing him as "boy" and "pretty knave," and the like, may be explained, partly by the force of habit — for he *was* a mere boy when he first became Lear's companion, and, it may be added, would from his very position naturally continue to be regarded and treated as a boy — and partly from his slight and fragile physique, which would make him appear more like an overgrown boy than a man.

Coxcomb. The fool's cap. Furness quotes Minsheu (s. v. *cockes-combe*, ed. 1617): "Englishmen use to call vaine and proud brag-gers, and men of meane discretion and judgement *Coxcombes*. Because naturall Idiots and Fooles haue, and still doe accustome themselues to weare in their Cappes, cock's feathers, or a hat with a necke and head of a cocke on the top and a bell thereon, &c., and thinke themselues finely fitted and proudly attired therewith, so we compare a presumptuous bragging fellow, and wanting all true Iudgement and discretion, to such an Idiote foole, and call him also Coxecombe."

102. *You were best.* It were best for you. The pronoun was originally the dative, but came to be regarded as a nominative.

104. *One's part that's*, etc. Abbott (*Grammar*, 81) says that " we never use the possessive inflection of the unemphatic *one* as an antecedent," as here; but the construction does not strike me as wholly unfamiliar now, at least colloquially.

106. *Thou 'lt catch cold*. That is, be turned out of doors and exposed to the weather.

108. *On 's*. Of his. *On* was often used for *of*, especially in contractions like this.

110. *Nuncle*. Probably a contraction of *mine uncle*, the customary appellation of the licensed fool to his superiors (Nares). *Nuncle* and *naunt* are said to be still in vulgar use in Yorkshire.

113. *Living*. Property. Cf. *W. T.* iv. 3. 104: "where my land and living lies." See also *Mark*, xii. 44, *Luke*, viii. 43, etc.

116. *The whip*. Whipping, as Douce has shown, was a common punishment of fools. Cf. *A. Y. L.* i. 2. 91, where Celia says to Touchstone, "you 'll be whipped for taxation [that is, satire] one of these days." See also 168 below.

118. *Lady the brach*. Cf. 1 *Hen. IV.* iii. 1. 240: "I had rather hear Lady, my brach, howl in Irish." A *brach* was a female hound. See also iii. 6. 69 below.

120. *A pestilent gall to me!* Moberly explains this as "a passionate remembrance of Oswald's insolence." Furness says: "This does not satisfy me, but I can offer nothing better." Why may it not refer to the Fool, who has just nettled his master into a hint of the whip? Cf. "A bitter fool!" just below.

126. *Owest*. Ownest. See on i. 1. 197 above.

128. *Trowest*. Apparently here = knowest. The usual meaning of *trow* was think or believe; but *trow you* was often = do you know? Cf. *A. Y. L.* iii. 2. 189: "Trow you who hath done this?" *T. of S.* i. 2. 165: "Trow you whither I am going?" etc.

129. *Set*. Stake, risk. Cf. *Rich. III.* v. 4. 9: "I have set my life upon a cast." *Throwest* seems to be = throwest *for;* but it may be = "hast won by thy last throw" (Schmidt).

136. *Nothing can be made of nothing*. See on i. 1. 85 above.

144–159. *That lord . . . snatching.* These lines are omitted in the folios; "perhaps for political reasons," says Johnson, "as they seemed to censure the monopolies."

150. *Motley.* The parti-colored dress of the professional fool. Cf. *A. Y. L.* ii. 7. 34, 58, etc. The word is = fool in *Sonn.* 110. 2 and *A. Y. L.* iii. 3. 79.

157. *A monopoly out.* That is, legally taken out, issued for my benefit. Warburton considered this "a satire on the gross abuses of monopolies at that time, and the corruption and avarice of the courtiers, who commonly went shares with the patentee." Steevens quotes sundry hits at the same abuse from other writers of the time.

165. *Thy ass.* An allusion to Æsop's fable of the man and his ass.

167. *If I speak*, etc. "If *I speak* on this occasion *like myself* — that is, like a fool, foolishly — let not *me* be whipped, but him who first finds it to be as I have said — that is, the king himself, who was likely to be soonest sensible of the truth and justness of the sarcasm, and who, he insinuates, deserved whipping for the silly part he had acted" (Eccles).

170. *Fools had ne'er less grace in a year.* "There never was a time when fools were less in favour; and the reason is that they were never so little wanted, for wise men now supply their place" (Johnson).

171. *Foppish.* Foolish; the only instance of the word in S. For the rhyme with *apish*, cf. that of *Tom* and *am* in ii. 3. 20, 21 below; also that of *corn* and *harm* in iii. 6. 42, 44. To these examples Ellis (*Early Eng. Pronunciation*, iii. 953) adds seven from other works of S. See *R. of L.* 554, *M. N. D.* ii. 1. 48, 54, 263, iii. 3. 348, v. 1. 303, and *L. L. L.* v. 2. 55.

176. *Used it.* Made a practice of it. Cf. *Ham.* iii. 2. 50.

179. *Then they*, etc. Steevens compares Heywood's *Rape of Lucrece*, 1608: —

> " When Tarquin first in court began,
> And was approved king,

> Some men for sodden joy gan weep,
> But I for sorrow sing."

191. *Thee.* Cf. *T. of A.* iv. 3. 277 : " Ay, that I am not thee; "
2 *Hen.* VI. iv. 1. 117 : " it is thee I fear," etc.

194. *Enter Goneril.* " The monster Goneril prepares what is
necessary, while the character of Albany renders a still more mad-
dening grievance possible — namely, Regan and Cornwall in perfect sympathy of monstrosity. Not a sentiment, not an image,
which can give pleasure on its own account is admitted. When-
ever these creatures are introduced, and they are brought forward
as little as possible, pure horror reigns throughout " (Coleridge).

What makes that frontlet on ? What causes that frown like a
frontlet on your brow ? A *frontlet* was a band of cloth worn at
night on the forehead to keep it smooth. Steevens quotes *The
Four P's,* 1569 (the Pardoner has asked why women are so long
dressing when they get up in the morning, and the Pedler replies,
with a play on the word *let* = hindrance) : —

> " Forsooth, women have many lettes,
> And they be masked in many nettes :
> As frontlettes, fyllettes, partlettes, and bracelettes ;
> And then theyr bonettes, and theyr poynettes.
> By these lettes and nettes, the lette is suche,
> That spede is small, when haste is muche."

Clarke cites Chapman, *Hero and Leander : —*

> " E'en like the forehead cloth that in the night,
> Or when they sorrow, ladies us'd to wear."

198. *An O.* A cipher. For "the allusion reversed," see *W. T.*
i. 2. 6 (Malone).

205. *A shealed peascod.* A shelled pea-pod ; a mere husk.
Shealed is only the old spelling of *shelled,* which some eds. give
instead. S. uses the verb nowhere else.

207. *Other.* For the plural, cf. *M. N. D.* iv. 1. 71 : " That he
awaking when the other do," etc. *Retinue* is accented on the

penult; the only instance in which S. uses the word in verse. So Milton in the two instances in his verse; and Tennyson regularly.

209. *Rank.* Gross; as in *Ham.* i. 2. 136, iii. 3. 36, etc.

210. *I had thought . . . To have found.* Cf. *Ham.* v. 1. 268, *Much Ado,* ii. 1. 261, etc.

213. *Put it on.* Promote or encourage it. Cf. *Ham.* v. 2. 394, etc.

214. *Allowance.* Permission, sanction. Cf. ii. 2. 108 below. Moberly remarks: "The rest of the sentence labours under a plethora of relatives. The meaning, however, is simple: 'If you instigate your men to riot I will check it, even though it offends you; as that offence, which would otherwise be a shame, would be proved by the necessity to be a discreet proceeding.' 'Yes,' replies the Fool, 'and so the young cuckoo, wanting the nest to itself, was under the regrettable necessity of biting off the head of its foster-mother the sparrow; which, under the circumstances, was not a shame, but an act of discretion.'"

215. *Scape.* Not "'scape," as usually printed, being found in contemporaneous prose.

216. *The tender of a wholesome weal.* The regard for a healthy commonwealth. Cf. 1 *Hen. IV. v.* 4. 49: —

> " Thou hast redeem'd thy lost opinion,
> And show'd thou mak'st some tender of my life."

For *wholesome,* cf. *Ham.* i. 5. 70, iii. 4. 65, *Macb.* iv. 3. 105, etc.; and for *weal, Macb.* iii. 4. 76, v. 2. 27, *Cor.* ii. 3. 189, etc.

218. *Which else,* etc. Which necessity would justify as discreet proceeding, though otherwise (that is, but for the necessity), it would be shameful.

222. *It head.* In the folio *its* occurs but once (*M. for M.* i. 2. 4), while *it 's* is found nine times. *It* as a genitive (or "possessive") occurs fourteen times (not counting its repetition in the same passage), in seven of which it precedes *own.* This *it* is an early provincial form of the old genitive. In our version of the Bible, *it*

is found only in *Leviticus*, xxv. 5, where the ed. of 1611 has "of it own accord."

For the allusion to the cuckoo laying its eggs in the nests of other birds, cf. *R. of L.* 849, 1 *Hen. IV.* v. 1. 60, etc.

223. *Darkling.* In the dark. S. found the almost identical image applied to the story of Lear as told by Spenser, *F. Q.* ii. 10. 30: —

> " But true it is that, when the oyle is spent,
> The light goes out, and weeke [wick] is throwne away:
> So when he had resignd his regiment,
> His daughter gan despise his drouping day,
> And wearie wax of his continuall stay."

226. *I would you would.* Cf. 1 *Hen. IV.* 3. 112, *M. N. D.* v. 1. 255, etc.

227. *Whereof . . . fraught.* Elsewhere in S. *fraught* is followed by *with*.

228. *Dispositions.* Moods, humours; as in 299 below. Cf. *A. Y. L.* v. 1. 113: "Now I will be your Rosalind in a more coming-on disposition," etc.

231. *Whoop, Jug! I love thee.* Probably a quotation from some old song, but having no special point here, unless perhaps to express ironically the Fool's estimation of Goneril. *Jug* was the old nickname for Joan, also used as a term of endearment.

234. *His notion weakens.* For *notion* = mind, cf. *Cor.* v. 6. 107 and *Macb.* iii. 1. 83; the only other instances of the word in S. *Discernings* and *lethargied* he uses nowhere else.

241. *Which.* Steevens takes this to be = *whom*, referring to Lear; but it may be "the commonest connective used improperly," as the illiterate sometimes use it now.

243. *This admiration.* That is, the astonishment you affect. We do not find the noun *savour* used elsewhere by S. in this metaphorical way; but cf. the verb in *L. L. L.* iv. 2. 165, *T. N.* v. 1. 322, *W. T.* ii. 3. 119, *Hen. V.* i. 2. 250, 295, etc.

244. *Other your new pranks.* For the order, cf. *2 Hen. IV.* iv. 4. 53: "With Poins and other his continual followers," etc.

248. *Debosh'd.* An old spelling of *debauched*, and the only one found in the folio in the four instances in which the word occurs.

250. *Shows.* Appears; as in 274 below.

Epicurism . . . lust . . . tavern . . . brothel. "An instance of what Corson calls a *respective construction*. The first word refers to the third, and the second to the fourth" (Furness). See on iv. 2. 65 below.

251. *Makes.* The singular verb with two singular subjects is not uncommon.

252. *Grac'd.* Full of grace, dignified. Cf. *Macb.* iii. 4. 41: "the grac'd person of our Banquo." *Speak for* = call for, demand. Cf. *Cor.* iii. 2. 41: "when extremities speak" (that is, call to action); *Temp.* ii. 1. 207: "the occasion speaks thee" (calls upon thee), etc.

255. *Disquantity.* Diminish; used by S. nowhere else. Cf. *disnatured* in 290 below.

256. *Depend.* Be dependent, continue in service.

257. *Besort.* Become, befit. Cf. the noun in *Oth.* i. 3. 239.

258. *Which.* Who; as often.

266. *Marble-hearted.* Cf. *marble-breasted* in *T. N.* v. 1. 127.

268. *Sea-monster.* The commentators have wasted much ink on the question whether S. refers to the hippopotamus or to the whale. If any particular monster is meant (which is doubtful), it may be that in *M. of V.* iii. 2. 57, or some other old classical story.

269. *Detested.* See on i. 2. 75 above.

270. *Choice and rarest.* Perhaps for *choicest and rarest.* Cf. *M. for M.* iv. 6. 13: "The generous and gravest citizens," etc.

273. *Worships.* Honour, dignity. Cf. *W. T.* i. 2. 314: "rear'd to worship" (that is, raised to honour), etc. For the plural, see on iv. 6. 35 below.

275. *An engine.* The rack. Steevens quotes Beaumont and

Fletcher, *Night-Walker*, iv. 5 : "Their souls shot through with adders, torn on engines."

279. *Dear.* Here apparently = precious. Cf. i. 1. 177 above, and iii. 1. 19 below.

287. *Derogate.* Degenerate, debased. For the form, cf. *felicitate*, i. 1. 70 above.

288. *Teem.* Bear children. Cf. *Rich. II.* v. 2. 91 : " my teeming date," etc. For the transitive use, see *Macb.* iv. 3. 176, etc.

290. *Thwart.* Perverse ; the only instance of the adjective in S. Cf. Milton, *P. L.* viii. 132 : " Mov'd contrary with thwart obliquities ; " and *Id.* x. 1075: "the slant lightning, whose thwart flame, driven down," etc. *Disnatur'd* = unnatural, wanting in natural affection. The word is used only once by S., like sundry other compounds with *dis-: dislimn, dismask, dispiteous, disorbed, disproperty, disquantity* (255 above), *disunite, disvalue, disvouch*, etc.

292. *Cadent.* Falling (Latin *cadens*) ; used by S. only here ; and *cadence* only in *L. L. L.* iv. 2. 126.

293. *Her mother's pains and benefits.* Her maternal pains and good offices, her loving attention to the training of her child.

295. *How sharper*, etc. Malone compares *Psalms*, cxl. 3.

299. *Disposition.* See on 228 above.

307. *Untented.* That cannot be probed, incurable. Cf. *detested* = detestable, i. 2. 75 above. For *tent* = a probe, cf. *T. and C.* ii. 2. 16 : —

> " the tent that searches
> To the bottom of the worst."

For the verb, see *Ham.* ii. 2. 626 : " I 'll tent him to the quick."

308. *Fond.* Foolish. See on i. 2. 46 above.

309. *Beweep.* Cf. *Sonn.* 29. 2 : " I all alone beweep my outcast state," etc.

313. *Comfortable.* In an active sense = ready to comfort. Cf. i. 4. 313 above and ii. 2. 166 below. See also *A. W.* i. 1. 86 : " Be comfortable to my mother," etc.

KING LEAR — 14

325-329. Ellis says that the last three rhymes are remarkable, especially the last, including the word *halter*. *Daughter* and *after* are also rhymed in *T. of S.* i. 1. 245, 246 and *W. T.* iv. 1. 27, 28. In the former of these two, the rhyme, as here in *Lear*, may be meant to be ridiculous.

332. *At point.* Ready, prepared for any emergency. Cf. iii. 1. 33 below and *Ham.* i. 2. 200.

333. *Buzz.* Whisper. Cf. *Hen. VIII.* ii. 1. 148 : —

> " did you not of late days hear
> A buzzing of a separation
> Between the king and Katherine?"

334. *Enguard.* Surround as with a guard, protect; used by S. only here.

335. *In mercy.* At his mercy. Cf. *M. of V.* iv. 1. 355 : —

> " And the offender's life lies in the mercy
> Of the duke only ; "

and *L. L. L.* v. 2. 856: "That lie within the mercy of your wit." " *In misericordia* is the legal phrase " (Malone).

337. *Still.* Ever. See on i. 1. 226 above.

338. *Taken.* That is, taken with harm, be harmed by others. *Harms* = causes of harm.

345. *Full.* Used adverbially; as often. Cf. *W. T.* i. 2. 129: "To be full like me," etc. *Particular* = personal, individual. Cf. v. 1. 30 below, and the noun in ii. 4. 290.

347. *Compact.* "Unite one circumstance with another so as to make a consistent account" (Johnson). *More* is metrically a dissyllable.

349. *This milky gentleness and course.* This weak gentleness of your course. For the construction, see on i. 2. 43 and 173 above. Cf. *T. of A.* iii. 1. 57 : "A faint and milky heart ; " and " milk-liver'd," iv. 2. 50 below.

351. *At task.* Liable to be "taken to task," as we say.

354. *Striving to better,* etc. Cf. *Sonn.* 103. 9 : —

> " Were it not sinful then, striving to mend,
>   To mar the subject that before was well ? "

356. *The event.* That is, the event will show ; *nous verrons.*

SCENE V. — 1. *Gloster.* The city of Gloucester, which S. chose to make the residence of the Duke of Cornwall and Regan, in order to give a probability to their setting out late from there on a visit to the Earl of Gloster, whose castle may be supposed to be near that city.

8. *Brains.* S. makes *brains* plural, except in *A. W.* iii. 2. 16: " The brains of my Cupid 's knocked out," where the intervening singular may perhaps account for the irregularity. As *brain* and *brains* were used indiscriminately (except in such phrases as " to beat out the brains "), it is not strange that the pronoun referring to the words should be used somewhat loosely, at least in vulgar parlance.

9. *Kibes.* Chilblains. Cf. *Temp.* ii. 1. 276, *Ham.* v. 1. 153, etc.

11. *Thy wit shall ne'er go slipshod.* " For you show you have no wit in undertaking your present journey."

14. *Shalt see.* The omission of *thou* as subject is common. *Kindly* here = " both affectionately and like the rest of her kind " (Mason).

15. *Crab.* That is, a crab apple. Cf. *M. N. D.* ii. 1. 48, etc.

20. *On 's.* See on i. 4. 108 above. Just below, in 20, we have *of* = on.

25. *I did her wrong.* Weiss remarks: " The beautiful soul of Cordelia, that is little talked of by herself, and is but stingily set forth by circumstance, engrosses our feeling in scenes from whose threshold her filial piety is banished. We know what Lear is so pathetically remembering; the sisters tell us in their cruellest moments; it mingles with the midnight storm a sigh of the daughterhood that was repulsed. In the pining of the Fool we detect it. Through every wail or gust of this awful symphony of madness, ingratitude, and irony, we feel a woman's breath."

34. *Be.* Often used in questions, perhaps on account of the doubt implied.

36. *The seven stars.* The Pleiades. Cf. 1 *Hen. IV.* i. 2. 16. The Pleiades have been familiar as household words from the earliest times, and "the seven stars" has always been the popular English name for them. *Moe* (= more) is regularly plural.

40. *To take 't again,* etc. I am inclined to agree with Johnson that Lear is here " meditating on his assumption of royalty " (Johnson), rather than on " his daughter's having in so violent a manner deprived him of those privileges which before she had agreed to grant him " (Steevens).

47. *O, let me not be mad,* etc. Dr. Bucknill remarks: "This self-consciousness of gathering madness is common in various forms of the disease. . . . A most remarkable instance of this was presented in the case of a patient, whose passionate, but generous, temper became morbidly exaggerated after a blow upon the head. His constantly expressed fear was that of impending madness; and when the calamity he so much dreaded had actually arrived, and he raved incessantly and incoherently, one frequently heard the very words of Lear proceeding from his lips: 'Oh, let me not be mad!'"

ACT II

SCENE I. — 1. *Save thee.* That is, God save thee. Cf. *T. G. of V.* i. 1. 70, *T. N.* iii. 1, 76, etc. For the full form, see *Much Ado,* iii. 2. 82, v. 1. 327, *A. Y. L.* v. 2. 20, etc.

9. *Ear-kissing.* With lips touching the hearer's ear. The quartos have "eare-bussing," in which there may be a play on *buzzing* (see on i. 4. 333 above).

11. *Toward.* In preparation, near at hand; as in iii. 3. 20 and iv. 6. 192 below,

18. *Queasy.* Delicate, to be handled nicely.

27. *Upon his party.* On his side. Delius thinks that in order to confuse his brother and urge him to flight, Edmund asks him first whether he has not spoken against Cornwall, and then, reversing the question, whether he has not said something on the side of Cornwall against Albany. Craig suggests that the meaning may be : "against Cornwall's party, which is soon to be opposed to that of Albany."

28. *Advise yourself.* Consider. Cf. *T. N.* iv. 2. 102: "Advise you what you say," etc.

31. *Quit you.* Acquit yourself. Cf. 1 *Corinthians*, xvi. 13.

32. *Yield! come before my father!* This is spoken loud so as to be heard outside.

35. *I have seen drunkards*, etc. Steevens quotes Marston, *Dutch Courtezan*, iv. 1 : "Nay, looke you ; for my owne part, if I have not as religiously vowd my hart to you, — been drunk to your healthe, swalowd flap-dragons, eate glasses, drunke urine, stabd arms, and don all the offices of protested gallantrie for your sake."

40. *Mumbling.* Either the participle with *of* added (cf. *Ham.* ii. 1. 92) or the verbal with *a* omitted; more likely the former.

43. *This way.* "A wrong way should be pointed to " (Capell).

47. *But that.* Following the *when* in 43. The construction is not uncommon. Cf. *Ham.* iv. 7. 160 : —

> " *When* in your motion you are hot and dry —
> As make your bouts more violent to that end —
> *And that* he calls for drink," etc.

51. *Loathly.* Loathingly ; the only instance of the adverb in S. The adjective occurs several times ; and so does the noun *loathness.*

52. *Motion.* A fencing term, meaning an attack as opposed to *guard* or parrying. Cf. the passage from *Ham.* in note on 47 above.

53. *Charges home,* etc. Cf. *Oth.* v. 1. 2: " Wear thy good rapier bare, and put it home," etc.

54. *Lanc'd.* The quartos have "lancht" or "launcht," but *lance* and *launch* seem to have been often used interchangeably.

55. *But when.* The quarto reading; the folios have "And when." Furness adopts Staunton's conjecture of "whe'r" (= whether) for *when*, which is very plausible; but there may be a change of construction in *Or whether*, or an ellipsis: *Or whether* (it was that he was) *gasted*, etc. *Best alarum'd* = thoroughly awakened. The verb occurs again in *Macb.* ii. 1. 53.

57. *Gasted.* Frightened. Nares cites an instance of *gast* as a participle from *Mirrour for Magistrates:* "Thou never wast in all thy life so ghast." *Gaster* was another form of the word. Cf. Gifford, *Dial. on Witches,* 1603: "If they run at him with a spit red hote, they gaster him so sore," etc. *Gastness* (= ghastliness) occurs in *Oth.* v. 1. 106.

60. *Dispatch.* That is, dispatch him ; or = Dispatch is the word. Cf. *death* in 65 just below.

61. *Arch.* Chief, master; used by S. only here. Steevens quotes Heywood, *If you Know*, etc. : "Poole, that arch, for truth and honesty."

67. *Pight.* Fixed, settled. Cf. *T. and C.* v. 10. 24 : —

> "You vile abominable tents,
> Thus proudly pight upon our Phrygian plains."

Straight-pight (= erect) occurs in *Cymb.* v. 5. 164. It was the old participle of *pitch ;* also the past tense, as in Spenser, *F. Q.* i. 2. 42 : —

> "Then brought she me into this desert waste,
> And by my wretched lovers side me pight."

Curst = harsh, sharp (as in *T. N.* iii. 2. 46); often = shrewish.

69. *Unpossessing.* Incapable of inheriting ; a bastard being, as Blackstone says, "nullius filius," and therefore of kin to nobody.

70. *If I would.* If I were disposed to, if I should. *Reposal* (used by S. only here) is analogous to *disposal.* "The words *virtue, or worth* are in loose construction with the rest of the

sentence; 'the reposure of any trust, (or the belief in any) virtue, or worth in thee'" (Wright).

72. *Faith'd.* Believed, credited; used by S. only here.

74. *Character.* Handwriting. See on i. 2. 60 above.

75. *Suggestion.* Prompting to evil ; the usual meaning of the word in S. The verb *suggest* is often used in a similar sense. For *practice* see on i. 2. 180 above.

76. *Dullard.* Cf. *Cymb.* v. 5. 265: "What, mak'st thou me a dullard in this act?" S. uses the word only twice.

77. *Not.* For the transposition (a common one) cf. iv. 2. 2 below.

78. *Pregnant.* Ready; or *about to appear* (in action, as truth, etc., according to the connection). This is a frequent metaphorical sense of the word.

79. *Strong.* Obdurate. For the bad sense of the word, cf. *Rich. II.* v. 3. 59: "O heinous, strong, and bold conspiracy; " and *T. of A.* iv. 3. 45: "strong thief." Here the word seems in perfect keeping with the *fasten'd* (= confirmed, hardened) which follows.

80. *I never got him.* He is no son of mine. For *get* = beget, cf. iii. 4. 146 below.

81. *Hark!* etc. A *tucket* (see stage-direction) was a set of notes on the trumpet, used as a signal for a march. The word is found in the text of *Hen. V.* iv. 2. 35.

82. *Ports.* Portals, gates; as in *T. and C.* iv. 4. 113, 138, *Cor.* i. 7. 1, v. 6. 6, etc.

83. *His picture,* etc. Lord Campbell remarks: "One would suppose that photography, by which this mode of catching criminals is now practised, had been invented in the time of Lear." Furness adds that photography has merely been called to our aid in continuing a practice common in the time of S.; and he cites the old play of *Nobody and Somebody,* 1606: —

> " Let him be straight imprinted to the life;
>   His picture shall be set on euery stall,

> And proclamation made, that he that takes him,
> Shall haue a hundred pounds of *Somebody*."

86. *Natural.* Here used in the double sense of *illegitimate* and as opposed to *unnatural*, which Gloster implies that Edgar is.

87. *Capable.* Capable of inheriting ; a legal use of the word.

99. *Consort.* Company, fellowship ; as in *T. G. of V.* iv. 1. 64: " Wilt thou be of our consort?" The word in this sense has the accent on the last syllable; but when it means a company of musicians (as in *T. G. of V.* iii. 2. 84 and 2 *Hen. VI.* iii. 2. 327), on the first.

101. *Put him on.* Prompted him to. See on i. 4. 213 above.

102. *Th' expense.* The spending ; as in *M. W.* ii. 2. 147: " after the expense of so much money ; " *Sonn.* 94. 6: " And husband nature's riches from expense," etc. For the accent of *revenue*, see on i. 1. 132 above.

109. *Bewray.* Disclose, betray. Cf. iii. 6. 111 below ; and see also *R. of L.* 1698, *Cor.* v. 3. 95, etc. For *practice*, cf. 75 above.

113. *Of doing.* With regard to doing.

114. *In my strength.* With my authority.

115. *Doth.* The singular verb is often used after two singular nominatives.

117. *Trust.* Trustworthiness; as in *Oth.* i. 3. 285: " A man he is of honesty and trust," etc.

121. *Threading*, etc. Cf. *Cor.* iii. 1. 127: " They would not thread the gates."

122. *Poise.* Weight, moment. Cf. *Oth.* iii. 3. 82: " full of poise and difficult weight."

126. *From our home.* That is, away from our home. Cf. *Macb.* iii. 4. 36: —

> " To feed were best at home ;
> From thence the sauce to meat is ceremony; "

127. *Attend dispatch.* Wait to be dispatched.

129. *Businesses.* The folio reading ; the quartos have " busi-

nesse." If the singular is adopted (as it is in many eds.) it must be a trisyllable. The plural is found in *A. W.* i. 1. 220, iii. 7. 5, iv. 3. 98, *W. T.* iv. 2. 15, and *K. John*, iv. 3. 158.

130. *Craves.* Demands. The relative often takes a singula-verb, though the antecedent be plural.

SCENE II.— 1. *Dawning.* Not elsewhere used by S. in such salutation.

6. *If thou lov'st me.* "A conventional phrase before a question or request, which Kent here takes literally" (Delius).

9. *Lipsbury pinfold.* No such place as *Lipsbury* is known. Nares suggests that it may be a coined term, referring to "the teeth, as being the pinfold within the *lips*." For *pinfold* = (a pound), cf. *T. G. of V.* i. 1 114: "You mistake; I mean the pound, — a pinfold;" Milton, *Comus*, 7: "Confin'd and pester'd in this pinfold here," etc.

16. *Three-suited.* Having but three suits of clothes; contemptuous, and in keeping with *beggarly*. Steevens cites Ben Jonson, *Silent Woman*, iv. 2: "wert a pitiful poor fellow . . . and hadst nothing but three suits of apparel." Wright says: "It is probable that three suits of clothes a year were part of a servant's allowance. In the *Silent Woman*, iii. 1, Mrs. Otter, scolding her husband whom she treats as a dependant, says, 'Who gives you your maintenance, I pray you? Who allows you your horse-meat and man's-meat, your three suits of apparel a year? your four pair of stockings, one silk, three worsted?'" *Hundred-pound* was also a term of reproach. Cf. Middleton, *Phœnix*, iv. 3: "Am I used like a hundred-pound gentleman?"

17. *Worsted-stocking.* In England in the time of Elizabeth silk stockings were worn by all who could afford them, and worsted or woolen ones were thought cheap and mean. Steevens quotes Beaumont and Fletcher, *The Captain*, iii. 3: "serving-men . . . with woolen stockings." Malone adds from Middleton, *Phœnix*, iv. 2: " Metreza Auriola keeps her love with half the cost that I am

at ; her friend can go afoot, like a good husband, walk in worsted stockings, and inquire for the six-penny ordinary." *Lily-livered* = white-livered, cowardly. Cf. *Macb.* v. 3. 15 : " Thou lily-liver'd boy." See on i. 4. 349 above.

18. *Action-taking* = resenting an injury by a lawsuit, instead of fighting it out like a man. *Superserviceable* = over-officious ; or, perhaps, above his work. Cf. iv. 6. 235 below.

19. *One-trunk-inheriting.* With all his belongings in a single trunk. *Inheriting* = possessing ; as often. Cf. *Temp.* ii. 2. 179, *R. and J.* i. 2. 30, etc.

25. *Addition.* Title. See on i. 1. 131 above.

27. *Rail on.* S. uses *rail on* or *upon* oftener than *rail at.*

33. *Sop o' the moonshine.* Probably an allusion to the old dish called " eggs in moonshine," for which Nares gives the receipt from a cook-book of the time. Clarke remarks that the threat is equivalent to " I 'll beat you flat as a pancake."

34. *Cullionly* = cullion-like, base. Cf. *Hen. V.* iii. 2. 22 : " Up to the preach, you dogs ! avaunt, you cullions ! " (Fluellen's speech). See also 2 *Hen. VI.* i. 3. 43. *Barber-monger* = one who deals much with barbers ; hence a fop. Cf. *A. and C.* ii. 2. 229 : " barber'd ten times o'er."

37. *Vanity the puppet's part.* " Alluding to the old moralities or allegorical plays, in which Vanity, Iniquity, and other vices were personified " (Johnson).

39. *Carbonado.* Literally, to cut a piece of meat crosswise for broiling. Cf. *W. T.* iv. 4. 268 : " to eat adders' heads and toads carbonadoed." For the noun, see 1 *Hen. IV.* v. 3. 61.

40. *Come your ways.* Come on ; used by S. oftener than *come your way.*

43. *Neat slave.* " Mere slave, very slave " (Johnson); "finical rascal " (Steevens). Furness is inclined to agree with Johnson, and to find a parallel instance in Ben Jonson, *Poetaster,* iv. 1 : " By thy leave, my neat scoundrel." It is perhaps an objection to Johnson's explanation that S. nowhere else has *neat* = pure, unmixed. Or

the other hand, he seems to use it contemptuously = spruce, finical, in 1 *Hen. IV.* i. 3. 33: " Came there a certain lord, neat, and trimly dress'd," etc.

46. *Goodman boy.* Cf. *R. and J.* i. 5. 79: " What, goodman boy ! " *Goodman* was sometimes used contemptuously; as in *M. for M.* v. 1. 328 : " Come hither, goodman baldpate," etc.

47. *Flesh.* To initiate. Cf. *K. John,* v. 1. 71, 1 *Hen. IV.* v. 4. 133, etc. See also *fleshment* in 125 below.

51. *Messengers.* Oswald is the messenger *from our sister,* Kent the messenger from *the king.*

55. *Disclaims in.* Disowns; elsewhere in S. without *in.* Cf. i. 1. 106 above. For *a tailor made thee,* cf. *Cymb.* iv. 2. 81 : —

> " No, nor thy tailor, rascal,
> Who is thy grandfather; he made those clothes,
> Which, as it seems, make thee."

63. *Ancient.* Aged, old; as in 128 below.

65. *Thou whoreson zed!* etc. Ben Jonson in his *Eng. Gram.* says: "Z is a letter often heard among us, but seldom seen." Farmer quotes Mulcaster: " Z is much harder among us, and seldom seen : — S is become its lieutenant-general. It is lightlie expressed in English, saving in foren enfranchisements." Baret, in his *Alvearie,* 1580, omits the letter.

67. *Unbolted.* Coarse, unrefined. Tollet says: " *Unbolted mortar* is mortar made of unsifted lime, and to break the lumps it is necessary to tread it by men in wooden shoes." For *bolted* = refined, see *Hen. V.* ii. 2. 137: " Such and so finely bolted didst thou seem ; " and *Cor.* iii. 1. 322: " In bolted language."

68. *Jakes.* A privy. S. uses the word only here, but it is implied in the play on *Ajax* in *L. L. L.* v. 2. 581.

69. *Wagtail.* The bird so called ; mentioned by S. nowhere else.

76. *The holy cords.* The natural ties between parents and chil-

dren. *A twain* = in twain. Cf. *L. C. 6*: "Tearing of papers, breaking rings a-twain."

77. *Intrinse.* Intricate, or tightly drawn; used by S. only here. It seems to be a contracted form of *intrinsicate*, which occurs only in *A. and C.* v. 2. 307 : —

> "With thy sharp teeth this knot intrinsicate
> Of life at once untie."

Malone notes that the word was a new one at this time, and quotes the preface to Marston's *Scourge of Villanie*, 1598: "new-minted epithets (as reall, intrinsecate, Delphicke)." *Smooth* = flatter, humour; as in *Rich. II.* i. 2. 169: "Sweet smoothing word ; " and *Id.* i. 3. 48: "smooth, deceive, and cog."

78. *Rebel.* The plural may be explained by the proximity of *lords*, or by the plural implied in *every*.

80. *Renege.* Deny: from the Late Latin *renego*, whence also we get *renegade* (through the Spanish). It occurs again in *A. and C.* i. 1. 8: "reneges all temper." The quartos spell the word "Reneag," which indicates the pronunciation. Nares quotes Du Bartas, *The Battail of Ivry* : —

> "All Europe nigh (all sorts of rights reneg'd)
> Against the Truth and Thee, un-holy Leagu'd."

Halcyon. Kingfisher. Steevens quotes Lupton's *Notable Things*, b. x.: "A lytle byrde called the Kings Fysher, being hanged vp in the ayre by the neck, his nebbe or byll wyll be alwayes dyrect or strayght against ye winde ; " and Marlowe, *Jew of Malta*, i. 1 : —

> "But now how stands the wind ?
> Into what corner peers my halcyon's bill ? "

According to Charlotte Smith's *Nat. Hist. of Birds* (quoted by Dyce), the belief in a connection between the halcyon and the wind still lingered among the common people of England in 1807.

81. *Vary.* The only instance of the noun in S.

83. *Epileptic.* "Distorted by grinning" (Dyce). Oswald is pale with fright, yet pretending to laugh.

84. *Smile.* Smile at; but probably a corruption. *As* = as if; as in iii. 4. 15 and v. 3. 203 below.

85. *Sarum.* The ancient name of Salisbury.

86. *Cackling.* "Oswald's forced laughter suggests to Kent the cackling of a goose" (Furness). *Camelot,* famed in the Arthurian legends, was Cadbury in Somersetshire, according to Selden; and near it, Hanmer says, "there are many large moors, upon which great numbers of geese are bred." Malory identifies Camelot with Winchester; and "Winchester goose" (1 *Hen. VI.* i. 3. 53, *T. and C.* v. 10, 55) was a cant term for a certain sore, to which Capell saw a quibbling reference here. Sundry other explanations have been suggested.

92. *Likes.* Pleases. See on i. 1. 195 above.

99. *Constrains the garb,* etc. "Forces his *outside,* or his *appearance,* to something totally *different from* his natural disposition" (Johnson). For the figurative use of *garb,* cf. *Hen. V.* v. 1. 80, *Cor.* iv. 7. 44, *Ham.* ii. 2. 390, and *Oth.* ii. 1. 315.

102. *So.* That is, be it so; a very common use of the word.

103. *These kind of knaves.* Cf. *T. N.* i. 5. 95: "These set kind of fools," etc. In *Id.* i. 2. 10 we find "and those poor number."

104. *More corrupter.* See on i. 1. 73 above.

105. *Silly-ducking.* The hyphen is in the folios. *Ducking* is contemptuous for bowing; as in *Rich. III.* i. 3. 49 and *T. of A.* iv. 3. 18. *Observants* = obsequious attendants. For *observance* = homage, cf. *M. W.* ii. 2. 203 and *A. Y. L.* v. 2. 102. So *observe* = pay homage; as in *T. of A.* iv. 3. 212: —

> " Hinge thy knee,
> And let his very breath whom thou 'lt observe
> Blow off thy cap."

106. *Nicely.* With the utmost exactness. Cf. v. 3. 146 below.

108. *Aspect.* An astrological term. See on i. 1. 106 and i. 2. 126 above. Cf. *Sonn.* 26. 10, 1 *Hen. IV.* i. 1. 97, etc. The accent in S. is always on the last syllable.

111. *Discommend.* Disapprove ; used by S. nowhere else.

113. *Accent.* Speech, language ; as in *M. N. D.* v. 1. 97, *J. C.* iii. 1. 113, etc.

114. *Though I should win,* etc. "Though I should win you, displeased as you now are, to like me so well as to entreat me to be a knave " (Johnson).

120. *Compact.* Joined with him, taking his part. Cf. *M. for M.* v. 1. 242 : "Compact with her that 's gone," etc.

121. *Being down, insulted. I* being down, *he* insulted, etc.

122. *Put upon him,* etc. Assumed such a show of manhood that he seemed a hero and won praises from the king.

123. *That worthied him.* As exalted him into a hero (Schmidt).

124. *For him attempting.* For venturing to attack him. Cf. *M. W.* iv. 2. 226 : " he will never . . . attempt us again," etc.

125. *In the fleshment of.* "In the first glory of" (Clarke). See on ii. 2. 47 above.

127. *Is their fool.* Is a fool compared with them.

132. *Do respect* is like *do homage, do reverence,* etc. Cf. i. 4. 108 above.

134. *Stocking.* Putting in the stocks ; as in ii. 4. 186 below.

137. *Till noon!* etc. Clarke remarks : "Very artfully is this speech thrown in. Not only does it serve to paint the vindictive disposition of Regan, it also serves to regulate dramatic time by making the subsequent scene where Lear arrives before Gloucester's castle and finds his faithful messenger in the stocks appear sufficiently advanced in the morning to allow of that same scene closing with the actual approach of 'night,' without disturbing the sense of probability. S. makes a whole day pass before our eyes during a single scene and dialogue, yet all seems consistent and natural in the course of progression."

139. *Being.* That is, *you* being. Cf. 121 above.

140. *Colour.* "Nature" (the quarto reading); as in *A. Y. L.* iii. 2. 435, etc.

141. *Bring away.* Bring here, bring along ; as in *M. for M.* ii. 1. 41, *T. of A.* v. 1. 68, etc. So *come away* = come here ; as in *Temp.* i. 2. 187, etc. In great houses movable stocks were kept for the correction of servants.

144. *Check.* Rebuke; as in *J. C.* iv. 3. 97, etc.

149. *Answer.* Cf. i. 1. 146 and i. 3. 11 above.

150. *More worse.* See on 104 above.

156. *Rubb'd.* Hindered ; a metaphor from the game of bowls. Cf. the noun in *Rich. II.* iii. 4. 4.

159. *A good man's fortune,* etc. Even a good man may have bad luck. Possibly, as Furness suggests, Kent may jocosely mean "that what is usually but a metaphor is with him a reality."

160. *Give you good morrow!* God give you good morning! For the full form, see *L. L. L.* iv. 2. 84, and for the contraction, *God ye good morrow, R. and J.* ii. 4. 116. The salutation was one "used only by common people" (Schmidt). *Good morrow* was considered proper only before noon.

162. *Approve the common saw,* etc. Prove the truth of the old saying, "Out of God's blessing into the warm sun." Malone cites Howell, *English Proverbs,* 1660: "He goes out of God's blessing to the warm sun, viz. from good to worse." The origin of the proverb is uncertain. The simplest explanation, perhaps, is that it was applied to those who were turned out of doors and exposed to the weather.

165. *This under globe.* Cf. *T. of. A.* i. 1. 44: "this beneath world; " and *Sonn.* 7. 2 : —

> " Lo in the orient when the gracious light
>   Lifts up his burning head, each under eye
>   Doth homage to his new-appearing sight."

166. *Comfortable.* Comforting. See on i. 4. 313 above.

167. *Nothing almost,* etc. The wretched are almost the only

persons who can be said to see miracles. "That Cordelia should have thought of him, or that her letter should have reached him, seems to him such a miracle as only those in misery experience" (Delius).

170. *My obscured course.* My disguise. *And shall find time,* etc. = and who (that is, Cordelia) will find opportunity in this abnormal state of affairs to set things right again. The style is disjointed, partly because he is soliloquizing, partly because he can hardly keep his eyes open for weariness.

171. *Enormous* (which has the same etymology as *abnormal*, except that *norma* is compounded with *e* instead of *ab*) is rightly explained by Johnson as = "unwonted, out of rule, out of the ordinary course of things."

172. *All weary*, etc. Here he gives way to his drowsiness, bids his eyes take advantage of their heaviness not to see how poor a resting-place he has, and, with a good-night prayer for better fortune, falls asleep. For *o'er-watched* (= worn out with watching), cf. *J. C.* iv. 3. 241: "Poor knave, I blame thee not; thou art o'er-watch'd."

For other interpretations of portions of the passage, as well as for the emendations that have been proposed, the curious reader may consult Furness.

SCENE III. — 2. *Happy.* Lucky, fortunate; as in iv. 6. 209 below.

3. *Port.* Harbour, refuge.

5. *Attend my taking.* Watch to capture me. For *does*, see on ii. 1. 115 above.

6. *Am bethought.* Think, intend; the only instance of the form in S. He generally uses the reflexive form; as in *J. C.* iv. 3. 251: "It may be I shall otherwise bethink me;" *T. N.* iii. 4. 327 "he hath better bethought him of his quarrel," etc.

7. *Most poorest.* See on i. 1. 73 above.

8. *In contempt of man.* Bringing a man into contempt.

10. *Elf all my hair.* Tangle my hair as elves were supposed to do that of sluttish persons. Cf. *R. and J.* i. 5. 91 : "the elf-locks in foul, sluttish hair."

11. *Presented.* Assumed. The verb is often = represent. Cf. *Temp.* iv. 1. 167 : "when I presented Ceres," etc.

14. *Bedlam beggars.* Steevens quotes from Dekker's *Belman of London*, of which three editions appeared in 1608, the same year in which *Lear* was first printed, the following description of "an Abraham man" : "He sweares he hath been in Bedlam, and will talke frantickely of purpose : you see pinnes stuck in sundry places of his naked flesh, especially in his armes, which paine he gladly puts himselfe to, only to make you believe he is out of his wits. He calls himselfe by the name of *Poore Tom*, and comming near any body cries out, *Poore Tom is a-cold.* Of these Abraham-men, some be exceeding merry, and doe nothing but sing songs fashioned out of their own braines: some will dance, others will doe nothing but either laugh or weepe : others are dogged, and so sullen both in loke and speech, that spying but a small company in a house, they boldly and bluntly enter, compelling the servants through feare to give them what they demand."

15. *Mortified.* Deadened, hardened. See the quotation from Dekker just above.

16. *Wooden pricks.* Skewers. "The *Euonymus*, of which the best skewers are made, is called *prick-wood*" (Mason).

17. *Object* Appearance, sight; as often. Cf. v. 3. 240 below. *Low* = lowly, humble.

18. *Pelting.* Paltry, petty. Cf. *M. N. D.* ii. 1. 91 : "every pelting (folio, 'petty') river," etc.

19. *Bans.* Curses; as in *T. of A.* iv. 1. 34 : "with multiplying bans." Elsewhere in S. the plural refers to the marriage bans; as in v. 3. 88 below.

20. *Turlygod.* So in all the early eds. Warburton conjectured "Turlupin," the name applied to a fraternity of gypsies or beggars in the 14th century. Douce says that this name was corrupted into

"Turlygood," the form adopted by many editors. Nares doubts whether *Turlygood* has any real connection with *Turlupin*, though, like that, it evidently means a kind of beggar.

21. *Edgar I nothing am.* Edgar I shall no longer be. The adverbial use of *nothing* is common.

SCENE IV. — 7. *Cruel.* A play upon *crewel*, or worsted, of which garters were often made. The pun occurs often in the old dramatists.

10. *At legs.* The expression is found in Dekker, Massinger, Middleton, and other writers of the time.

11. *Nether-stocks.* Short stockings. Cf. 1 *Hen. IV.* ii. 4. 131: "I'll sew nether-stocks." For *stocks* = stockings, see *T. N.* i. 3. 144.

13. *To set thee. As* to set thee. See on i. 4. 38 above.

24. *Upon respect.* Upon consideration, deliberately. Cf. *K. John,* iv. 2. 214: "More upon honour than advised respect."

25. *Resolve me.* Inform me, explain to me. Cf. *Rich. III.* iv. 2. 26: "I will resolve your grace." *Modest* = reasonable, becoming. Cf. iv. 7. 5 below, where *modest* is exactly explained by "Nor more nor clipp'd, but so," that is, not too much nor too little, but just the measure (Latin *modus*).

26. *Usage.* Treatment; the only sense in which S. uses the word.

27. *Coming.* Relating to *thou.*

28. *Commend.* Commit, deliver; as in *Macb.* i. 7. 11, etc.

33. *Spite of intermission.* Not waiting for me to receive my answer. Cf. *Macb.* iv. 3. 232: "Cut short all intermission."

34. *Presently.* Immediately; as often. Cf. 114 below.

35. *Meiny.* Retinue, attendants. The word occurs repeatedly in Chaucer, and also in Spenser. Cf. *F. Q.* iii. 12. 23: "That all his many it affraide did make," etc. See also Cotgrave, *Fr. Dict.*: "Mesnie : f. A meynie, familie, household, household companie, or seruants."

41. *Display'd so saucily.* Made so impudent a display; the only instance of the intransitive verb in S.

42. *Drew.* That is, *I* drew my sword.

52. *Dolours.* For the play on the word, cf. *Temp.* ii. 1. 18 and *M. for M.* i. 2. 50.

53. *Tell.* "Count, or recount; according to the sense in which *dolours* is understood" (Wright).

54. *Mother.* Used as synonymous with *Hysterica passio*, or what we call *hysteria*. Ritson quotes Harsnet, *Declaration*, where Master Richard Mainy, who was persuaded by the priests that he was possessed of the devil, deposes as follows: "The disease I spake of, was a spice of the *Mother*, where-with I had beene troubled (as is before mentioned) before my going into Fraunce: whether I doe rightly terme it the *Mother* or no, I know not."

61. *How chance?* How chances it? Cf. *C. of E.* i. 2. 42: "How chance thou art returned so soon?" etc.

65. *To an ant*, etc. See *Proverbs*, vi. 6–8. "If, says the Fool, you had been schooled by the ant, you would have known that the king's train, like that sagacious animal, prefer the summer of prosperity to the colder season of adversity, from which no profit can be derived" (Malone).

75. *Sir.* Cf. *Temp.* v. 1. 69: "a loyal sir;" *T. N.* iii. 4. 81: "some sir of note," etc.

82. *Perdy.* A corruption of *par Dieu.* Cf. *Hen. V.* ii. 1. 52, etc.

85. *Deny.* Refuse; as often. Cf. *Rich. III.* v. 3. 343, etc.

86. *Fetches.* Shifts, pretexts. Cf. *Ham.* ii. 1. 38: "a fetch of warrant," etc.

87. *Images.* Signs, tokens. The word may be metrically a dissyllable. See p. 165 above.

89. *Quality.* Temper, disposition; as in 134 below.

90. *Unremovable.* Immovable. We find *irremovable* in *W. T.* iv. 4. 518, and *unremovably* in *T. of A.* v. 1. 227.

103. *Office.* Service, duty. Cf. 176 below. "The strong inter-

est now felt by Lear, to try to find excuses for his daughter, is most pathetic" (Coleridge).

107. *More headier.* See on i. 1. 73. These double comparatives and superlatives occur with more than usual frequency in this play. *Heady* here is "not *headstrong*, but *headlong, impetuous.*" Cf. *Hen. V.* i. 1. 34, etc.

111. *Remotion.* Removal (from their own house to Gloster's castle). Cf. *T. of A.* iv. 3. 346: "All thy safety were remotion, and thy defence absence."

112. *Practice.* Artifice. See on i. 2. 180 above.

114. *Presently.* See on 34 above.

116. *Till it cry sleep to death.* Till the clamour murders sleep.

119. *Cockney.* The word here seems to mean a *cook*, though it may be only a *cockney* cook (the noun being understood), or a London cook; perhaps an allusion to some familiar story of the time. Tyrwhitt cites passages from *Piers the Plowman* and *The Turnament of Tottenham*, in which the word also appears to be = cook; but Whalley, Malone, and Douce explain it differently. S. uses it only here and in *T. N.* iv. 1. 15, where it appears to be used in the modern sense.

120. *Knapped.* The word meant to "strike smartly," as well as to break in pieces (as in *Psalms*, xlvi. 10, Prayer Book version: "knappeth the spear in sunder"). Cf. Bacon, *Nat. Hist.* 133: "Knap a pair of tongs some depth within the water, and you shall hear the sound of the tongs."

122. *'Twas her brother*, etc. Absurd cruelty and absurd kindness are kindred follies.

128. *Thy mother's tomb.* The only reference to her in the play. In the old drama she is mentioned as "our (too late) deceast and dearest queen."

129. *Sepulchring.* Cf. *R. of L.* 805: "May likewise be sepulchred in thy shade;" and *T. G. of V.* iv. 2. 118: "Or at the least, in hers sepulchre thine." In both passages the accent is on the

penult, as here. The noun has the modern accent in S. except in *Rich. II.* i. 3. 196. Milton makes the same distinction.

131. *Naught.* Bad, wicked; usually spelt *naught* in the early eds. when it has this sense, but *nought* when = nothing.

132. *Sharp-tooth'd unkindness.* Cf. i. 4. 295 above. For the allusion to the vulture of Prometheus, cf. 2 *Hen. IV.* v. 3. 145, 1 *Hen. VI.* iv. 3. 47, etc.

134. *Quality.* Disposition, nature. Cf. 89 above.

135. *Take patience.* Cf. *W. T.* iii. 2. 232: "take your patience to you." See also *Hen. VIII.* v. 1. 106.

136. *You less know how*, etc. One of the peculiar "double negatives" explained by Schmidt, p. 1420. The meaning is: "You are apter to depreciate her than she to scant her duty." Furness asks: "Is the levity ill-timed that suggests that perhaps Regan's speech puzzles poor old Lear himself quite as much as his commentators, and he has to ask her to explain: 'Say, how is that ?'"

143. *O, sir, you are old*, etc. Coleridge remarks: "Nothing is so heart-cutting as a cold, unexpected defence or palliation of a cruelty passionately complained of, or so expressive of thorough hard-heartedness. And feel the excessive horror of Regan's 'O, sir, you are old !' — and then her drawing from that universal object of reverence and indulgence the very reason for her frightful conclusion — 'Say you have wrong'd her.' All Lear's faults increase our pity for him. We refuse to know them otherwise than as means of his sufferings and aggravations of his daughters' ingratitude."

145. *Confine.* S. accents the noun on either syllable.

148. *Make return.* Return, go back; as in *T. G. of V.* ii. 7. 14, *M. for M.* iv. 3. 107, *T. N.* i. 4. 22, etc. S. does not use the phrase in the modern sense (= make requital).

150. *The house.* "The order of families, duties of relation" (Warburton). Steevens cites Chapman, *Blind Beggar of Alexandria*, 1598: "Come up to supper; it will become the house

wonderful well." Schmidt compares the horror of Coriolanus (*Cor.* v. 3. 56) when his mother kneels to him.

152. *Age is unnecessary.* An ironical apology for his useless existence.

154. *Unsightly tricks.* This refers to Lear's kneeling. According to Davies (quoted by Furness), "Garrick threw himself on both knees, with his hands clasped, and in a supplicating tone repeated this touching, though ironical, petition."

156. *Abated.* Deprived. The construction is not found elsewhere in S.

157. *Strook.* The early eds. have "strooke" or "stroke," as in many other passages; oftener than "struck," which modern editors generally print here. For the participle the early eds. have *struck, strook* or *strooke, stroke, strooken, stroken, strucken* (see i. 4. 82 above), and *stricken.*

160. *Ingrateful top.* Ungrateful head. S. uses *ingrateful* much oftener than *ungrateful.* See on 90 above. For *top*, cf. *A. W.* i. 2. 43: "and bowed his eminent top to their low ranks," etc. *Her young bones* = her unborn infant. Cf. the old play of *King Leir :* —

> "Alas, not I : poore soule, she breeds yong bones,
> And that is it makes her so tutchy sure."

161. *Taking.* Malignant, bewitching ; as in iii. 4. 60 below. Cf. also *Ham.* i. 1. 163: "No fairy takes, nor witch hath power to harm."

165. *Fall.* Malone made the verb transitive (= cause to fall, humble), as it often is ; but I have no doubt that it is intransitive. As Wright remarks, this is more in keeping with *drawn* and *blast.* It is also the sense in which S. uses it in similar passages ; as in *Temp.* ii. 2. 2 (a strikingly parallel imprecation) : —

> "All the infections that the sun sucks up
> From fogs, fens, flats, on Prosper fall, and make him
> By inch-meal a disease ! "

See also *M. N. D.* ii. 1. 90, *A. W.* i. 1. 79, *Macb.* iv. 1. 105, iv. 3. 227, etc.

169. *Tender-hefted.* The folio reading; the quartos having "tender hested." Neither is easily explained. As *hefts* = heavings in *W. T.* ii. 1. 45, Steevens thought *tender-hefted* might mean 'whose bosom is agitated with tender passions.' The only other sense of *heft* (not found in S.) is *haft* or handle; whence some make the compound = "held by tenderness," "tender, gentle, to touch or to approach," "set in a tender handle or delicate bodily frame," etc. On the other hand, *hest* = command, and *tender-hested*, it is said, may be = "governed by gentle dispositions." All these interpretations are unsatisfactory. There is probably some corruption in the passage, but *tender-hearted*, the only emendation that has been proposed, is "tolerable and not to be endured." S. could never have written "tender-hearted nature."

171. *Do comfort and not burn.* Malone compares *T. of A.* v. 1. 134: "Thou sun, that comfort'st, burn!"

173. *Sizes.* Allowances. Wright says: "The words *sizar* and *sizing* are still well known in Cambridge; the former originally denoting a poor student, so called from the *sizes* or allowances made to him by the college to which he belonged." For *bandy* see on i. 4. 87 above.

181. *Approves.* Confirms; as in i. 1. 179 and ii. 2. 162 above.

183. *Easy-borrow'd.* "Borrowed without the trouble of doing anything to justify it" (Moberly).

186. *Stock'd.* See on ii. 2. 134 above.

189. *Allow.* Approve of; as in the Prayer Book version of *Psalms*, xi. 6: "The Lord alloweth the righteous" (Upton).

198. *Less advancement.* "A still worse, or more disgraceful situation" (Percy). It appears to be, as Schmidt terms it, "an undisguised sneer."

207. *To wage.* That is, to wage combat, to contend; not elsewhere used by S. in this sense without an object.

209. *Necessity's sharp pinch!* This is explained as in apposition

with what precedes, and perhaps correctly. It may, however, be
an exclamation that has no syntactical connection with what precedes. It may mean, Is *this* the pinch to which Necessity brings
me ? Or it is barely possible that it is a sarcastic reference to the
excuse which Regan has given for not receiving him — that she is
away from home, and has not the means of entertaining him.
Schmidt points it as an anacoluthon, "Necessity's sharp pinch —,"
leaving us to guess at what Lear would have said, but for the sudden turn in the tide of his passion. On *the wolf and owl*, cf. *R.
of L.* 165 : —

> " No comfortable star did lend his light;
> No noise but owls' and wolves' death-boding cries."

212. *Knee.* Kneel before. The verb occurs again in *Cor.* v.
1. 5 : —
> "A mile before his tent fall down, and knee
> The way into his mercy."

214. *Sumpter.* A pack-horse. S. uses the word only here.

221. *Boil.* Spelt "Bile" or "Byle" in the early eds., as in
other printing of the time ; doubtless indicating the pronunciation.

222. *Embossed.* Tumid ; as in *A. Y. L.* ii. 7. 67 : " And all the
embossed sores and headed evils," etc. The *emboss* in *A. W.* iii.
6. 107, as Furnivall has shown, is of different origin (Old Fr. *em-
boser = emboîter*). This is Cotgrave's " Emboister : To imbox, in-
close, insert, fasten, put, or shut vp, as within a box."

226. *High-judging Jove.* Cf. Milton's " all-judging Jove " (*Lycidas*, 82).

237. *Sith.* See on i. 1. 175 above. *Charge* = expense ; as in
K. John, i. 1. 49 : "this expedition's charge," etc.

240. *Hold amity.* Keep friendship. Cf. " hold friendship " in
L. L. L. ii. 1. 141. " Hold antipathy " occurs in ii. 2. 89 above.

243. *Slack ye.* Neglect you. Cf. i. 3. 10 above.

247. *Notice.* Attention, recognition. Cf. *Cymb.* ii. 3. 45, 65,
etc.

249. *My guardians.* The guardians under me of my realms.

251. *With.* By. Cf. 303 below.

254. *Well-favour'd.* Well in *favour*, or features. Cf. *Much Ado*, iii. 3. 15, *T. N.* i. 5. 169, etc.

255. *Not being the worst*, etc. Steevens compares *Cymb.* v. 5. 215 : —

> " It is I
> That all the abhorred things o' the earth amend
> By being worse than they."

259. *What need*, etc. How need, or why need, etc. Cf. *J. C.* ii. 1. 123: " What need we any spur but our own cause ? "

262. *O, reason not*, etc. " Observe that the tranquillity which follows the first stunning of the blow permits Lear to reason " (Coleridge).

263. *Are in the poorest*, etc. Have in their poverty something that may be called superfluous.

268. *Need—.* " To imagine how Shakespeare would have ended this sentence, one must be a Shakespeare. The poor king stops short in his definition ; it is too plain that his true need is patience " (Moberly).

269. *Patience, patience I need!* Perhaps, as Malone conjectured, the repetition of *patience* was a slip of the printer. If so, *patience* would be a trisyllable. Abbott would put *you heavens* in a separate line, making the first *patience* a dissyllable, the second a trisyllable.

272. *Stirs.* See on i. 1. 234 and ii. 1. 115 above.

274. *To bear.* *As* to bear. See on i. 4. 38 above.

283. *Flaws.* " A *flaw* signifies a crack, but is here used for a small broken particle " (Malone).

284. *Or ere.* A reduplication, *or* being = before. Cf. *Temp.* i. 2. 11, v. i. 103, etc.

287. *Bestow'd.* Lodged; as often. Cf. iv. 6. 269 below.

288. *Hath.* For the omission of the subject, see on ii. 4. 42 above. Cf. 299 below.

290. *For his particular.* As to him personally, so far as he himself is concerned. Cf. *Cor.* iv. 7. 13: —

> "Yet I wish, sir —
> I mean for your particular — you had not
> Join'd in commission with him;"

299. *Ruffle.* Bluster. The word is used figuratively (= be turbulent) in *T. A.* i. 313: "To ruffle in the commonwealth of Rome."

303. *With.* See on 251 above.

304. *Incense.* Instigate, provoke; as in *J. C.* i. 3. 13, etc.

305. *His ear abus'd.* Cf. *A. W.* v. 3. 295: "She does abuse our ears."

ACT III

SCENE I. — 6. *The main.* The mainland. Elsewhere in S. it means the sea. Cf. *Sonn.* 64. 7: "the watery main;" *K. John,* ii. 1. 26: "England, hedg'd in with the main," etc.

On *curled waters,* cf. 2 *Hen. IV.* iii. 1. 23: —

> "Who take the ruffian billows by the top,
> Curling their monstrous heads," etc.

8. *Eyeless.* Blind, undiscerning. Cf. the literal use in iii. 7. 96 below.

9. *Make nothing of.* Treat with contempt (as we still use the expression), not "annihilate," as some explain it.

10. *His little world of man.* Probably an allusion to the ancient notion of man as the *microcosm,* or little world, containing in miniature the elements of the *macrocosm,* or the universe. Cf. *Rich. II.* v. 5. 9: "And these same thoughts people this little world." See also *L. C.* 7.

12. *Cub-drawn.* Sucked dry by her cubs, and made hungry by

it. Cf. *A. Y. L.* iv. 3. 115: "A lioness, with udders all drawn dry;" and *Id.* iv. 3. 127: "the suck'd and hungry lioness."

14. *Unbonneted.* Cf. *Oth.* i. 2. 23; and for *bonnet* = cap, see *Rich. II.* i. 4. 31, etc.

15. *Take all.* Cf. *M. W.* i. 3. 84: "then Lucifer take all!" 2 *Hen. VI.* iii. 1. 307: "nay, then, a shame take all!" etc.

17. *Heart-strook.* See on ii. 4. 157 above.

18. *Note.* Observation, or knowledge. Cf. ii. 1. 85 above.

23. *Who seem no less.* Who seem nothing else than *servants*, and not the *spies* that they really are.

24. *Speculations.* Close observers. Schmidt, in his *Lexicon* (p. 1421), gives more than sixty instances in S. of this use of the abstract for the concrete; and Furness adds *discretion* in ii. 4. 146 below.

25. *Intelligent.* Giving information. Cf. iii. 5. 12 and iii. 7. 12 below. *What hath been seen,* etc.; that is, to note and report, etc.

26. *Snuffs.* Huffs, offence-taking. Cf. "taking it in snuff" (*L. L. L.* v. 2. 22) and the play upon the expression in 1 *Hen. IV.* i. 3. 41. *Packings* = plottings. Cf. *T. of S.* v. 1. 121: "Here's packing, with a witness, to deceive us all!"

29. *Furnishings.* "Colours, external pretences" (Johnson).

30. *Power.* Army; as often, both in the singular and the plural, Cf. iii. 3. 13, iv. 2. 17, iv. 3. 50, iv. 4. 21, etc., below.

31. *Scatter'd.* "Divided, unsettled, disunited" (Johnson); not elsewhere used in this sense by S.

32. *Feet.* Footing, landing.

33. *At point.* See on i. 4. 332 above.

34. *To show their open banner.* To begin active hostilities.

36. *To make.* As to make. See on i. 4. 38 and ii. 4. 13 above.

39. *Plain.* Complain. Cf. *Rich II.* i. 3. 75, etc.

43. *I will talk further with you.* This implies a courteous postponement or dismissal of a request; hence Kent's reply (Delius).

45. *Out-wall.* Exterior. Cf. *wall* in *T. N.* i. 2. 48, and *K. John,* iii. 3. 20.

48. *That.* S. generally uses the possessive pronoun with *fellow* = companion.

52. *To effect.* As to effect, in importance.

53. *Pain.* Labour, effort (*will be* or *lies* being understood). S. uses both *pain* and *pains* in this sense ; now we use only the latter.

SCENE II. — 2. *Hurricanoes.* Water spouts. Cf. *T. and C.* v. 2. 172 : —

> " the dreadful spout
> Which shipmen do the hurricano call."

Nares quotes Drayton, *Mooncalf*, 168 : —

> " And downe the shower impetuously doth fall,
> Like that which men the Hurricano call."

3. *Cocks.* That is, the weathercocks.

4. *Thought-executing.* Doing execution with the rapidity of thought.

5. *Vaunt-couriers.* Forerunners, precursors ; originally "the foremost scouts of an army." Cf. *Temp.* i. 2. 201 : —

> " Jove's lightnings, the precursors
> O' the dreadful thunder-claps."

8. *Germens.* Seeds; as in *Macb.* iv. 1. 59. Cf. *W. T.* iv. 4. 489 : —

> " Let nature crush the sides o' the earth together,
> And mar the seeds within."

Spill = destroy : Cf. *Ham.* iv. 5. 20 : "It spills itself," etc. See also Spenser, *F. Q.* iii. 7. 54 : Badd her commaund my life to save or spill ; " and *Id.* v. 10. 2 : "As it is greater prayse to save then spill," etc.

10. *Court holy-water.* " Ray, among his proverbial phrases, mentions *court holy-water* to mean *fair words*. The French have the same phrase : *Eau benite de cour* " (Steevens). Cotgrave, *Fr.*

Dict., has " *Eau beniste de Cour.* Court holy water ; complements, faire words, flattering speeches," etc.

13. *Pities.* For the ellipsis of the relative, cf. i. 4. 62 above.

15. *Fire.* A dissyllable ; as in *Rich. II.* i. 3. 294, ii. 1. 34, v. 1. 48, etc.

18. *Subscription.* Submission, obedience ; the only instance of the noun in S. Cf. the use of the verb in i. 2. 19 above and iii. 7. 65 below.

23. *High-engender'd.* *High* = in the heavens; as in *high-judging*, ii. 4. 226 above. *Battles* = battalions ; as in *J. C.* v. i. 4. etc.

27. *That makes his toe*, etc. Makes that his last object which should be his first (Capell). Furness paraphrases the quatrain thus : " A man who prefers or cherishes a mean member in place of a vital one shall suffer enduring pain where others would suffer merely a twinge. Lear had preferred Regan and Goneril to Cordelia."

31. *For there was never yet*, etc. " This is the Fool's way of diverting attention after he has said something a little too pointed; the idea of a very pretty woman making faces in a looking-glass raises a smile " (Furness). For *made mouths*, cf. *Ham.* ii. 2. 381, iv. 4. 50, etc.

39. *Gallow.* Affright ; the only instance of the word in S. According to Nares, the word in the corrupt form of *gally* is still used in the West of England.

43. *Carry.* Bear, sustain. Cf. *R. and J.* iv. 5. 120 : " I will carry no crotchets."

44. *Affliction.* Used for " any painful sensation " (Schmidt).

45. *Pudder.* The folio spelling, followed by Furness and some other editors ; but the majority read "pother," as Furness notes. Charles Lamb preferred *pudder*, and uses it in his remarks on this play. Cf. *Cor.* ii. 1. 234, where the old eds. have " poother."

49. *Simular.* Simulator; the only instance of the noun in S. The adjective occurs in *Cymb.* v. 5. 200: " with simular proof enough " (that is, pretended, counterfeited).

52. *Has.* One of many examples of the verb in the third person

with a relative whose antecedent is of the first or second person. *Practis'd on* = plotted against. Cf. the noun in i. 2. 180 above.

53. *Continents.* That which contains or encloses; the original sense of the word, and the usual one in S. Cf. *Ham.* iv. 4. 64, etc. *Concealing continents* = "shrouds of secrecy" (Herford). *Cry grace* = cry for grace or pardon. Cf. *cry you mercy* (*M. W.* iii. 5. 27) and *cry you pardon* (*Oth.* v. 1. 93).

54. *Summoners.* The officers that summon offenders before a tribunal.

56. *Gracious my lord.* Cf. iii. 4. 1 below.

59. *More harder.* See on i. 1. 73 above.

60. *Demanding.* Inquiring, asking. Cf. v. 3. 63 below.

62–68. *My wits begin to turn,* etc. Dr. Bucknill remarks: "The import of this must be weighed with iv. 6. 100–104, when Lear is incoherent and full of delusion. Insanity arising from mental and moral causes often continues in a certain state of imperfect development; . . . a state of exaggerated and perverted emotion, accompanied by violent and irregular conduct, but unconnected with intellectual aberration, until some physical shock is incurred, — bodily illness, or accident, or exposure to physical suffering; and then the imperfect type of mental disease is converted into perfect lunacy, characterized by more or less profound affection of the intellect, by delusion or incoherence. This is evidently the case in Lear, and although we have never seen the point referred to by any writer, and have again and again read the play without perceiving it, we cannot doubt from these passages, and especially from the second, in which the poor madman's imperfect memory refers to his suffering in the storm, that S. contemplated this exposure and physical suffering as the cause of the first crisis in the malady. Our wonder at his profound knowledge of mental disease increases, the more carefully we study his works ; here and elsewhere he displays with prolific carelessness a knowledge of principles, half of which would make the reputation of a modern psychologist."

65. *The art.* "The alchemy or transforming power" (Moberly).

69. *He that has and,* etc. Cf. *T. N.* v. 1. 398 fol. "This may have been the same song, but changed by the Fool to suit the occasion" (Furness).

74. *I'll speak a prophecy,* etc. The whole of this speech is probably an interpolation. Cf. *Ham.* iii. 2. 42: "And let those that play your clowns speak no more than is set down for them," etc. The *prophecy* is an imitation of one formerly ascribed to Chaucer, but now regarded as spurious.

87. *Merlin.* Cf. 1 *Hen. IV.* iii. 1. 150: "the dreamer Merlin and his prophecies."

SCENE III. — 5. *Neither . . . or.* For the use with more than two particulars, cf. *M. for M.* iv. 2. 108: "neither in time, matter, or other circumstance," etc.

13. *Home.* Fully. See on ii. 1. 53 above, and cf. iii. 4. 16 below.

14. *Footed.* On foot; or perhaps = "landed," which is the quarto reading. Cf. iii. 7. 45 below. *Look* = look for, "seek" (the quarto reading). Cf. *A. Y. L.* ii. 5. 34: "He hath been all this day to look you."

20. *Toward.* At hand. See on ii. 1. 11 above.

21. *Forbid thee.* Forbidden thee; the usual form of the participle in S. Cf. v. 1. 47 below.

SCENE IV. — 6. *Think'st 't is much.* Cf. *Temp.* i. 2. 252: "Thou dost, and think'st it much to tread the ooze," etc.

7. *Invades.* See on i. 1. 139 above.

15. *As.* As if. Cf. v. 3. 203 below.

16. *Home.* See on ii. 1. 53 and iii. 3. 13 above.

26. *Poverty.* The abstract for the concrete. See on iii. 1. 24 above.

31. *Loop'd.* Full of holes. For *loop* = hole, see 1 *Hen. IV.* iv. 1. 71: "all sight-holes, every loop," etc.

35. *Superflux.* Superfluity; which is the word S. uses elsewhere.

37. *Fathom and half,* etc. Probably Steevens is right in supposing that Edgar talks as if taking soundings at sea.

54. *Knives under his pillow,* etc. That is, to tempt him to suicide. Steevens quotes *Dr. Faustus,* 1604 : —

> " Swords, poisons, halters, and envenom'd steel,
> Are laid before me to dispatch myself."

57. *Four-inched bridges.* The old bridges of a single beam or plank across small streams, intended for pedestrians but sometimes used by horsemen.

58. *Thy five wits.* Cf. *T. N.* iv. 2. 92 : " Alas, sir, how fell you besides your five wits ? "

59. *Do de, do de, do de* is " perhaps intended to express the teeth-chattering sound emitted by one who shivers with cold " (Clarke).

60. *Star-blasting.* Cf. *Ham.* i. 1. 162 : " then no planets strike," etc. For *taking,* see on ii. 4. 161 above.

62. *Now, and there,* etc. " He catches at the fiend, as he would at flies " (Moberly).

68. *Pendulous.* Impending, overhanging. Cf. *T. of A.* iv. 3. 108 : —

> " Be as a planetary plague when Jove
> Will o'er some high-vic'd city hang his poison
> In the sick air."

Schmidt quotes *The Birth of Merlin* (which has been attributed to S.), iv. 1 : " Knowest thou what pendulous mischief roofs thy head ? "

72. *Lowness* = abject condition. In *A. and C.* ii. 7. 22 it is used literally (= small elevation), and in *Id.* iii. 11. 63 it is = meanness. *Unkind* is accented on the first syllable, as usual *before* a noun. See on i. 1. 254 above.

74. *Should have,* etc. This probably refers to the sticking of pins into the arms. In Edwin Booth's *Prompt-book* there is a stage-direction : " Draws a thorn, or wooden spike, from Edgar's

arm, and tries to thrust it into his own; " and after line 76 : " Edgar seizes Lear's hand and takes away the thorn " (Furness).

75. *Judicious.* Wise, or just.

76. *Pelican.* Alluding to the fable that the young of the pelican were fed with blood from its own breast. Cf. *Rich. II.* ii. 1. 126 and *Ham.* iv. 5. 146.

77. *Pillicock.* Suggested by *pelican.* In Ritson's *Gammer Gurton's Garland* we find the nursery rhyme : —

> " Pillycock, Pillycock sat on a hill;
> If he 's not gone, he sits there still."

The word was often used as a term of endearment. Dyce quotes Florio : " *Pinchino*, a prime-cocke, a pillicocke, a darlin, a beloued lad."

78. *Loo, loo !* Craig says that this is " a cry to excite dogs " which he has heard in Cardigan. Cf. *T. and C.* v. 7. 10 : " Now, bull ! now, dog ! Loo, Paris, loo ! " Schmidt explains it in the same way.

82. *Commit.* The word seems to have been applied particularly to incontinence (Malone). Schmidt compares *Oth.* iv. 2. 72 fol.

87. *Curled my hair.* Curling the hair seems to have been the mark of a swaggerer, for in Harsnet's *Declaration* we are told that the devil was said to appear " sometimes like a Ruffian, with curled haire." Cf. *T. of A.* iv. 3. 160 : " Make curl'd-pate ruffians bald." *Gloves in my cap ;* that is, as the favour of a mistress. Cf. *Rich. II.* v. 3. 17 : —

> " And from the common'st creature pluck a glove,
> And wear it as a favour."

See also *T. and C.* iv. 4. 73, v. 2. 79, etc.

92. *Light of ear.* " Foolishly credulous " (Schmidt).

93. *Hog in sloth*, etc. In the *Ancren Riwle*, the seven deadly sins are typified by seven wild animals; the lion being the type of pride, the serpent of envy, the unicorn of wrath, the bear of sloth,

the fox of covetousness, the swine of greediness, and the scorpion of lust.

99. *Suum, mun, nonny.* The nonsensical burden of a song. Cf. *Ham.* iv. 5. 165 and *Much Ado*, ii. 3. 76. *Dolphin my boy* is probably a quotation from a song. Farmer quotes Ben Jonson, *Bartholomew Fair*, v. 3 : "he shall be Dauphin my boy."

100. For *sessa* (a word of doubtful origin and meaning) cf. *T. of S.* ind. 1. 6: "let the world slide; sessa!"

101. *Thou wert better.* See on i. 4. 102 above. Cf. *2 Hen. IV.* i. 2. 245: "I were better to be eaten to death with a rust," etc.

105. *The cat.* That is, the civet cat. Cf. *A. Y. L.* iii. 2. 70.

106. *Sophisticated.* Adulterated, not genuine; as now often used. The word is used by S. only here.

107. *Unaccommodated.* Unsupplied with conveniences ; the only instance of the word in S. Cf. *accommodated* in *2 Hen. IV.* iii. 2. 72: "a soldier is better accommodated than with a wife ; " and see also iv. 6. 81 below.

108. *Off, off,* etc. "The latent madness against which Lear has been struggling bursts into violence at sight of the strange and awful object which Edgar has made of himself, and he longs to reduce himself, like him, to a state of absolute and unmitigated nature " (Moberly).

109. *Unbutton here.* Furness remarks : "It has been suggested to me by an eminent novelist and dramatist in London that these words are properly a stage-direction."

111. *Naughty.* Bad; used in a much stronger sense than now. Cf. iii. 7. 37 below. See also on ii. 4. 131 above.

112. *Wide.* The early eds. and most modern ones have "wild." Jennens suggested the change, on the ground that *wide* is better opposed to *little ;* and Walker, who says that "*wild* is in the manner of modern, not Elizabethan poetry," gives other instances from S. and contemporaneous writers of the same misprint of *wild* for *wide.*

114. *A walking fire.* **That is,** Gloster with his torch approaching in the distance.

115. *Flibbertigibbet.* This name, like that of the other demons here, is from Harsnet, who says : " Frateretto, Fleberdigibet, Hoberdidance, Tocobatto, were four deuils of the round, or Morrice, whom Sara in her fits, tuned together, in measure and sweet cadence." It had come to be used figuratively even in that day, for Cotgrave gives it as one of the definitions of *Coquette :* " a fisking, or fliperous minx, a cocket or tatling housewife; a titifill, a flebergebit."

116. *Walks.* Often = go away. Cf. *Cymb.* i. 1. 176: " Pray, walk awhile." See also *M. for M.* iv. 5. 12, *W. T.* i. 2. 172, *Oth.* iv. 3. 4, and iv. 7. 83 below.

117. *The web and the pin.* An old name for cataract in the eye. Cf. *W. T.* i. 2. 291 : " Blind with the pin and web."

120. *Saint Withold.* The folios have " Swithold." The name is a corruption of *St. Vitalis.* *Old* (the reading of the early eds.) = " wold," which is another form of the word.

121. *Her nine-fold.* That is, her nine imps, or familiars (Capell).

124. *Aroint thee.* Evidently implying aversion, and = " Away with thee ! " but of doubtful origin. Cf. *Macb.* i. 3. 6.

126. *What 's he ?* Who 's he? Cf. v. 3. 120, 126, 166 below.

130. *Tadpole.* The old eds. have " tod pole," " Tod-pole," " Tod-pool," or " toade pold; " but the modern spelling was then in use. Cotgrave has " Gyrine : the frog tearmed, a Tadpole." *The wall-newt and the water* = the lizard common on stone walls in Europe and the water-newt. For the ellipsis in *water*, cf. *M. for M.* iii. 2. 9 : " furred with fox and lamb-skins."

132. *Sallets.* Salads. Cf. *2 Hen. VI.* iv. 10. 9. It is used figuratively in *Ham.* ii. 2. 462.

133. *Ditch-dog* = a dead dog thrown into a ditch. For *mantle*, cf. *Temp.* iv. 1. 182 : " Filthy-mantled pool."

134. *Whipped from tithing to tithing.* A *tithing* is the same in the country as a ward in the city. A statute of the time of Eliza-

beth enacted that vagabonds or "tramps" should be publicly
whipped and sent from parish to parish.

135. *Hath.* The quartos read "hath had." Schmidt remarks:
"*Hath had* probably accords with the fact, but what have facts to
do with madness ? Tom hath three suits and six shirts ; — where
are they ? who has taken them from him ?"

138, 139. Capell cites the old romance of *Sir Bevis of North-
ampton* (referred to in *Hen. VIII.* i. 1. 38) : —

> " Rattes and myce and suche smal dere
> Was his meate that seuen yere."

Deer was sometimes used in the general sense of game. Malone
quotes Barclay, *Eclogues*, 1570 : —

> " Everie sorte of dere
> Shrunk under shadowes abating all their chere."

140. *Smulkin.* Another name from Harsnet's category of
devils, like *Modo* and *Mahu* just below.

143. *The prince of darkness*, etc. Cf. Sir John Suckling (who
may be quoting from *Lear*), *Goblins*, ii. 1 : —

> " The prince of darkness is a gentleman,
> Mahu, Mahu is his name."

145. *Our flesh and blood*, etc. Clarke remarks : "One of Shakespeare's subtle touches. Some tone or inflection in Edgar's voice
has reached the father's heart, and bitterly recalls the supposed un-
filial conduct of his elder son, and he links it with that of Lear's
daughters. Edgar, instinctively feeling this, perseveres with his
Bedlam cry, to drown the betrayed sound of his own voice, and
maintain the impression of his assumed character."

149. *To obey.* That is, by my obeying. *Obey in all*, etc. is =
obey your daughters in all their hard commands.

153. *Is.* Cf. ii. 1. 115 above.

159. *Prevent.* Avoid ; perhaps with something of its original
sense of anticipating. *To kill vermin*, as Clarke remarks, is "an

instance of Shakespeare's dexterous mode of indicating points that would be treated by other writers of his time with revolting coarseness."

161. *Importune.* Accented regularly by S. on the penult.

168. *Late.* Lately; as in i. 4. 195 above.

171. *I do beseech your grace,* —. " Here Gloster attempts to lead Lear towards the shelter he has provided in the farm-house adjoining the castle ; but the king will not hear of quitting his 'philosopher.' Gloster then induces the Bedlam-fellow to go into the hovel, that he may be out of Lear's sight ; but Lear proposes to follow him thither, saying, 'Let's in all.' Kent endeavours to draw Lear away, but, finding him resolved to 'keep still with' his 'philosopher,' begs Gloster to humour the king, and 'let him take the fellow' with him. Gloster accedes, and bids Kent himself take the fellow with them in the direction they desire to go ; and this is done. We point out these details, because, if it be not specially observed, the distinction between the 'hovel' and the 'farm-house' would hardly be understood. The mention of 'cushions' and a 'joint-stool' in scene vi. shows it to be some place of better accommodation than the 'hovel;' and probably some cottage or farmhouse belonging to one of Gloster's tenants" (Clarke). For *cry you mercy*, see on iii. 2. 53 above.

177. *Soothe.* Humour. Cf. *C. of E.* iv. 4. 82: "Is't good to soothe him in these contraries?" The word in S. always means either to humour or to flatter.

182. *Child Rowland.* The use of *Child* as the title of a young knight is familiar to every reader of the old English ballads and of Spenser. Byron has adopted it in *Childe Harold.* The ballad quoted here has never been discovered. Fragments of a Scottish version of the story are given by Jamieson in his *Illustrations of Northern Antiquities,* and in Professor Child's *English and Scottish Ballads.* Browning's poem suggested by the passage is well known.

183. *His word.* That of the giant in the old story.

SCENE V. — 3. *Censured.* Judged, estimated ; as often. Cf. *J. C.* iii. 2. 16: "Censure me in your wisdom," etc. *Nature* = natural affection. He refers to his giving information against his father. See iii. 3. 21 above.

4. *Fears me.* Makes me fear, frightens me. Cf. *T. of S.* i. 2. 211: "Fear boys with bugs," etc.

8. *A provoking merit.* "A merit he felt in himself which irritated him against a father that had none" (Mason). Some take *provoking merit* to refer to Gloster, not to Edgar.

11. *To be just.* Of being just. See on iii. 4. 149 above.

12. *Approves* = proves. See on ii. 4. 181 above. *An intelligent party to,* etc. = a party intelligent to (or knowing to), etc. Cf. iv. 1. 3 below.

21. *Comforting.* "Giving aid and comfort to ; " as the legal phrase still is.

23. *Persever.* The spelling of the first three folios, indicating the old pronunciation of the word, the only one in S.

24. *Blood.* Equivalent to *nature* in 4 above, and opposed like that to *loyalty.*

SCENE VI. — 4. *Have.* The reading of all the early eds., changed in most modern ones to "hath" or "has." It is one of the instances of "confusion of proximity" so common in S.

6. *Frateretto.* See on iii. 4. 115 above.

7. *Innocent.* He is addressing the Fool. Cf. *A. W.* iv. 3. 213: "a dumb innocent that could not say him nay."

10. *A yeoman.* A freeholder, but not a gentleman. Cf. *1 Hen. VI.* ii. 4. 81, 85, 95, and *1 Hen. IV.* iv. 2. 16.

19. *A horse's health.* "A horse is above all other animals subject to disease" (Johnson). Cf. *T. of S.* i. 2. 81: "though she have as many diseases as two and fifty horses."

21. *Justicer.* Cf. 56 below, and *Cymb.* v. 5. 214: "Some upright justicer." Boswell quotes Lambard's *Eirenarcha :* "And of this it commeth that M. Fitzherbert (in his treatise of the Justices

of Peace) calleth them *justicers* (contractly for *justiciars*) and not *justices*, as we commonly, and not altogether unproperly, doe name them."

22. *Sapient.* Used by S. nowhere else.

24. *Wantest thou eyes*, etc. "Do you want eyes to gaze at and admire you during trial, madam ? The fiends are there to serve your purpose" (Clarke).

25. *Come o'er*, etc. Cf. Chappell, *Popular Music of the Olden Time:* "The allusion is to an English ballad by William Birch [1558], entitled, 'A songe betwene the Quenes Majestie and Englande,' a copy of which is in the library of the Society of Antiquaries. England commences the dialogue, inviting Queen Elizabeth in the following words : —

> 'Come over the born, Bessy, come over the born, Bessy,
> Swete Bessy, come over to me.'"

Halliwell-Phillipps gives the music of the song from a MS. of the 16th century in the British Museum.

30. *Hoppedance.* See on iii. 4. 115 above.

31. *White herring.* According to some authorities, this means fresh herring; but in the North of England pickled herring are so called. On *Croak not*, etc., Malone quotes Harsnet : "One time shee remembereth, that shee having the said croaking in her belly, they said it was the devil that was about the bed, that spake with the voice of a toad."

38. *Bench.* Used again in *W. T.* i. 2. 314, where it is = raise to authority. *Of the commission ;* that is, a justice of the peace. Cf. *2 Hen IV.* iii. 2. 97: "my cousin Silence, in commission with me."

41. *Sleepest*, etc. Steevens quotes an old play, *The Interlude of the Four Elements :* "Sleepyst thou, wakyst thou, Geffery Coke?"

43. *Minikin.* Small and pretty ; used by S. only here.

45. *Pur.* This may be only an imitation of a cat. *Purre* is, however, one of Harsnet's devils.

52. *Cry you mercy*, etc. A proverbial expression, found in Ray's *Proverbs*. Steevens quotes Lyly, *Mother Bombie*, 1594: "I crie you mercy, I tooke you for a joynt stoole." For *cry you mercy*, cf. iii. 4. 171 above.

54. *Store.* If this is what S. wrote, it must be = substance or material.

57. *Thy five wits.* See on iii. 4. 58 above.

69. *Brach.* See on i. 4. 118 above. *Lym* is Hanmer's correction of the "him" or "Him" of the quartos and "Hym" of the folios. The word meant a *lime-hound*, or a hound led in a *lime*, or leash.

70. *Tike.* A small dog, or cur. Cf. *Hen. V.* ii. 1. 31. Nares gives *trindle-tail* as "a corruption of *trundle-tail*, or *curly-tail*," and cites Beaumont and Fletcher, *Love's Cure*, iii. 3: —

> "Like a poor cur, clapping his trindle tail
> Between his legs."

73. *Hatch.* A half-door, or the lower half of a divided door; common now in English cottages. Cf. *K. John* i. 1. 171, v. 2. 138, etc.

74. *Sessa !* See on iii. 4. 100 above.

75. *Thy horn is dry.* "A horn was usually carried about by every Tom of Bedlam, to receive such drink as the charitable might afford him, with whatever scraps of food they might give him" (Malone). Aubrey, in his MS. *Natural History of Wiltshire*, in describing "Bedlam beggars," says: "they wore about their necks a great horn of an oxe in a string or bawdric, which, when they came to an house for almes, they did wind; and they did putt the drink given them into this horn, whereto they did putt a stopple."

76. *Anatomize Regan.* That is, dissect her after executing her. Cf. *A. Y. L.* i. 1. 162, ii. 7. 56, etc.

79. *Entertain.* Take into service, engage. Cf. *T. G. of V.* ii. 4. 110: "Sweet lady, entertain him for your servant; " *Much Ado*, i. 3. 60: "entertained for a perfumer," etc. So *entertainment* = service; as in *A. W.* iii. 6. 13, iv. 1. 17, etc.

81. *Persian.* Perhaps a reminiscence of the Persian robes of an embassy sent to England early in James I.'s reign.

84. Bucknill remarks here: " Lear is comparatively tranquil in conduct and language during the whole period of Edgar's mad companionship. It is only after the Fool has disappeared, and Edgar has left to be the guide of his blind father, that the king becomes absolutely wild and incoherent. The singular and un-doubted fact is, that few things tranquillize the insane more than the companionship of the insane. It is a fact not easily explicable, but it is one of which, either by the intuition of genius, or by the information of experience, S. appears to be aware."

85. *And I'll go to bed at noon.* White remarks: "About the middle of the play the Fool suddenly disappears, making in reply to Lear's remark, ' We'll go to supper in the morning,' the fitting rejoinder, ' And I'll go to bed at noon.' Why does he not return? Clearly for this reason: he remains with Lear during his insanity, to answer in antiphonic commentary the mad king's lofty ravings with his simple wit and homespun wisdom: but after that time, when Lear sinks from frenzy into forlorn imbecility, the Fool's utterances would have jarred upon our ears. The situation be-comes too grandly pathetic to admit the presence of a jester, who, unless he is professional, is nothing. Even Shakespeare could not make sport with the great primal elements of woe. And so the poor Fool sought the little corner where he slept, turned his face to the wall, and went to bed in the noon of his life for the last time — *functus officio.*"

89. *Upon.* Against. We may still say " an attack upon him."

94. *Thine, and all,* etc. Thine and *that of* all, etc. As Abbott remarks, the Elizabethan writers object to scarcely any ellipsis that can be readily supplied from the context.

95. *Assured loss.* Assurance, or certainty, of loss ; or *stand in* = stand in danger of, are exposed to. Cf. 100 below.

98. *Balm'd.* Anointed with healing balm, healed. Elsewhere (*T. of S.* ind. i. 1. 48 and *Per.* iii. 2. 65) it is used of fragrant

applications. *Sinews* = nerves; as in *V. and A.* 903, and some-times in other writers of the time.

99. *Convenience.* A quadrisyllable.

100. *Stand in hard cure.* Will be hard to cure. Cf. *Oth.* ii. 1. 51: "Stand in bold cure."

106. *Sufferance.* Suffering; as often in S. Cf. *J. C.* ii. 1. 115, etc.

107. *Bearing.* Endurance of suffering.

108. *Portable.* Bearable, endurable; as in *Macb.* iv. 3. 89: "all these are portable."

110. *Childed* is not found elsewhere in S. For *father'd*, cf. *J. C.* ii. 1. 297 and *Macb.* iv. 2. 27.

111. *The high noises.* "The loud tumults of approaching war" (Steevens). *Bewray* = disclose, discover. See on ii. 1. 109 above. Johnson paraphrases the passage thus: "Attend to the great events that are approaching, and make thyself known when that *false opinion* now prevailing against thee shall, in consequence of *just proof* of thy integrity, revoke its erroneous sentence and recall thee to honour and reconciliation."

113. *Repeals.* Recalls. Cf. *J. C.* iii. i. 51, etc.

114. *What will hap.* Happen what will.

SCENE VII. — 2. *Letter.* Cf. iii. 5. 11 above.

7. *Revenges.* For the plural, cf. ii. 4. 277 above.

10. *Festinate.* Speedy. The word is used by S. only here, but *festinately* is one of Armado's affectations in *L. L. L.* iii. 1. 6.

12. *Swift and intelligent.* Prompt in conveying information. See on iii. 1. 25 above.

13. *My lord of Gloster.* "Meaning Edmund, newly invested with his father's titles" (Johnson). Cf. iii. 5. 18 above. Oswald in 14 refers to the old earl.

17. *Questrists.* Seekers, searchers (Fr. *questeur*). The word is not found elsewhere. Cf. *questant* in *A. W.* ii. 1. 16.

18. *Lord's dependants.* Some editors print "lords dependants"

(= dependant lords) ; but, as Furness remarks, it clearly means *Gloster's* dependants. There were no *lords* dependent on the king, but only certain *knights*. The question in 46 below doubtless refers to Gloster's agency in giving Lear an escort of some of his own followers.

24. *Pass upon.* "That is, pass a judicial sentence" (Johnson). It is still a legal term (Furness).

26. *Do a courtesy to.* Yield to, obey. Cf. *M. for M.* ii. 4. 175: "Bidding the law make court'sy to their will."

28. *Ingrateful.* See on ii. 4. 160 above.

29. *Corky.* "Dry, withered, husky" (Johnson) ; used by S. only here. Harsnet has the expression: "an old corkie woman."

37. *Naughty.* A striking instance of the old strong meaning of the word. See on iii. 4. 111 above.

39. *Quicken.* Come to life. Cf. *Oth.* iii. 3. 277, etc.

40. *My hospitable favours.* The features of me your host. Cf. *1 Hen. IV.* iii. 2. 136: "And stain my favours in a bloody mask ; " where most editors read "favour." Steevens quotes *David and Bethsabe*, 1599 : "To daunt the favours of his lovely face."

43. *Simple-answer'd.* Plain in your answer. Cf. *better-spoken* in iv. 6. 10 below.

45. *Footed.* See on iii. 3. 14 above.

54. *I am tied*, etc. An allusion to bear-baiting. Cf. *Macb.* v. 7. 1 : —

> "They have tied me to a stake; I cannot fly,
> But, bear-like, I must fight the course; "

Course was the technical term for a bout or round in the baiting. Cf. Brome, *Antipodes :* "two ten-dog courses at the great bear."

60. *Buoy'd up.* Lifted itself up. The verb occurs nowhere else in S. For the noun, see iv. 6. 19 below.

61. *Stelled.* Fixed, as Schmidt explains it ; not = starry (from *stella*), as some make it. Cf. *R. of L.* 1444 and *Sonn.* 24. 1.

62. *Holp.* Often used by S. both as past tense and participle of *help.*

63. *Stern.* The quartos have "dearn" (= dreadful), which some editors adopt. The word occurs in *Per.* iii. prol. 15 : " By many a dearn and painful perch."

65. *All cruels else subscribe.* The quartos have "subscrib'd." As Furness remarks, this is "the most puzzling phrase" in the play. If we follow the folio, we may as well put the words into the address to the porter, as Furness does. He suggests two para-phrases ("acknowledge the claims of all creatures, however cruel they may be at other times," or "give up all cruel things else — that is, forget that they are cruel"), and the second may be right. "As in i. 2. 19, Lear *subscribed* his powers, so here the porter should *subscribe all cruels*, that is, he should surrender, yield, give up whatsoever was cruel in the poor beasts, and see only their claim to his compassion ; " or, more concisely, " condone all cruelties." For the general meaning of the passage, cf. iv. 7. 36 fol. below.

67. *See 't shalt thou never !* Coleridge asks : " What can I say of this scene ? — There is my reluctance to think Shakespeare wrong, and yet —." Elsewhere he says : " I will not disguise my conviction that in this one point the tragic in this play has been urged beyond the outermost mark and *ne plus ultra* of the dramatic."

77. *What do you mean ?* Furness asks : " Should not this be given to Cornwall ? " So S. may have intended.

78. *Villain.* In its literal sense of serf. Moberly remarks : " As a villain could hold no property but by his master's sufferance, had no legal rights as against his lord, and was (perhaps) incapable of bearing witness against freemen, that one should raise his sword against his master would be unheard-of presumption, for which any punishment would be admissible. The lord's making war against his superior lord would entail no such consequences."

87. *Quit.* Requite ; as often. Cf. *Ham.* v. 2. 68, etc.

89. *Overture.* Disclosure. Cf. *W. T.* ii. 1. 172: "without more overture."

91. *O.* Monosyllabic exclamations sometimes take the place of a foot in the verse. Cf. iv. 2. 26 below.

98. *Untimely.* Adverbial ; as in *Ham.* iv. 1. 40: "untimely done," etc.

101. *Old course of death.* Ordinary course of death, a natural death. Wordsworth (*Shakespeare's Knowledge and Use of the Bible*) compares *Numbers*, xvi. 29.

103. *Bedlam.* Lunatic ; as in *K. John*, ii. 1. 83: "Bedlam, have done."

105. *Allows itself to.* Allows itself to be turned to, or employed in.

106. *Flax and whites of eggs.* A common remedy in that day.

ACT IV

SCENE I.— 3. *Dejected thing of fortune.* Thing cast down by fortune.

4. *Esperance.* Hope; as in *T. and C.* v. 2. 121: "An esperance so obstinately strong."

7. *Unsubstantial.* Cf. *R. and J.* v. 3. 103. *Insubstantial* occurs in *Temp.* iv. i. 155. See on ii. 4. 160 above.

9. *Owes nothing to thy blasts.* Need not care for them ; or, has nothing to thank them for.

12. *Life would not yield to age.* "We so hate life that we gladly find ourselves lapsing into old age, and approaching death, which will deliver us from it (Moberly).

20. *Our means secure us.* "The advantages we enjoy make us careless" (Schmidt). For *secure,* cf. *T. of A.* ii. 2. 185 : —

> " Canst thou the conscience lack
> To think I shall lack friends ? Secure thy heart; "

and *Oth.* i. 3. 10: "I do not so secure me in the error," etc. Wright explains the passage thus: "Things we think meanly of, our mean or moderate condition, are our security;" and he adds that he knows of no instance of the verb *secure* = to render careless. *I* know of no instance of *means* = mean things, or "moderate condition." Knight says: "The means, such as we possess, are our securities, and, further, our mere defects prove advantages." Sundry emendations have been suggested, but the old text is probably right, and the choice of explanations lies between Schmidt's and Knight's.

21. *Commodities.* Advantages. Cf. 2 *Hen. IV.* i. 2. 278.

22. *Abused.* Deceived, deluded; as often. Cf. *Cymb.* iii. 4. 123, etc.

37. *They kill us for their sport.* Wordsworth (*Shakespeare's Knowl. of Bible*) says: "I very much doubt whether S. would have allowed any but a heathen character to utter this sentiment."

39. *Angering itself and others.* "He at the same time displeases himself and the person he endeavours to amuse" (Heath).

46. *Times'.* The plural, not the singular. Cf. *M. for M.* iii. 2. 288: "Making practice on the times;" *M. of V.* ii. 9. 48: "the chaff and ruin of the times," etc. But the singular is similarly used; as in *T. G. of V.* iii. 1. 86, *Macb.* v. 8. 24, *Ham.* iii. 2. 27, etc. *When madmen lead the blind* = "when enthusiasts madden the ignorant."

52. *Daub it.* Disguise; as in *Rich. III.* iii. 5. 29: "So smooth he daub'd his vice with show of virtue."

61. *Flibbertigibbet.* Cf. iii. 4. 115 above. *Mopping and mowing* = making faces or grimaces. The two words have the same meaning, and are often thus conjoined. Cf. *Temp.* iv. 1. 47: —

> " Each one, tripping on his toe,
> Will be here with mop and mow," etc.

63. *Chambermaids.* Probably an allusion to Harsnet's account of three chambermaids in the family of Mr. Edmund Peckham.

Perhaps, as Moberly thinks, there may be a general reference to chambermaids " who perform these antics before their mistress's dressing-glass."

67. *Makes thee the happier.* " That is, because my wretchedness now teaches me to compassionate those who are in distress " (Wordsworth). Cf. Dido's " Non ignara mali miseris succurrere disco."

68. *Superfluous.* Having more than enough. Cf. *A. W.* i. 1. 116 : "Cold wisdom waiting on superfluous folly." See also ii. 4. 260 above.

69. *That slaves,* etc. " Who, instead of paying the deference and submission due to your ordinance, treats it as his slave, by making it subservient to his views of pleasure or interest " (Heath).

74. *There is a cliff,* etc. The *cliff,* now known as *Shakespeare's Cliff,* is just outside of the town of Dover, to the southwest. It has been somewhat diminished in height by frequent landslips, but is still about 350 feet high. The surge still chafes against the pebbles, and the samphire-gatherer is still let down in a basket to pursue his perilous trade ; but the cliff is not so perpendicular, noi do objects below seem so small, as one would infer from the poet's description. Probably he did not mean to give a picture of this particular cliff, but delineated one " in his mind's eye," and more or less ideal. The South Eastern Railway now runs through the Dover cliff in a tunnel 1331 yards long.

75. *Confined.* Restrained, kept back by the *cliff.*

SCENE II. — 1. *Welcome.* She welcomes him to her house after reaching it in his company (Delius). *Our mild husband* is contemptuous.

2. *Not.* For the transposition, see on ii. 1. 77 above, and cf. 53 below.

8. *Sot.* Fool (like the Fr. *sot*); the only meaning in S. So *sottish* = foolish, in the one instance in which he uses it, *A and C.* iv. 15. 79.

11. *What like, offensive.* Ellipses in antithetical sentences are common.

12. *Cowish.* Cowardly; used by S. only here.

14. *Answer.* That is, a manly answer to a challenge; as in *Ham.* v. 2. 179 and *T. and C.* i. 3. 332.

16. *Powers.* Forces. See on iii. 1. 30 above.

19. *Like.* Likely; as in i. 1. 296 above and iv. 7. 95 below.

22. *Decline your head.* Either that she may put a chain round his neck (Delius), or to receive the kiss.

24. *Conceive.* Understand; as in *Temp.* iv. 1. 50, etc.

26. *O.* See on iii. 7. 91 above.

29. *I have been worth the whistle.* There was a time when you would not have waited so long without coming to meet me. Steevens quotes Heywood's *Proverbs:* "A poore dogge that is not woorth the whystlyng."

31. *Fear* = fear for; as in v. 1. 16 below.

32. *That nature,* etc. That nature which despises its origin cannot be restrained within any bounds whatever, but is capable of any depravity. For *it* possessive, cf. i. 4. 222 above.

34. *Sliver.* Cf. *Macb.* iv. 1. 28: "Sliver'd in the moon's eclipse." The word is in common use in this country, but apparently obsolete (or provincial) in England. *Disbranch* is used by S. only here.

35. *Material.* Furnishing matter, nourishing. Schmidt remarks: "From Shakespeare's use of *material* elsewhere, in the sense of *full of matter,* and hence of *importance,* it is not easy to explain it here." But here it is = "full of matter," in a sense in which S. often uses *matter* (= substance, materials). *Perforce* = of necessity; used only with *must* in this sense. Cf. 49 below. It is often = by force; as in i. 4. 305 and i. 5. 40 above.

36. *Deadly use.* Ruin, or destruction; like the use made of wood when dead (that is, for burning).

39. *Filths.* Cf. *T. of A.* iv. 1. 6: "To general filths," etc. *Savour* = have a taste or relish for.

42. *Head-lugg'd.* Led by the head. Cf. 1 *Hen. IV.* i. 2. 82·
" a lugged bear."

43. *Madded.* Cf. *Rich. II.* v. 5. 61 : " This music mads me,"
etc. S. does not use *madden.*

47. *Tame.* Schmidt thinks the word suspiciously " weak "; but
S. often uses it in the sense of " subdue " or " crush " (see
Schmidt's *Lexicon*); as in *K. John*, v. 2. 74 : " And tame the sav-
age spirit of wild war," etc. See also iii. 6. 18 above.

50. *Milk-liver'd.* See on ii. 2. 17 above.

54. *Fools do those villains*, etc. I am inclined to agree with
Furness that this probably refers to Albany himself, not to Gloster
or Lear as others explain it. " She cannot refer to Gloster, because
Albany is ignorant of what had been done to him, and she herself
had left Gloster's castle before the blinding was accomplished;
and it is difficult to believe that she refers to Lear."

55. *Where's thy drum ?* That is, why are you not rallying your
forces ?

56. *Noiseless.* With no sound of warlike preparation.

58. *Moral.* Moralizing. Cf. *Much Ado*, v. 1. 30, *A. Y. L.* ii.
7. 29, etc.

60. *Proper deformity.* Native depravity. Cf. 2 *Hen. IV.* iv.
1. 37 : —

" if damn'd commotion so appear'd
In his true native and most proper shape."

62. *Self-cover'd.* Whose natural (feminine) self is covered or
concealed. The meaning then is : Thou perverted creature, who
hast lost thy proper self (either thy womanly self, or thy self as it
has seemed to me, the ideal of my affection) and hast become a
fiend, *do* not thus make a monster of thyself. Were it becoming
in me to yield to the angry impulse, I could tear thee limb from
limb; but, fiend though thou art, thy woman's shape doth shield
thee. " Is it over-refinement to suppose that this revelation to
Albany of his wife's fiendlike character transforms, in his eyes,
even her person? She is changed, her true self has been covered ;

now that she stands revealed, her whole outward shape is be-
monstered. No woman, least of all Goneril, could remain un-
moved under such scathing words from her husband. Goneril's
'feature' is quivering and her face distorted with passion. Then
it is that Albany tells her not to let her evil self, hitherto covered
and concealed, betray itself in all its hideousness in her outward
shape" (Furness). No emendation is necessary, but several have
been proposed. For *feature* = bodily shape in general, figure, form,
cf. *Ham.* iii. 1. 167; and for *blood* = passion, anger, *L. L. L.* i. 2. 32.

65. *To dislocate and tear Thy flesh and bones.* That is, to tear
thy flesh and dislocate thy bones. The construction is used by S.
many times (cf. i. 4. 250 above); and sometimes, as here, without
preserving the proper order of the corresponding words. Cf.
Cymb. iii. 1. 3 : —

> "And will to ears and tongues
> Be theme and hearing ever; "

A. and C. iv. 15. 25 : —

> " If knife, drugs, serpents have
> Edge, sting, or operation," etc.

For the proper order, cf. *Macb.* i. 3. 60 : —

> " Who neither beg nor fear
> Your favours nor your hate ; "

W. T. iii. 2. 164 : —

> "Though I with death and with
> Reward did threaten and encourage him," etc.

68. *Your manhood now !* Sarcastic: " This is your manhood,
is it ? " Moberly paraphrases thus: " A nice notion you have of
manhood ! "

73. *Remorse.* Pity, compassion ; as very often. Cf. *Temp.* v.
1. 76, *Macb.* i. 5. 45, etc.

74. *Oppos'd.* Opposed himself. For *oppose against,* cf. *W. T.* v.
1. 46 : —

> " 'T is your counsel
> My lord should to the heavens be contrary,
> Oppose against their wills."

It is often used reflexively; as in *K. John*, iii. 1. 170, *Rich. II.* iii. 3. 18, etc. *Bending . . . to* = turning against.

75. *To.* In the direction of, against.

78. *Pluck'd.* A favourite word with S. It occurs six times in the present play.

79. *Justicers.* See on iii. 6. 21 above. *Nether* = committed on earth (opposed to *above*).

80. *Venge.* Not to be printed " 'venge," as in many eds. It is the Fr. *venger* (Latin *vindicare*), but has now given place to *avenge* and *revenge*. Cf. *vengeance* and *vengeful*.

83. *One way*, etc. " Goneril's plan was to poison her sister, — to marry Edmund, — to murder Albany, — and to get possession of the whole kingdom. As the death of Cornwall facilitated the last part of her scheme, she was pleased at it; but disliked it, as it put it in the power of her sister to marry Edmund " (Mason).

85. *The building in my fancy.* Cf. *Cor.* ii. 1. 216 : —

> " my very wishes
> And the buildings of my fancy."

86. *Another way.* Really the same as the *One way* in 83, the *other* way — which she did *not* like — being introduced by the *But*.

90. *Back again.* That is, going back again.

SCENE III. — This scene is omitted in the folios.

Enter . . . a Gentleman. "The same whom he had sent with letters to Cordelia " (Johnson).

8. *Who.* For *whom*, as often. Cf. i. 4. 25 above and v. 3. 250 below.

11. *Letters.* Letter; as often. Cf. *M. of V.* iv. 1. 108. *M. W.* iii. 3. 148, *M. for M.* iv. 3. 97, etc.

14. *Trill'd.* Trickled: used by S. only here. Cf. *Brit. Pastorals*, ii. 4: "And chilly drops trill o'er his staring eyes."

16. *Who.* See on i. 1. 107 and i. 2. 47 above, and cf. 19 below.

21. *A better way.* A much disputed passage. Clarke says: "It means that her mingled 'smiles and tears' expressed her feelings in 'a better way' than either 'patience or sorrow' could do separately; each of which 'strove who should express her goodliest.' The words 'her smiles and tears were like a better way,' moreover, include comparison with the opening phrase of the speech, 'Not to a rage'; showing that her emotion vented itself in nothing like rage, but ('a better way') in gentle 'smiles and tears,' compounded of both 'patience and sorrow.'" Various emendations have been suggested. *Smilets* is "a purely Shakespearian diminutive" used only here.

24. *As pearls,* etc. Steevens takes the poetry out of the passage by the following note, which might have been written by a jeweller's apprentice: "This idea might have been taken from the ornaments of the ancient carcanet or necklace, which frequently consisted of table *diamonds* with *pearls* appended to them, or, in the jeweller's phrase, *dropping* from them. Pendants for the ear are still called *drops.*"

31. *Let pity not be believed!* That is, believed to exist.

33. *And, clamour-moisten'd,* etc. The quartos read "And clamour moistened her." Capell gave "And clamour moisten'd" = allayed with tears her grief ready to burst out into *clamour,* as winds are allayed by rain. Moberly explains it, "Shed tears upon her cry of sorrow." Walker makes *clamour-moisten'd* refer to eyes; or, as Furness puts it, "her eyes that were heavenly and wet with wailing." Furness prefers this explanation, but believes the passage to be corrupt — as it probably is. For the construction he compares *Hen. V.* ii. 2. 139: "the full-fraught man and best endued."

34. *It is the stars,* etc. Cf. i. 2. 105 fol. above.

35. *Conditions.* Nature, disposition. Cf. i. 1. 292 above.

36. *Self mate and mate.* "The same husband and wife" (Johnson). For *self,* cf. i. 1. 64 above.

37. *Spoke not.* Have not spoken. Cf. *Hen. V.* iv. 7. 58: "I was not angry since I came to France," etc.

44. *Elbows.* Perhaps = pushes him aside (Schmidt). The word is a puzzling one, and probably one of the corruptions of this corrupt scene, "perhaps the most corrupt throughout Shakespeare's plays" (Furness).

47. *Dog-hearted.* Inhuman, brutal. Craig, in his note on this passage, says that " S. rarely, if ever, says anything good of the dog;" but see the description of the hounds in *M. N. D.* iv. 1. 118 fol.; the talk of the hunters in *T. of S.* ind. 1. 16 fol.; Page's defence of his greyhound against the criticism of Slender (*M. W.* i. 1. 96 fol.); the classification of dogs in *Macb.* iii. 1. 92 fol.; "the cunning hounds" in *V. and A.* 687, etc. S. evidently loved dogs as he did horses, though he naturally often makes his characters refer to them with the ordinary contemptuous and derogatory metaphors taken from the meaner types of the animal.

51. *'T is so, they are afoot.* "So it is that they are on foot" (Johnson); "they are actually on foot" (Malone).

53. *Some dear cause.* Some important business. Cf. i. 4. 279 above.

SCENE IV. — 3. *Fumiter.* Fumitory; the common name for plants of the genus *Fumaria.* Cf. *Hen. V.* v. 2. 45: "The darnel, hemlock, and rank fumitory."

4. *Burdocks.* The quartos have "hor-docks," and the folios "Hardokes" or "Hardocks." *Burdocks* is Hanmer's emendation, adopted by most of the editors. The common burdock (*Lappa officinalis,* Wood) grows abundantly by roadsides and in waste places both in England and in this country. *Hemlock* is one of the ingredients of the witches' cauldron, in *Macb.* i. 4. 25. See also the quotation from *Hen. V.* just above. *Nettles* are often mentioned by S.; as in *W. T.* i. 3. 329, *Rich. II.* iii. 2. 18, *Hen. V.* i. 1. 60, etc.

Cuckoo-flowers. Cf. *cuckoo-buds* in *L. L. L.* v. 2. 906. According to Beisly, the *Lychnis flos-cuculi* is here meant; but that has "rose-coloured flowers," while the *cuckoo-buds* in *L. L. L.* are " of yellow hue." Ellacombe thinks that either the cowslip or the buttercup is meant, and he is inclined, with Dr. Prior, to decide on the latter.

5. *Darnel.* The *Lolium temulentum.* Cf. *Hen. V.* v. 2. 45 and 1 *Hen. VI.* iii. 2. 44. According to Ellacombe, in the time of S. *darnel,* like *cockle,* was used as "a general name for any hurtful weed." *Idle* = unprofitable, worthless ; opposed to *sustaining.*

6. *Century.* A company of a hundred men ; as in *Cor.* i. 7. 3. In the only other instance of the word in S. (*Cymb.* iv. 2. 391 : "a century of prayers "), it means simply a hundred.

8. *Can.* Cf. *Temp.* iv. 1. 27 : "Our worser genius can," etc.

10. *Helps.* Heals, cures; as in *R. of L.* 1822, *Temp.* ii. 2. 97, *T. G. of V.* iv. 2. 47, etc. *Take* is 3d pers. imperative, or "subjunctive imperative."

11. *Means.* For the singular use, cf. *M. of V.* ii. 1. 19, *W. T.* iv. 4. 632, 865, etc. Dr. Kellogg (*Shakespeare's Delin. of Insanity,* p. 26) remarks : "The reply of the Physician is significant, and worthy of careful attention, as embracing a brief summary of almost the only true principles recognized by modern science, and now carried out by the most eminent physicians in the treatment of the insane. We find here no allusion to the scourgings, the charms, the invocation of saints, etc., employed by the most eminent physicians of the time of S. ; neither have we any allusion to the rotary chairs, the vomitings, the purgings by hellebore, the showerings, the bleedings, scalp-shavings, and blisterings, which, even down to our own times, have been inflicted upon these unfortunates by 'science falsely so called,' and which stand recorded as imperishable monuments of medical folly; but in place of all this, S., speaking through the mouth of the Physician, gives us the principle, simple, truthful, and universally applicable."

14. *Simples.* Medicinal herbs. Cf. *A. Y. L.* iv. 1. 16: "compounded of many simples," etc.

15. *Anguish.* Generally used in S. of physical pain. Cf. iv. 6. 6 below.

17. *Aidant and remediate.* Helpful and healing. S. uses neither adjective elsewhere; but we find *aidance* in *V. and A.* 330 and 2 *Hen. VI.* iv. 4. 17.

19. *Ungovern'd.* Unbridled ; as in *T. G. of V.* iv. 1. 45 : "the fury of ungovern'd youth."

26. *Important.* Importunate. Cf. *Much Ado*, ii. 1. 74, *A. W.* iii. 7. 21, etc.

27. *Blown.* Inflated, swollen. Cf. *A. and C.* v. 2. 352.

28. *Aged.* Abbott makes the word here a monosyllable, and seems to think that the only alternative is to make *our* a dissyllable; but why not scan thus: "But love, | dear love, | and our a- | ged fa- | ther's right "?

SCENE V. — 13. *Nighted.* Darkened. The word occurs again in *Ham.* i. 2. 68 : "thy nighted colour."

20. *By word.* By word of mouth, orally. *Belike* = it is likely, it may be.

22. *Madam, I had rather —.* Johnson says: "I know not well why S. gives to Oswald, who is a mere factor of wickedness, so much fidelity. He now refuses the letter; and afterwards, when he is dying, thinks only how it may be safely delivered." Verplanck remarks : "S. has here incidentally painted, without the formality of a regular moral lesson, one of the very strange and very common self-contradictions of our enigmatical nature. Zealous, honourable, even self-sacrificing fidelity, — sometimes to a chief or leader, sometimes to a party, a faction, or a gang, — appears to be so little dependent on any principle of virtuous duty that it is often found strongest among those who have thrown off the common restraints of morality. It would seem that when man's obligations to his God or his kind are rejected or forgotten, the most abandoned mind still craves something for the exercise of its natural social sympathies, and as it loses sight of nobler and truer

duties becomes, like the Steward, more and more 'duteous to the vices' of its self-chosen masters."

25. *Œillades.* Amorous glances. The word is spelled "aliads" in the quartos, and "Eliads" or "Iliads" in the folios. Cf. *M. W.* i. 3. 68: "Page's wife, who even now gave me good eyes too, examined my parts with most judicious œillades."

26. *Of her bosom.* In her confidence. Cf. *J. C.* v. 1. 7: "I am in their bosoms."

29. *Take this note.* Take note of this, attend to what I say. It could not have been a letter, because when Oswald was afterward killed by Edgar, and his pockets rifled, only one letter was found, and that was Goneril's. See iv. 6. 245 below.

35. *Desire her call,* etc. Tell her to help herself, if she can.

SCENE VI. — The materials of this scene are taken from Sidney's *Arcadia.* See p. 173 fol. above.

3. *Horrible.* For the adverbial use, cf. *T. N.* iii. 4. 196: "swear horrible; " 1 *Hen. IV.* ii. 4. 402: "horrible afeard," etc.

10. *You're better-spoken ;* like *well-spoken* in *T. G. of V.* i. 2. 10. Cf. Orlando's comment on Rosalind's speech in *A. Y. L.* iii. 2. 359.

13. *Choughs.* The *Corvus monedula.* Cf. *M. N. D.* ii. 2. 21 and *Macb.* iii. 4. 12.

14. *Gross.* Big, large. Cf. the quibble in 1 *Hen. IV.* ii. 4. 250: "These lies are like their father that begets them; gross as a mountain, open, palpable."

15. *Sampire.* The spelling of the early eds. and more in keeping with its derivation (from the Fr. " l' herbe de *Saint-Pierre* ") than the modern *samphire.* Gerarde, in his *Herbal,* gives as one of its Italian names, *Herba di San Pietro.* He says: " Rocke Sampier groweth on the rocky cliffes at Douer." Malone says: "This personage is not a mere creature of Shakespeare's imagination, for the gathering of samphire was literally a *trade* or common occupation in his time, it being carried and cried about the streets, and much used as a pickle." Cf. Drayton, *Polyolbion,* xviii. : —

> " Rob Dover's neighbouring cleeves of samphire, to excite
> His dull and sickly taste, and stir up appetite."

18. *Yond.* Not to be printed " yond'," as it often is.   It is not
a contraction of *yonder*.

19. *Cock.* Cockboat; the only mention of it in S.

21. *Unnumber'd.* Innumerable ; as in *J. C.* iii. 1. 63: " The
skies are painted with unnumber'd sparks." Cf. *untented* in i. 4. 291
above. For *idle,* cf. iv. 4. 5 above. *Pebble* is used collectively;
but some eds. adopt the harsh reading, " pebbles chafes."

23. *Deficient.* Defective, failing ; used by S. only here and in
Oth. i. 3. 63: " Being not deficient, blind, or lame of sense."

27. *Upright.* So near the edge of the cliff it would be dangerous to leap even upwards.

35. *Sights.* For the plural, cf. *Rich. II.* iv. 1. 314: " Whither
you will, so I were from your sights." Such plurals are common in
S. when more than one person is meant.

38. *Opposeless.* Not to be opposed ; used by S. only here.

39. *My snuff,* etc. Cf. *A. W.* i. 2. 59 : —

> " ' Let me not live,' quoth he,
> ' After my flame lacks oil, to be the snuff
> Of younger spirits ' "

(that is, to be called a snuff by them).

42. *Conceit.* Imagination ; as in *Ham.* iii. 4. 114, etc. " The
illusion may be so strong," Edgar says, " as actually to cause
death."

47. *Pass.* Pass away, die ; as in v. 3. 315 below. Cf. *2 Hen.
VI.* iii. 3. 25: " let him pass peaceably."

50. *Fathom.* S. uses both *fathom* and *fathoms* in the plural.
Cf. *A. Y. L.* iv. 1. 210: " how many fathom deep ; " *T. and C.*
i. 1. 50: " how many fathoms deep," etc.

53. *At each.* Joined end to end.

54. *Fell* also occurs as the participle in *T. A.* ii. 4. 50 and *T. of
A.* iv. 3. 265.

57. *Bourn.* Boundary. Cf. *Temp.* ii. 1. 152: "Bourn, bound of land," etc.

58. *A-height.* To the height, aloft. We find "a-high" in *Rich. III.* iv. 4. 86. *Shrill-gorg'd* = shrill-throated. For *gorge* = throat, stomach, cf. *Oth.* ii. 1. 236, etc.

71. *Whelk'd.* Protruding, like *whelks*. Cf. *Hen. V.* iii. 6. 108: "His face is all bubukles, and whelks, and knobs," etc. *Enridged* is used by S. only here. Cf. *V. and A.* 820: "Whose ridges with the meeting clouds contend; " and *R. of L.* 1439: "with swelling ridges."

73. *Clearest.* This has been variously defined as "open and righteous," "purest," and "clear-sighted." As Schmidt remarks, it seems to combine the ideas of "bright, pure, and glorious." In *Lycidas*, 70, "clear spirit " is = "noble mind " in 71.

74. *Men's impossibilities.* What men call impossibilities. Capell cites *Luke*, xviii. 27.

80. *Free.* Sound. Cf. *M. of M.* i. 2. 44: "whether thou art tainted or free," etc.

81. *Safer.* Sounder, saner. Cf. *M. for M.* i. 1. 72: "safe discretion; " *Cor.* ii. 3. 226: "safer judgment," etc. *Accommodate* = equip, furnish. Cf. *unaccommodated*, iii. 4. 107 above.

87. *There's your press-money*, etc. As Capell notes, Lear's mad thoughts are running upon war and warlike exercises, the enlisting of soldiers, the training of bowmen, etc. *Press-money* was the money given to a soldier when he was *pressed* into service. Cf. *2 Hen. IV.* iii. 2. 296, where Wart receives "a tester," or sixpence.

88. *A crow-keeper.* One who keeps off crows from a field. Cf. *R. and J.* i. 4. 6: "Scaring the ladies like a crow-keeper."

A clothier's yard. Steevens compares the old ballad of *Chevy-Chace:* "An arrow of a cloth-yard long."

92. *Brown bills.* Halberds used by foot-soldiers. Cf. *2 Hen. VI.* iv. 10. 13: "For many a time, but for a sallet, my brain-pan had been cleft with a brown bill." They were browned to protect them from rust.

Well flown, bird!   The phrase is taken from falconry, but Lear uses it figuratively of the arrow. The *clout* was the white mark in the centre of the target. Cf. *L. L. L.* iv. 1. 136: "he 'll ne'er hit the clout."

93. *The word.* The watchword; as in *Rich. III.* v. 3. 349 and many other passages.

94. *Marjoram.* The plant *Origanum marjorana.* Cf. *A. W.* iv. 5. 17, etc.

98. *And told me,* etc. Told me that I had the wisdom of age before I had attained to that of youth (Capell).

100. *Ay and no too,* etc. Clarke says: "Lear first exclaims indignantly: 'To say "ay" and "no" to everything I said!' recollecting the facility with which his courtiers veered about in their answers to suit his varying moods, just as Osric does to Hamlet; and then he goes on to say that this kind of 'ay' and 'no' too is no good divinity."

103. *Peace.* Hold its peace. Cf. *Oth.* v. 2. 219: —

" *Iago.* Come, hold your peace.
   Emilia.   'T will out, 't will out ! I peace ! "

107. *Trick.* Peculiarity. Cf. *K. John,* i. 1. 85: "He hath a trick of Cœur-de-Lion's face;" 1. *Hen. IV.* ii 4. 446: "a villanous trick of thine eye," etc.

109. *Subject.* Probably collective; as in *M. for M.* iii. 2. 145: "The greater file of the subject held the duke to be wise."

115. *Civet.* Cf. iii. 4. 105 above.

119. *Piece.* Nearly = masterpiece, or model (Schmidt). Cf. *Temp.* i. 2. 56: "a piece of virtue;" *W. T.* iv. 4. 32: "a piece of beauty," etc. *This great world* = the *macrocosm,* as opposed to the *microcosm,* or "little world of man" (iii. 1. 10), implied in what precedes.

122. *Squiny.* Squint. Wright says the word is still used in Suffolk; and, as Furness adds, in this country also. I have heard a New England mother say to a boy, "Don't squiny up your eyes."

126. *It is.* Emphatic; as in *Macb.* i. 3. 141: "and nothing is But what is not."

129. *The case.* The empty socket. Cf. *W. T.* v. 2. 14: "to tear the cases of their eyes."

130. *Are you there with me?* Is that what you mean? Cf. *A. Y. L.* v. 2. 32: "O, I know where you are." Furness compares "take me with you" in *R. and J.* iii. 5. 140.

134. *Feelingly.* In a heartfelt way. Lear takes it to mean "only by feeling, as I have no eyes." *Simple* = of low estate. Cf. *A. and C.* v. 2. 342: "a simple countryman," etc.

138. *Handy-dandy.* A children's game, in which, by a sort of sleight of hand, a thing is passed quickly from one hand to the other. Douce quotes an old MS., *A free discourse*, etc.: "They . . . play with your majestie as men play with little children at handye dandye, which hand will you have, when they are disposed to keep any thinge from them."

146. *Through tatter'd clothes great vices do appear.* "When looked at through tattered clothes, all vices appear great" (Furness).

147. *Robes and furr'd gowns hide all.* Cf. *R. of L.* 93: "Hiding base sin in plaits of majesty." *Plate* = clothe in plate armour.

150. *Able.* Warrant, answer for. Cf. Middleton, *Game at Chess*: "That 's safe, I 'll able it."

156. *Matter.* Meaning, sense. Cf. *Ham.* ii. 2. 95: "More matter with less art ;" *Much Ado*, ii. 1. 344: "all mirth and no matter," etc. *Impertinency* = what is not *pertinent*, or to the purpose. Douce says that the word was not used in the sense of *rude* or *unmannerly* till the middle of the 17th century, nor in that of *saucy* until a considerable time afterward. Cf. *impertinent* in *Temp.* i. 2. 138.

162. *Wawl.* Used by S. only here. Cf. *caterwaul.*

165. *This'.* This is. The early eds. have "this a " or "This a." *Block* = the fashion of a hat, from the *block* on which it was shaped.

Cf. *Much Ado*, i. I. 77. Lear probably had no hat on his head, but only his fantastic crown of weeds. Furness says that in Edwin Booth's *Prompt Book*, there is the stage-direction, "Lear takes Curan's hat;" which is certainly better than to suppose that he took his own.

166. *A delicate stratagem*, etc. Malone says: "This 'delicate stratagem' had actually been put in practice fifty years before S. was born, as we learn from Lord Herbert's *Life of Henry the Eighth:* 'the ladye Margaret, . . . caused there a juste to be held in an extraordinary manner; the place being a fore-room raised high from the ground by many steps, and paved with black square stones like marble; while the horses, to prevent sliding, *were shod with felt* or flocks [the Latin words are *feltro sive tomento*]: after which the ladies danced all night.'"

169. *Then, kill, kill*, etc. Formerly the word given in the English army when an onset was made (Malone). Cf. *V. and A.* 652: "in a peaceful hour doth cry, 'kill, kill.'" See also *The Mirrour of Magistrates:* "Our Englishmen came boldly forth at night, crying, 'St. George, Salisbury, kill, kill!'"

173. *The natural fool of fortune.* One *born* to be the sport of fortune. Cf. *R. and J.* iii. I. 129: "I am fortune's fool."

174. *A surgeon.* The word that S. uses elsewhere, but we find *chirurgeonly* in *Temp.* ii. I. 140.

175. *Cut to the brains.* Cf. *Acts*, v. 33: "cut to the heart."

177. *A man of salt.* A man of tears. Cf. *K. John*, v. 7. 45, *Ham.* i. 2. 154, and *Cor.* v. 6. 93.

181. *Smug.* Spruce. Cf. *M. of V.* iii. I. 43, I *Hen. IV.* iii. I. 102, etc.

185. *There's life in 't.* The case is not yet desperate.

186. *Sa, sa, sa, sa.* "An exclamation inciting to swift running" (Schmidt).

191. *Speed you.* May you speed, or prosper. Cf. *T. G. of V.* iv. 4. 112: "I would not have him speed," etc.

192. *Toward.* See on ii. I. 11 above.

193. *Vulgar.* Commonly known. Cf. *A. and C.* iii. 13. 119: " vulgar fame," etc.

194. *Which.* Who. See on i. 4. 258 above.

196. *The main descry,* etc. " The main body is expected to be descried every hour " (Johnson).

201. *My worser spirit.* Cf. iv. 7. 7 below and *Temp.* iv. 1. 27: " Our worser genius." S. uses *worser* often, and sometimes adverbially ; as in *A. and C.* ii. 5. 90: " I cannot hate thee worser than I do," etc.

205. *Feeling.* Heartfelt, or touching ; or perhaps combining both senses. Cf. *W. T.* iv. 2. 8: " To whose feeling sorrows I might be some allay."

206. *Pregnant.* Disposed, ready. See on ii. 1. 78 above.

207. *Biding.* Abiding-place, abode. Cf. *R. of L.* 550: " from their biding."

209. *To boot, and boot.* Over and above my thanks. Herford sees a double meaning: " to boot, in addition (to my thanks), and (the bounty of heaven) be your help."

212. *Thyself remember.* Recollect thy past sins, and commend thyself to heaven.

213. *Now let,* etc. Clearly addressed to Oswald, as Furness explains it; not to Edgar, as some suppose.

218. *Chill.* I will (in the Somersetshire dialect) contracted from *ich will,* as *chud* from *ich would* or *ich should.* In Grose's *Provincial Glossary, chell* is said to be used for *I shall* in Somerset and Devon, and *cham* for *I am* in Somerset.

220. *Gait.* Way; now confined to northern dialects.

224. *Che vor ye.* I warn you. *Ise* = I shall; still used in the western part of Somersetshire, and pronounced *ice,* as it is spelt in the folios (Wright). *Costard* = head; literally a kind of apple. Cf. *Rich. III.* i. 4. 159 and *M. W.* iii. 1. 14. *Ballow* is a northern word = pole, cudgel.

226. *Out, dunghill!* Cf. *K. John,* iv. 3. 87: " Out, dunghill! dar'st thou brave a nobleman?"

228. *Foins.* Thrusts in fencing; the only instance of the noun in S. For the verb, see *M. W.* ii. 3. 24, *Much Ado*, v. 1. 84, etc.

231. *Letters.* Applied to a single letter, as in i. 5. 1 above. Malone says it is used like the Latin *epistolæ*, but he probably meant *litteræ*, as *epistola* is a quasi-singular only in post-classical writers.

238. *Father.* Often used as an address to any old man. Cf. *Macb.* ii. 4. 4, *M. of V.* ii. 2. 76, etc.

241. *Deathsman.* Executioner; as in *R. of L.* 1001, 2 *Hen. VI.* iii. 2. 217, etc. Edgar is sorry that he anticipated the hangman.

242. *Leave, gentle wax.* Cf. *Cymb.* iii. 2. 35: "Good wax, thy leave."

243. *We'd rip their hearts.* Cf. *Cymb.* iii. 5. 86: —

> "I 'll have this secret from thy heart, or rip
> Thy heart to find it."

244. *Their papers.* For the ellipsis, cf. iv. 2. 11 above.

247. *Fruitfully.* Abundantly, fully; as in *A. W.* ii. 2. 73, the only other instance of the adverb in S.

254. *O indistinguish'd space,* etc.   "O, unmarked, boundless range of woman's will!" Schmidt makes *undistinguished* (the 2d quarto reading) = "incalculable, unaccountable." *Indistinguished* occurs nowhere else in S., and *undistinguished* only in *L. C.* 20. For *space*, cf. i. 1. 51 above.

257. *Rake up.* Cover by raking up the earth. Cf. the New England phrase, "to rake up a fire," that is, cover it with ashes. *Unsanctified* = wicked; as in *Macb.* iv. 2. 81. Steevens thought it referred to his burial "in ground unsanctified" (*Ham.* v. 1. 252). S. has the word only these three times.

258. *Mature.* Accented here on the penult, because coming before a noun.

260. *Death-practis'd.* Whose death is plotted. Cf. *practise* = plot, in iii. 2. 52 above.

263. *Ingenious.* Conscious; or, perhaps, sensitive, acute. Cf.

Ham. v. 1. 271: "thy most ingenious sense;" where it seems to mean "keen intellect."

264. *Distract.* Cf. *J. C.* iv. 3. 155: "she fell distract," etc.

269. *Bestow.* Lodge. See on ii. 4. 287 above.

SCENE VII. — 5. *Modest.* Moderate. See on ii. 4. 25 above.

6. *Suited.* Dressed. Cf. *M. of V.* i. 2. 79, *T. N.* v. 1. 241, etc.; also Milton, *Il. Pens.* 122: "Till civil-suited Morn appear."

7. *Weeds.* Garments. Cf. *M. N. D.* ii. 2. 71: "Weeds of Athens he doth wear," etc. *Memories* = memorials; as in *A. Y. L.* ii. 3. 3, etc. For *worser*, see on iv. 6. 201 above.

9. *My made intent.* The intention or plan I have formed. *Shortens* = mars, prejudices.

13. *Sleeps.* For the ellipsis of the subject, see on ii. 4. 42 above.

16. *The untun'd*, etc. Cf. *Ham.* iii. 1. 166: "Like sweet bells jangled out of tune, and harsh." The metaphor in *wind up* is taken from a stringed instrument.

17. *Child-changed.* Either "changed to a child," as some explain it; or "changed by the conduct of his children," as others understand it.

24. *Temperance.* Self-restraint, calmness. Cf. *Macb.* iv. 3. 92, etc.

25. *Music.* Dr. Bucknill says: "This seems a bold experiment, and one not unfraught with danger. The idea that the insane mind is beneficially influenced by music is, indeed, an ancient and general one; but that the medicated sleep of insanity should be interrupted by it, and that the first object presented to the consciousness should be the very person most likely to excite profound emotion, appear to be expedients little calculated to promote that tranquillity of the mental functions which is, undoubtedly, the safest state to induce, after the excitement of mania. A suspicion of this may have crossed Shakespeare's mind, for he represents Lear in imminent danger of passing into a new form of delusion."

26. *Restoration hang*, etc. Let restoration hang upon my lips the medicine to cure thee.

32. *Oppos'd against.* Cf. ii. 4. 174 above.

33. *Dread-bolted.* Clarke calls attention to the number of compound words in this play.

35. *Perdu.* Forlorn one ; according to Reed and others, an allusion to the *enfants perdus,* or soldiers sent on a desperate service. Craig refers it to the *sentinelle perdu* of the old French army, a sentinel placed in a very perilous position ; and the *watch* favours this interpretation. *Perdu* in this sense is found in Beaumont and Fletcher (*Little French Lawyer,* ii. 2) and Tourneur (*Atheist's Tragedy,* ii. 65).

36. *Mine enemy's dog,* etc.. Verplanck remarks : " The late J. W. Jarvis, the artist, used often to quote these lines as accumulating in the shortest compass the greatest causes of dislike to be overcome by good-natured pity. It is not merely the personal enemy, for whom there might be human sympathy, that is admitted to the family fireside, but his dog, and that a dog who had himself inflicted his own share of personal injury, and that too upon a gentle being from whom it was not possible that he could have received any provocation."

39. *To hovel.* The only instance of the verb in S. ; and the noun occurs only in this play (iii. 2. 56 fol. and iii. 4. 174).

40. *Short.* If this is what S. wrote, it must be = scanty, insufficient.

42. *Concluded all.* Come to an end altogether. See on i. 1. 95 above.

47. *That. So* that ; as often.

53. *Abus'd.* Deceived ; as in 77 below and iv. 1. 22 above. Cf. *Ham.* ii. 2. 632 : " Abuses me to damn me."

60-75. *I am a very foolish,* etc. Dr. Ray says : " A more faithful picture of the mind, at the moment when it is emerging from the darkness of disease into the clear atmosphere of health restored, was never executed than this of Lear's recovery. Generally, recovery from acute mania is gradual, one delusion after another giving away, until, after a series of struggles, which may occupy

KING LEAR — 18

weeks or months, between the convictions of reason and the suggestions of disease, the patient comes out a sound, rational man. In a small proportion of cases, however, this change takes place very rapidly. Within the space of a few hours or a day he recognizes his true condition, abandons his delusions, and contemplates all his relations in an entirely different light."

61. *Not an hour more or less.* Sir Joshua Reynolds and Steevens thought this must be an interpolation; but Lear is not yet in his perfect mind.

70. *And so I am, I am.* "Never surely was the passionate weeping of a reticent woman more perfectly expressed in brief written words than these and the 'No cause, no cause' that follow. They so admirably portray the *suppressed* weeping natural to such a character as Cordelia's; concentrated and undemonstrative, yet intensely loving and earnest" (Clarke).

77. *Abuse.* Deceive; as in iv. 1. 22 above.

78. *Rage.* Insanity; as in *C. of E.* iv. 3. 89, etc.

80. *Even o'er.* "That is, to reconcile it to his apprehension" (Warburton).

82. *Till further settling.* Till he becomes calmer. Dr. Brigham (*Amer. Jour. of Insanity,* July, 1844) remarks: "We confess, almost with shame, that, although near two centuries and a half have passed since S. thus wrote, we have very little to add to his method of treating the insane as thus pointed out. To produce sleep, and to quiet the mind by medical and moral treatment, to avoid all unkindness, and, when the patients begin to convalesce, to guard, as he directs, against anything likely to disturb their minds and to cause a relapse, is now considered the best and nearly the only essential treatment." For the old-time treatment of insanity, see *A. Y. L.* iii. 2. 421 : "a dark house and a whip." Cf. *T. N.* iii. 4. 148, v. 1. 350, and *C. of E.* iv. 4. 97, v. 1. 247.

83. *Walk.* Withdraw. See on iii. 4. 107 above.

95. *Arbitrement.* Decision. Cf. *Rich. III.* v. 3. 89 : —

> " the arbitrement
> Of bloody strokes and mortal-staring war."

97. *Throughly.* Thoroughly ; as in *Temp.* iii. 3. 14, *M. of V.* iv. 1. 173, etc.

ACT V

SCENE I. — 4. *His constant pleasure.* His settled resolution. Cf. " constant will " in i. 1. 38 above.

5. *Miscarried.* Lost, killed ; as often. Cf. 44 below.

6. *Doubted.* Suspected, feared. So *doubtful* = suspicious, in 12 below.

7. *Intend upon.* Intend for, intend to confer upon. Elsewhere S. has *intend to* or *toward.* Cf. 66 below.

9. *Honour'd.* Honourable, virtuous.

11. *Forfended.* Forbidden. Elsewhere used by S. only in such phrases as *God forfend, heaven forfend,* etc.

12. *Conjunct.* Intimately connected. See on ii. 2. 120 above.

13. *Bosom'd.* Cf. " of her bosom " in iv. 5. 26 above. *As far as we call hers* = " *Hers* in the full sense of the word."

16. *Fear me not.* Fear not for me. See on iv. 2. 31 above.

18. *Had rather.* Good English now as then. *Be-met* = met ; used by S. only here.

25. *It toucheth us,* etc. Because the French are invaders of his country, not merely the supporters of Lear.

26. *Bolds.* Encourages. The verb is found nowhere else in S., but we have *bolden* in *A. Y. L.* ii. 7. 91 and *Hen. VIII.* i. 2. 55.

27. *Make oppose.* Cause or compel to fight against us.

28. *Reason'd.* Discussed, talked about. Cf. ii. 4. 262 above and *M. of V.* ii. 8. 27.

30. *Particular.* Private, personal. Cf. i. 4. 345 above. See also the noun in ii. 4. 290 above.

32. *The ancient of war.* Veteran soldiers.

36. *Convenient.* Becoming, proper. Cf. iv. 5. 31 above.

37. *I know the riddle.* I understand your game ; you want to keep watch of me.

44. *Miscarry.* See on 5 above. Here the meaning is plain from what follows.

50. *O'erlook.* Look over. See on i. 2. 33 above.

53. *Discovery.* Reconnoitring. Cf. *Macb.* v. 4. 6.

54. *Greet the time.* Meet the emergency.

56. *Jealous.* Suspicious ; as in i. 4. 71 above.

61. *Carry out my side.* Be a winner in the game. Cf. *Cor.* v. 3. 13 : " which side should win," etc.

63. *Countenance.* Authority. Cf. 2 *Hen. IV.* iv. 2. 13 : " abuse the countenance of the king; " and just below (24) : " the countenance and the grace of heaven."

65. *Taking-off.* Cf. *Macb.* i. 7. 20 : " his taking-off."

68. *For my state*, etc. For it concerns me to defend my state, etc. For *stands upon*, cf. *Rich. II.* ii. 3. 138, *A. and C.* ii. 1. 50, etc. *Shall = they* shall ; a " confusion of construction."

SCENE II. — 2. *For your good host.* That is, for your shelter. The tree is compared to a host, or one who takes us under his roof.

5. Mr. Spedding would begin act v. here. See *New Shaks. Soc. Transactions* for 1877–1879, p. 15.

11. *Ripeness is all.* Cf. *Ham.* v. 2. 232: "If it be now, 't is not to come; if it be not to come, it will be now; if it be not now, yet it will come : the readiness is all."

SCENE III. — 3. *Censure.* Judge, pass sentence upon. See on iii. 5. 3 above.

7. *These daughters and these sisters.* " A bitter sarcasm in simplest words, thoroughly characteristic in the woman of quiet expression with intense feeling " (Clarke).

13. *Gilded butterflies.* "Gay courtiers" (Craig). Cf. Beaumont and Fletcher, *The Coronation*, i. 1: "The gay flies that buzz about the court."

17. *As if we were God's spies.* "As if we were angels commissioned to survey and report the lives of men, and consequently endowed with the power of prying into the original motives of action and the mysteries of conduct" (Johnson).

18. *Packs.* Combinations, coalitions. Cf. *M. W.* iv. 2. 123: "a knot, a ging, a pack, a conspiracy," etc.

20–25. *Upon such sacrifices*, etc. Dr. Bucknill says: "This is not mania, but neither is it sound mind. It is the emotional excitability often seen in extreme age, as it is depicted in the early scenes of the drama, and it is precisely true to the probabilities of the mind's history that this should be the phase of infirmity displaying itself at this moment. Any other dramatist than S. would have represented the poor old king quite restored to the balance and control of his faculties. The complete efficiency of filial love would have been made to triumph over the laws of mental function. But S. has represented the exact degree of improvement which was probable under the circumstances, namely, restoration from the intellectual mania which resulted from the combined influence of physical and moral shock, with persistence of the emotional excitement and disturbance which is the incurable and unalterable result of passion exaggerated by long habitude and by the malign influence of extreme age."

23. *Like foxes.* Alluding to the practice of smoking foxes out of their holes. Steevens cites Harrington's *Ariosto:* —

> "Ev'n as a Foxe, whom smoke and fire doth fright,
> So as he dare not in the ground remaine,
> Bolts out, and through both smoke and fires he flieth
> Into the Tariers mouth, and there he dieth."

24. *Good-years.* An expression of doubtful origin (see the *New Eng. Dict.*), which "came to be used in imprecatory phrases as

denoting some undefined malefic power or agency." The old explanation (making it = the pox) is pronounced "quite inadmissible." *Flesh and fell* = flesh and skin. For *fell*, cf. *A. Y. L.* iii. 2. 55 and *Macb.* v. 5. 2.

28. *This note.* The warrant for the execution of Lear and Cordelia.

33. *Thy great employment,* etc. The important business intrusted to you does not admit of debate. *Sword* = soldier.

36. *Write happy.* Count yourself lucky, congratulate yourself; perhaps a hint of reward.

37. *Carry it.* Conduct the business, manage it. Cf. *Much Ado,* iv. 1. 212: "this well carried," etc.

41. *Strain.* Race, lineage. Cf. *J. C.* v. 1. 39: "the noblest of thy strain," etc.

43. *Opposites.* Opponents; as in *Ham.* v. 2. 62, etc.

48. *Retention.* Confinement, custody. The words *and appointed guard* are omitted in the folios.

50. *The common bosom.* The affection of the common people.

51. *Our impress'd lances.* The soldiers we have pressed into our service. *Our eyes which* = the eyes of us who. Cf. "their greater pleasures . . . that" in 2 above.

66. *Immediacy.* Being next in authority to me. Malone well compares *Ham.* i. 2. 109: "most immediate to our throne."

69. *Your addition.* The title you have given him. Cf. ii. 2. 25 above.

70. *Compeers.* Is the peer of, is equal with. The verb is not found elsewhere in S., and the noun occurs only in *Sonn.* 86. 7.

71. *That were the most,* etc. The quartos give this speech to Goneril.

73. *Look'd but a-squint.* Steevens cites Ray, *Proverbs:* "Love being jealous makes a good eye look a-squint."

74. *I am not well.* The poison which Goneril has given her (cf. 97 and 227 below) begins to work.

75. *Stomach.* Wrath, passion. Cf. the quibble in *T. G. of V.* i. 2. 68 : —

> " I would it were,
> That you might kill your stomach on your meat,
> And not upon your maid."

77. *The walls are thine.* It has been a matter of dispute whether this refers to Regan's castle (cf. 247 below), or whether it is used figuratively = " I surrender at discretion." The latter view seems the more probable.

80. *The let-alone,* etc. " Whether he shall not or shall, depends not on your choice " (Johnson).

84. *On capital treason.* Both *on* and *of* are used by S. with the cause of the arrest. Cf. *Rich. II.* iv. 1. 151 : " Of capital treason we arrest you here," etc.

90. *An interlude !* " Our play has plot within plot ! " (Moberly).

98. *What.* Whoever. Cf. *Hen. VIII.* ii. 1. 65 and v. 3. 47 : " Be what they will," etc.

104. *Virtue.* Valour (the Latin *virtus*); as in *Cor.* i. 1. 41 : " even to the altitude of his virtue."

108. *Come hither, herald.* For the formalities of the contest here, cf. *Rich. II.* i. 3.

113. *Supposed.* Pretended. Cf. *M. W.* iv. 4. 61 : " the supposed fairies." See also 3 *Hen. VI.* iii. 3. 223, iv. 1. 93, etc.

120. *What are you ?* Who are you? See on iii. 4. 126 above ; and cf. 125 and 166 below.

125. *Cope.* For the transitive use, cf. *A. Y. L.* ii. 1. 67 : " cope him in these sullen fits," etc.

130. *The privilege of mine honours.* The right of my *profession* (as a knight) to draw my sword against a traitor.

132. *Maugre.* In spite of. Cf. *T. N.* iii. 1. 163, etc.

133. *Fire-new.* Fresh from the mint. Cf. *T. N.* iii. 2. 23, etc.

136. *Conspirant.* " Conspirer " (*Macb.* iv. 1. 91). Elsewhere S. uses *conspirator.*

143. *In wisdom,* etc. Because if his adversary was not of equal

rank, he might have declined the combat. Hence the herald proclaimed (111), "If any man of quality or degree," etc. (Malone). Cf. also 154 below.

145. *And that.* And since that. *Say* = assay, taste, proof; alluding to the formality of *giving the say* at the royal table. See on i. 2. 42 above.

146. *What safe and nicely,* etc. The delay which by the laws of knighthood I might properly and with due regard to punctilio make, I scorn to make. We may consider *safe and nicely* as an instance like "fresh and merrily" in *J. C.* ii. 1. 224; for, though S. sometimes uses *safe* adverbially, he has *safely* much oftener.

149. *Hell-hated.* Abhorred like hell. Cf. "hell-black," iii. 7. 60 above.

150. *Which.* As to which.

153. *Save him,* etc. "Albany desires that Edmund's life may be spared at present, only to obtain his confession, and to convict him openly by his own letter" (Johnson). For *practice,* see on i. 2. 180 above.

157. *Hold, sir.* Addressed to Edmund.

161. *O!* Omitted in the quartos; but, as Furness notes, it is the groan that breaks from Albany at the revelation of his wife's abandoned effrontery, and is as needful to the character as it is to the rhythm.

163. *Govern.* Restrain, control; as often.

167. *This fortune on me.* The luck to conquer me.

170. The second *more* may be dissyllabic, as Abbott makes it.

172. *The gods,* etc. Wordsworth quotes the Apocryphal *Book of Wisdom,* xi. 16 : "Wherewithal a man sinneth, by the same also shall he be punished."

176. *The wheel.* That is, of fortune. Cf. ii. 2. 175 above. On the passage cf. *J. C.* v. 3. 25 : —

> " This day I breathed first: time is come round,
> And where I did begin there shall I end;
> My life is run his compass."

179. *Split my heart.* Cf. *Rich. III.* i. 3. 300 (see also v. 1. 26) : " When he shall split thy very heart with sorrow," etc. See also *A. and C.* v. 1. 24.

183. *List.* For the transitive use, cf. *Hen. V.* i. 1. 43, *Ham.* i. 3. 30, etc.

191. *Rings.* Sockets ; the *case* of iv. 6. 129 above.

194. *Fault.* Furness thinks Delius is right in giving this the meaning of " misfortune ; " but possibly Edgar now blames himself for not making himself known to his father sooner.

196. *Good success.* Good result, or issue. See on i. 2. 140 above.

198. *Flaw'd.* Broken. Cf. ii. 4. 283 above.

203. *As.* As if. See on iii. 4. 15 above, and cf. 215 below.

204. *More, more woful.* Cf. *K. John,* iv. 2. 42 : " And more, more strong," etc. See also *Cor.* iv. 6. 63.

205. *Dissolve.* Weep. Cf. *Rich. II.* iii. 2. 108 : " all dissolv'd to tears."

207. *But another*, etc. " One more such circumstance only, by amplifying what is already too much, would add to it and so exceed what seemed to be the limit of sorrow." For this gerundial use of the infinitive, see iii. 5. 12 above.

209. *Top.* See on i. 2. 16 above.

210. *Big.* Loud. Cf. *A. Y. L.* ii. 7. 161 : " His big manly voice," etc.

218. *Puissant.* Always a dissyllable in S., but *puissance* is sometimes a trisyllable.

219. *Began to crack.* Cf. *Rich. III.* iv. 4. 365 : "till heart-strings break."

220. *Tranc'd.* As in a trance, apparently dead ; like *entranced* in *Per.* iii. 2. 94.

222. *Enemy king.* Cf. *Cor.* iv. 14. 171 : " this enemy town," etc.

224. *What kind of help?* " I find something very expressive of the versatile and vigilant character of Edgar in this inquiry " (W. W. Lloyd).

236. *Manners.* S. makes the word either singular or plural, like *news, tidings,* etc.

243. *After.* For the adverbial use, cf. *Temp.* ii. 2. 10, iii. 2. 158, etc.

247. *My writ.* Cf. 28 above.

250. *To who?* Cf. *Oth.* i. 2. 52: "To who?" *Id.* iv. 2. 99: "With who?" etc. See also on iv. 3. 8 above.

253. *Haste thee.* *Thee* is apparently used for *thou* in this expression (Abbott).

257. *Fordid.* Destroyed. Cf. *Ham.* ii. 1. 103, v. 1. 244, etc. See also 293 below.

264. *Stone.* Apparently = crystal, or polished stone.

265. *The promis'd end.* The predicted doomsday. On the next line, cf. *Macb.* ii. 3. 83: "The great doom's image."

266. *Fall and cease!* "Fall, heavens, and let all things cease!" (Capell). Delius takes *fall* and *cease* as nouns in apposition with *horror*, which had occurred to me as a possible interpretation. Moberly and Schmidt also adopt this view. For *cease* as a noun, cf. *Ham.* iii. 3. 15: "cease of majesty." For other explanations of this perplexing little speech, see Furness.

267. *This feather stirs!* Cf. 2 *Hen. IV.* iv. 5. 31: —

> "By his gates of breath
> There lies a downy feather which stirs not.
> Did he suspire, that light and weightless down
> Perforce must move."

272. *I might have sav'd her.* They have distracted his attention for a moment, or he might have saved his child.

274. *Her voice,* etc. "This wonderfully quiet touch seems to complete the perfection of Cordelia's character, evidently the poet's best-loved creation, his type of the ideal Englishwoman. Her voice was the outward signature of her graciously tempered nature. Burke's description of his wife is a master's variation on Shakespeare's theme: 'Her eyes have a mild light, but they awe you

when she pleases; they command, like a good man out of office, not by authority, but by virtue. Her smiles are inexpressible. Her voice is a soft, low music, not formed to rule in public assemblies, but to charm those who can distinguish a company from a crowd. It has this advantage, you must be close to her to hear it'" (Moberly).

278. *Biting falchion.* Cf. *M. W.* ii. 1. 136: "I have a sword, and it shall bite upon my necessity."

279. *Made them skip.* Cf. *M. W.* ii. 1. 236: "I have seen the time, with my long sword I would have made you four tall fellows skip like rats."

286. *He's a good fellow*, etc. Lear's mind is wandering again.

290. *Your first of difference.* "Your first turn of fortune " (Schmidt). Cf. *Macb.* v. 2. 11: "their first of manhood."

292. *Nor no man else.* "Welcome, alas! here's no welcome for me or any one " (Capell).

293. *Fordone.* See on 257 above.

294. *Desperately.* In desperation.

299. *Decay.* Capell and Steevens refer this to Lear (= "this piece of decayed royalty, this ruined majesty "); but Delius and Furness are probably right in taking it as = "the collective misfortunes which this scene reveals."

303. *Boot.* More than that. Cf. iv. 6. 209 above.

306. *O, see, see !* These words are occasioned by seeing Lear again embrace the body of Cordelia (Capell).

307. *My poor fool.* Cordelia; not his Fool, as some have thought. For *poor fool* as a term of endearment, cf. *W. T.* ii. 1. 118, etc. Furness gives nearly three pages of notes on the passage, at the end of which he says: "Very reluctantly I have come to the conviction that this refers to Cordelia." I sympathize fully with his regret that it cannot be referred to Lear's "poor fool and knave " (iii. 2. 67), but to my mind the context settles the question beyond a doubt. There is no room for a divided sorrow here; Lear's thoughts can never wander more from his dead daughter.

311. *Pray you, undo this button.* The *Quarterly Review* (April, 1833) remarks: "The intense excitement which Lear had undergone, and which lent for a time a supposititious life to his enfeebled frame, gives place to the exhaustion of despair. But even here, where any other mind would have confined itself to the single passion of parental despair, S. contrives to indicate by a gesture the very train of internal physical changes which are causing death. The blood gathering about the heart can no longer be propelled by its enfeebled impulse. Lear, too weak to relieve the impediments of his dress, which he imagines cause the sense of suffocation, asks a by-stander to 'undo this button.'"

315. *Pass.* See on iv. 6. 47 above.

316. *Tough.* The epithet seems to be suggested by the unyielding force of the *rack*.

322. *Sustain.* As Jennens remarks, "the play would best end here."

323. *A journey.* That is, to another world.

324. *Master.* "Lear. It would be hard to find in S. a reference to God as *master*" (Schmidt).

325. *The weight,* etc. The folios and some modern eds. (perhaps rightly) give this speech to Edgar. Schmidt thinks that the first two lines may belong to Edgar, and the last two to Albany.

327, 328. *The oldest,* etc. "Age and fulness of sorrows have been the same thing to the unhappy Lear; his life has been prolonged into times so dark in their misery and so fierce in their unparalleled ingratitude and reckless passion, that even if we live as long as he has (which will hardly be), our existence will never light on days as evil as those which he has seen " (Moberly).

APPENDIX

LEAR'S INSANITY

WHETHER Lear is insane at the beginning of the play is a question (incidentally referred to in the notes above) which has been much discussed. Coleridge believed that the method by which the old king tests the affection of his daughters is only "a trick;" and that "the grossness of his rage is in part the natural result of a silly trick suddenly and most unexpectedly baffled and disappointed." Others have thought it simply a proof that the old man is in his dotage, though not verging upon insanity; but several eminent alienists agree in the opinion that the mind of the aged monarch is already unbalanced.

Dr. Amariah Brigham ("Shakespeare's Illustrations of Insanity," in *Amer. Jour. of Insanity,* July, 1844) says: "Lear's is a genuine case of insanity from the beginning to the end; such as we often see in aged persons. On reading it we cannot divest ourselves of the idea that it is a real case of insanity correctly reported. Still, we apprehend, the play, or *case*, is generally misunderstood. The general belief is, that the insanity of Lear originated solely from the ill-treatment of his daughters, while in truth he was insane before that, from the beginning of the play, when he gave his kingdom away, and banished, as it were, Cordelia and Kent, and abused his servants. The ill-usage of his daughters only aggravated the disease, and drove him to raving madness. Had it been otherwise, the case, as one of insanity, would have been inconsistent and very unusual. Shakespeare and Walter Scott prepare those whom they represent as insane, by education and other circumstances, for the disease, — they predispose them to insanity, and thus its outbreak is not unnatural. In the case of Lear the insanity is so evident before he received any abuse from his daughters that, professionally speaking, a feeling of regret arises that he was not so considered and so treated. He was unquestionably very troublesome, and by his 'new pranks,' as his daughter calls them, and rash and variable conduct, caused his children much trouble, and introduced much discord into their households. In fact, a little feeling of commiseration for his daughters at first arises in our minds from these circumstances, though to be sure they form no excuse for their subsequent bad conduct. Let it be remembered they exhibited no marked disposition to ill-treat or neglect him until after the conduct of himself and his knights had become outrageous. Then they at first reproved him, or rather asked him to change his course in a mild manner. . . . This, however, caused an unnatural and violent burst of rage, but did not *originate* his insanity, for he had already exhibited symptoms of it, and it would have progressed naturally even if he had not been thus addressed.

" Lear is not after this represented as constantly deranged. Like most persons affected by this kind of insanity, he at times converses rationally.

" In the storm-scene he becomes violently enraged, exhibiting what may be seen daily in a mad-house, a paroxysm of rage and violence. It is not until he has seen and conversed with Edgar, 'the philosopher and learned Theban,' as he calls him, that he becomes a real maniac. After this, aided by a proper course of treatment, he falls asleep, and sleep, as in all similar cases, partially restores him. But the violence of his disease and his sufferings are too great for his feeble system, and he dies, and dies deranged. The whole case is instructive, not as an interesting story merely, but as a faithful history of a case of *senile insanity*, or the insanity of old age."

Dr. Isaac Ray, another expert in insanity (*Amer. Jour. of Insanity*, April, 1847), recognizes in Lear " a strong predisposition to insanity, which, if it had not been developed by the approach of old age or the conduct of his daughters, would have been by something else." His conduct in the first scene "indicates an ill-balanced mind, if not the actual invasion of disease." Dr. Ray adds: "The development of the early stage of Lear's insanity, or its incubation, as it is technically called, is managed with masterly skill, the more surprising as it is that stage of the disease which attracts the least attention. And the reason is that the derangement is evinced, not so much by delusions or gross improprieties of conduct, as by a mere exaggeration of natural peculiarities, by inconsistencies of behaviour, by certain acts for which very plausible reasons are assigned, though they would never have been performed in a perfectly sound state of mind, by gusts of passion at every trifling provocation, or by doing very proper things at unseasonable times and occasions. With his own free will and accord he gives away his kingdom, but finds it difficult to sink the monarch in the private citizen. He attaches to his person a band of riotous retainers, whose loose and lawless behaviour is destructive to the peace and good order of his daughter's household. . . . Under such an infliction it is not strange that she should remonstrate, and, had not the divine light already begun to flicker, he would have acknowledged the justice of the reproof. As it is, however, instead of admitting some share of the fault, he attributes the whole of it to her, flies into a passion, pours upon her head the bitterest curses, upbraids her with the vilest ingratitude, and forthwith proclaims his wrongs to the public ear. . . . Another lifelike touch is given to the picture in Lear's attributing all his troubles to filial ingratitude, not being aware, of course, that he was on the high road to insanity long before he had any reason to doubt their kindness. In fact, nothing is more common than for the patient, when telling his story, to fix upon some event, and especially some act of his friends, as the cause of his troubles, which occurred long subsequently to the real origin of his disorder, and might have had but an accidental connection with it."

Dr. J. C. Bucknill (*The Mad Folk of Shakespeare*, 1867) takes similar ground. He is severe upon the critics for " refusing to see the symptoms of insanity in Lear until the reasoning power itself has become undeniably alienated." They "have completely over- looked the early symptoms of his insanity, and, according to the custom of the world, have postponed its recognition until he is running about a frantic raving madman."

I am inclined to adopt this opinion of professional judges of insanity, not only because they are so much better acquainted with the subject than I can pretend to be, but also because it perfectly clears up the difficulties of the opening scene of the play. We must say, it seems to me, either that Lear's mind is enfeebled by age and he has lapsed into second childhood, or that he is begin- ning to show symptoms of the insanity which subsequently mani- fests itself past a doubt. This latter explanation is, on the whole, the more natural and probable. If he were in his dotage, we should not look for the occasional evidences of sound judgment that afterward appear ; but these, as Dr. Brigham has said, are not unusual in the insane. They are more likely to appear in a mind that is deranged than in one that is hopelessly weakened by age.

It is an interesting fact that the first writer to call attention to the evidences of Lear's incipient insanity at the opening of the play was a woman ; and that this woman was the author of the first critical work on Shakespeare from an American pen. This work, entitled *Shakespeare Illustrated*, was in three volumes, pub- lished in 1753–1754. The dedication to the Earl of Orrery was written by Dr. Johnson, the lady, Mrs. Charlotte Lennox, being then a resident of London, as she had been from the age of fif- teen, though born in New York, of which city her father, Colonel James Ramsay, was lieutenant-governor. Besides her work on Shakespeare, she wrote plays, novels, biographies, and translations from the French.

The authorities on Lear's insanity from whom I have quoted also tell us that Edgar's madness is as clearly a sham as that of Lear is a reality. Edgar imposes upon those about him, as he might deceive most persons ; but Dr. Brigham or Dr. Ray or Dr Bucknill would soon detect the simulation, as they and other experts have done in hundreds of cases of assumed insanity. They soon see the method in the madness, however shrewdly it may be disguised. How marvellous the knowledge of the human mind which enabled Shakespeare to delineate not only its natural workings in almost every conceivable type of man or woman, but also to discriminate thus nicely between its morbid action and the imitation of such action!

It was the same wonderful insight into our mental nature in its diseased conditions that enabled him to see what even the medical men of his age, as of all earlier time, had failed to discern, that is, the proper treatment of insanity. A passage in *As You Like It* (iii. 2. 421) epitomizes the wisdom of the olden time on this subject in a single sentence: "Love is merely a madness, and, I tell you, deserves as well a dark house and a whip as madmen do." A dark house and a whip! This was the usual treatment of lunatics until long after the time of Shakespeare—indeed, almost down to our own day ; and the barbarous practice still lingers in the management of a certain class of cases in some asylums. Dr. Brown, a high authority of less than a century ago, seriously maintained that "the patient ought to be struck with fear and terror, and driven in his state of insanity to despair ; as a remedy against over muscular excitement the labour of draught cattle should be imposed on him ; the diet should be the poorest possible, and his drink only water." Compare this with the treatment of poor mad Lear in the last scene of act iv., and note Dr. Brigham's com ments upon it (see on iv. 7. 82 above).

CORDELIA : HER CHARACTER AND HER FATE

Lear, in his best days, must have been every inch a king, but one only fitted to be an absolute monarch. His preëminent trait is a strong *will* that can tolerate no limitations or restraints. In his old age, and with the shadow of insanity already resting upon him, this wilfulness becomes a blind, unreasoning arrogance and obstinacy which in the end proves his destruction. His daughters are all as wilful as he is, for Cordelia is no exception. Goneril and Regan are depraved by nature, and their self-will works itself out in filial ingratitude, conjugal infidelity, and reckless criminality. They let nothing stand in the way of their evil desires and purposes. Goneril poisons her sister to remove an obstacle from her path, and when detected and exposed destroys herself — wilful and defiant to the last.

Cordelia, with all her virtues, is as wilful as her bad sisters, and this is her ruin no less than their obstinacy in wickedness is theirs. By how slight a concession to her father's persistent demand for some stronger assurance of her love might she have saved herself from banishment and him from all the woes that his misunderstand' ing of her reticence brings upon him and upon her! But she has resolved to say "Nothing" in reply to his question: —

> "What can you say to draw
> A third more opulent than your sisters?"

and "Nothing" is the utmost that she *will* say. Lear loves her and pleads with her: "Nothing will come of nothing; speak again;" but her only answer is: —

> "Unhappy that I am, I cannot heave
> My heart into my mouth. I love your majesty
> According to my bond, no more nor less."

But the *cannot* is simply *will not;* and how exasperatingly cold and formal the whole speech is! "I love *your majesty* according to my *bond,*" and according to the strict letter of the bond, "no more nor less." Shylock's insistence upon the literal interpretation of his bond is not more unfeeling or inexorable. Contrast it with the tenderness of the king's preface to the appeal which has provoked her —

though her sisters' effusive professions of affection have been the
first cause — to this cold and repellent demeanour: —

> " Now, our joy,
> Although our last and least, to whose young love
> The vines of France and milk of Burgundy
> Strive to be interess'd, what can you say," etc.

What yearning of paternal fondness, inviting, almost entreating,
some reciprocal expression of filial love from her! He has addressed no such tender words to Goneril and Regan — mere com-
monplaces of courtesy in contrast to that spontaneous outburst of
fatherly affection for his "joy," his " last and least," his pet Cordelia.

Mrs. Jameson, who dwells enthusiastically on the beauty of the
character, says: "If Cordelia were not thus portrayed, this deliberate coldness would strike us verging on harshness or obstinacy." I
think it must so strike us, charming as she otherwise is. but we
judge the fault as gently as we can. We try to regard it as partially
due to the fact that she had already begun to look with favour
upon the King of France, who had long been one of her suitors.
This new affection, which we may imagine to have been less exact-
ing and unreasonable than her poor old father's, had already won
that half of her love to which she refers when she says: —

> " Why have my sisters husbands, if they say
> They love you all ? Haply, when I shall wed,
> That lord whose hand must take my plight shall carry
> Half my love with him, half my care and duty.
> Sure, I shall never marry like my sisters,
> To love my father all."

Well said, indeed, but not wisely just then! It was a pity that
one who was so sparing of speech should say what could only add
to her father's irritation instead of the loving conciliatory words
that would have set all right again.

But when we reflect that Shakespeare did not choose his incidents, but was simply dramatizing an old and familiar story, we

cannot but admire the skill with which he manages this troublesome point. It is *necessary* that Cordelia shall offend her father and be disinherited. At the same time, she must not do it in such a way as to forfeit our sympathy and appear to deserve the severe judgment of her father. Shakespeare therefore makes her behaviour the natural result of her temperament and the position in which she is placed; and we feel that she is lovely and loving even when she allows herself to seem cold and "untender."

Though the delineation of Cordelia is so distinct and complete, it is remarkable that she has so little to say in the course of the drama. After the few sentences she speaks in the first scene, she disappears from the stage until nearly the close of the fourth act, and in the remainder of the play her speeches are few and brief. Counting half-lines and less as whole lines, she has but 46 lines in the first scene and 69 more in the latter scenes — 115 in all out of 3336 lines, or little more than 3 per cent of the whole, to state it mathematically. Was ever a prominent character painted with so few strokes, and yet so vividly and so perfectly? Could any one but Shakespeare have done it?

But why must Cordelia die? "This veiled angelic form with the tender beauty of her loving, maidenly soul, and yet so manly in her resolution and self-reliance, with her deep, peaceful heart which is so strong and pure in feeling, with her silent love and self-denial, with her heroic loyalty — does her death not seem like that of an innocent victim, and, though not without a motive, does it not appear unreasonable and devoid of all internal necessity?" Ulrici, who asks this question, replies to it thus: "She is as well aware of the violence, the impetuosity, and domineering spirit of her father as Goneril is; and yet she continues — regardless of his repeated entreaties to consider what she is saying — to reply in her obviously offensive and provoking manner, and finally to give an explanation which could only irritate him even more, as it contained a distinct reproach against himself and his demands. What she must have expected, must have foreseen, occurs: Lear bursts out into a fit of rage; she does nothing to check or calm it, but lets its full force fall upon her. She thus draws upon her own head a share of the great misery which must follow her disinheritance ; nay, to a certain extent she is chiefly to blame for the whole of the terrible catastrophe; it could not have happened had she not been disinherited and banished. By her own fault, therefore, she has become entangled in the tragic fate which is hanging over her father's house ; she herself called it forth, and has also to fall with it. Her transgression, when compared with the crimes of those around her, does indeed appear next to nothing; and she has atoned for it by the love and devotion with which she hastens to the assistance of her aged father, and by which she saves, tends, and cures him. But it was she who unfettered the power of evil, and consequently she too is involved in the general destruction." In the words of another critic: "Does not the rain fall on the just and the unjust? Yes; and so does the rain of ruin. The whirlwind, when once it rages, does not pick and choose its victims. Goneril's spite will not spare Cordelia when once it has a chance of venting itself upon her; the chance comes, and it does not spare her. Let Lear bemoan his folly as he may, yet, alas! alas! he cannot cancel it!"

But throughout the play, "amidst the continual disorder and confusion in the natural and the moral world," we feel "a continual consciousness of eternal order, law, and good. The feeling of the play, to those who rightly consider it, is high and calm; " for the final impression it makes upon us is that of the ultimate triumph of good over evil — the eternal truth that God is in heaven, and that in the end all will be well — *there*, if not here on earth.

TATE'S VERSION OF THE PLAY

In 1681 Nahum Tate brought out a version of *Lear*, in which — to say nothing of minor changes — the ending of the play was made a happy instead of a tragic one. Neither Lear nor Cordelia dies, and the latter marries Edgar. This was the *Lear* " which held the stage for a hundred and sixty years, and in which all our greatest actors, Garrick, Kemble, Kean, and others, won applause," and which was discarded only about fifty years ago. Verplanck considers that Charles Lamb has hit the reason of this: " If he is right, then the real secret of the prolonged popularity of Tate's distortion of *King Lear* is to be found in the fact that the grand and terrible passion of the original is too purely spiritual for mere dramatic exhibition, because it belongs to that highest region of intellectual poetry which can be reached only by the imagination, warmed and raised by its own workings; while, on the contrary, it becomes chilled and crippled by attention to material and external imitation." Lamb says:—

"The Lear of Shakespeare cannot be acted. The contemptible machinery by which they mimic the storm which he goes out in is not more inadequate to represent the horrors of the real elements than any actor can be to represent Lear; they might more easily propose to personate the Satan of Milton upon a stage, or one of Michael Angelo's terrible figures. The greatness of Lear is not in corporal dimension, but in intellectual; the explosions of his passion are terrible as a volcano; they are storms turning up and disclosing to the bottom that sea, his mind, with all its vast riches. It is his mind which is laid bare. This case of flesh and blood seems too insignificant to be thought on, even as he himself neglects it. On the stage we see nothing but corporal infirmities and weakness, the impotence of rage; while we read it, we see not Lear, but we are Lear,—we are in his mind, we are sustained by a grandeur which baffles the malice of daughters and storms; in the aberrations of his reason, we discover a mighty irregular power of reasoning, immethodized from the ordinary purposes of life, but exerting its powers, as the wind blows where it listeth, at will upon the corruptions and abuses of mankind. What have looks or tones to do with that sublime identification of his age with that of the *heavens themselves,* when, in his reproaches to them for conniving at the injustice of his children, he reminds them that 'they themselves are old'? What gesture shall we appropriate to this? What has the voice or the eye to do with such things? But the play is beyond all art, as the tamperings with it show; it is too hard and stony; it must have love scenes and a happy ending, It is not enough that Cordelia is a daughter, she must shine as a lover too. Tate has put his hook in the nostrils of this Leviathan, for Garrick and his followers, the showmen of the scene, to draw the mighty beast about more easily. A happy ending! — as if the living martyrdom that Lear had gone through — the flaying of his feelings alive — did not make a fair dismissal from the stage of life the only decorous thing for him. If he is to live and be happy after, if he could sustain this world's burden after, why all this pudder and preparation — why torment us with all this unnecessary sympathy? As if the childish pleasure of getting his gilt robes and sceptre again could tempt him to act over again his misused station; as if, at his years and with his experience, anything was left but to die."

THE TIME-ANALYSIS OF THE PLAY

This is summed up by Mr. P. A. Daniel, in his paper "On the Times or Durations of the Action of Shakspere's Plays" (*Transactions of New Shakspere Society,* 1877–1879, p. 220) as follows: —

"Day 1. Act I. sc. i.
   " 2. Act I. sc. ii.
       An *Interval* of something less than a fortnight.
   " 3. Act I. sc. iii. iv. and v.
   " 4. Act II. sc. i. and ii.
   " 5. Act II. sc. iii. and iv. ; Act III. sc. i.–vi.
   " 6. Act III. sc. vii. ; Act IV. sc. i.
   " 7. Act IV. sc. ii.
       Perhaps an *Interval* of a day or two.

Day 8. Act IV. sc. iii.
" 9. Act IV. sc. iv. v. and vi.
" 10. Act IV. sc. vii.; Act V. sc. i.–iii."

LIST OF CHARACTERS IN THE PLAY

The numbers in parentheses indicate the lines the characters have in each scene.

Lear: i. 1(122), 4(131), 5(22); ii. 4(161); iii. 2(43), 4(68), 6(31); iv. 6(106), 7(32); v. 3(54). Whole no. 770.

King of France: i. 1(32). Whole no. 32.

Burgundy: i. 1(12). Whole no. 12.

Cornwall: i. 1(1); ii. 1(14), 2(32), 4(12); iii. 5(12), 7(38). Whole no. 109.

Albany: i. 1(1), 4(11); iv. 2(43); v. 1(14), 3(87). Whole no. 156.

Kent: i. 1(44), 4(37), 5(2); ii. 2(104), 4(32); iii. 1(41), 2(17), 4(18), 6(15); iv. 3(29), 7(16); v. 3(24). Whole no. 379.

Gloster: i. 1(25), 2(61); ii. 1(30), 2(15), 4(12); iii. 3(20), 4(23), 6(15), 7(33); iv. 1(44), 6(63); v. 2(3). Whole no. 344.

Edgar: i. 2(11); ii. 1(1), 3(21); iii. 4(74), 6(47); iv. 1(33), 6(119); v. 1(12), 2(10), 3(78). Whole no. 406.

Edmund: i. 1(3), 2(128); ii. 1(63), 2(1); iii. 3(6), 5(14); iv. 2(1); v. 1(31), 3(76). Whole no. 323.

Curan: ii. 1(11). Whole no. 11.

Oswald: i. 3(3), 4(6); ii. 2(27); iii. 7(6); iv. 2(10), 5(12), 6(16). Whole no. 80.

Old Man: iv. 1(12). Whole no. 12.

Doctor: iv. 4(5), 7(13). Whole no. 18.

Fool: i. 4(109), 5(31); ii. 4(43); iii. 2(40), 4(13), 6(16). Whole no. 252.

Captain: **v.** 3(6). Whole no. 6.

Gentleman: i. 5(1); ii. 4(5); iii. 1(17); **iv.** 3(34), 6(16), 7(9); v. 3(5). Whole no. 87.

Herald: v. 3(10). Whole no. 10.

1st Servant: iii. 7(9). Whole no. 9.

2d Servant: iii. 7(5). Whole no. 5.

3d Servant: iii. 7(5). Whole no. 5.

Knight: i. 4(16). Whole no. 16.

Messenger: iv. 2(17), 4(2). Whole no. 19.

Goneril: i. 1(31), 3(25), 4(66); ii. 4(15); iii. 7(2); iv. 2(39); v. 1(7), 3(16). Whole no. 201.

Regan: i. 1(17); ii. 1(23), 2(8), 4(59); iii. 7(19); iv. 5(33); v. 1(14), 3(18). Whole no. 191.

Cordelia: i. 1(46); iv. (24), 7(40); v. 3(5). Whole no. 115.

In the above enumeration, parts of lines are counted as whole lines, making the total in the play greater than it is. The actual number in each scene is as follows: i. 1(312), 2(200), 3(27), 4(371), 5(56); ii. 1(131), 2(180), 3(21), 4(312); iii. 1(55), 2(97), 3(26), 4(189), 5(26), 6(122), 7(108); iv. 1(82), 2(98), 3(57), 4(29), 5(40), 6(293), 7(98); v. 1(69), 2(11), 3(326). Whole no. in the play, 3336.

INDEX OF WORDS AND PHRASES
EXPLAINED